COLLEAGUES

COLLEAGUES

RICHARD B. RUSSELL AND HIS APPRENTICE, LYNDON B. JOHNSON

John A. Goldsmith

MERCER UNIVERSITY PRESS
MACON, GEORGIA

ISBN 0-86554-617-7   MUP/P176

Copyright ©1998
Mercer University Press, Macon, Georgia 31210-3960 USA
All rights reserved
Printed in the United States of America

The paper used in this publication meets the minimum require-
ments of American National Standard for Information Sciences—
Permanence of Paper for Printed Library Materials, ANSI Z39.48-
1984.

Library of Congress Cataloging-in-Publication Data

Goldsmith, John Alan, 1920
    Colleagues: Richard B. Russell and his apprentice, Lyndon B.
Johnson / by John A. Goldsmith
        xxi + 243 pp.   6 x 9" (15 x 22 cm.)
    Includes bibliographical references and index.
    ISBN 0-86554-617-7 (alk. Paper).
    1. Legislators—United States—Biography. 2. Presidents—United
States—Biography. 3. Russell, Richard B. (Richard Brevard), 1897-
1971. 4. Johnson, Lyndon B. (Lyndon Baines), 1908-1973. 5.
United States—Politics and government—1945-1989. I. Title.
    E747.G63 1998
    973.923'092'2—dc20
    [B]   93-28938
                                                                CIP

Manufactured in the United States of America

For Romie, Alan, and Grego,
who encouraged—and endured

". . . because he was a new senator then and I had been there for years, he rather put himself under my tutorage, or he associated with me, you might say. That sounds better."

— *Richard B. Russell, interviewed for the television special "Georgia Giant," WSB-TV Atlanta, 1970*

CONTENTS

ACKNOWLEDGMENTS

I am deeply indebted to many people, especially the staffs of the Russell and Johnson libraries, for their patient help in research for this book; but my thanks go first to former members of the staffs of Richard B. Russell and Lyndon B. Johnson. They offered encouragement while providing information and kept me on the job. In another era it was said that no man is a hero to his valet, and aides to public figures do acquire special insights into the character that underlies public personas. To a very large extent, mine has been a staff-assisted effort, and I have profited from those special insights.

Two individuals have been especially helpful in this regard. Proctor Jones was one of the last young Georgians whom Dick Russell brought to Washington to complete their education while working at the Capitol. By the time the Russell-Johnson relationship was deteriorating, Jones had become a personal assistant and companion to the ailing Russell. He gave me the extensive, previously unpublicized, oral history interview that he had recorded for the Russell Library, and he has met with me often to discuss its contents.

George Reedy was a senior colleague of mine when I joined the United Press Senate staff in 1946. Not long after Lyndon Johnson became a senator, George left United Press to join Johnson's staff. He worked for Johnson, on and off, during most of the next twenty years and became close to Dick Russell as well. In several meetings, and in more than twenty letters responding to my questions, he has talked to me about these men and these events.

Other members of the Russell and Johnson staffs whom I had known as a reporter have also been extremely helpful. From the Russell staff, Bill

Bates (also formerly with UP and UPI), Charles Campbell, Bill Darden, Bill Jordan, Earl Leonard, Powell Moore, and Barboura Raesly have my sincere thanks, as does D. W. Brooks, who, although not a staff member, was Russell's longtime adviser on farm policies and farm legislation. From the Johnson staff, counsel Harry McPherson was generous with his time, as was Tom Johnson (no relation to Lyndon), who went from the White House to the ranch with the retiring president in 1968. Horace Busby, Douglas Cater, and Eugene Rostow were speakers in a 1990 series of LBJ seminars presented by the Smithsonian Institution (as were newsmen Hugh Sidey, Doug Kiker, and Ray Scherer).

I am indebted as well to members of the Russell family. Richard B. Russell III, the senator's nephew, generously took me in hand on a couple of visits to Winder. At age 93, the late Ina Russell Stacy, an older sister, made time in her still busy life to talk to me twice, and I am sorry that I will not be able to send her a copy of this book as I promised. Two of the senator's younger brothers, Dr. Alex Russell and Prof. Fielding Russell, also found time to talk to me.

Much of my research was done at the Richard B. Russell Memorial Library, a part of the University of Georgia Libraries in Athens, Georgia. There, archivist Sheryl Vogt and her staff were patient, friendly, and immensely helpful to an inexperienced researcher, producing correspondence, other files, and the many notes Dick Russell made after meetings and telephone conversations. In addition, many of the book's newspaper references stem from the library's more than 100 scrapbooks that document Russell's career.

At the Lyndon Baines Johnson Library, Harry Middleton and his staff, especially in the Reading Room, were similarly helpful in locating, in that very large collection, correspondence and other material that relates to the Russell-Johnson friendship.

At both libraries (and later, from both, by mail) I was able to borrow and read transcripts of interviews granted by associates of the two principals for the libraries' oral history collections. These interviews were particularly helpful because they were, for the most part, conducted soon after the events they describe. (And Merle Miller, for his book *Lyndon: An Oral Biography*, conducted additional oral history interviews for which I am grateful.)

My local library, the John Marshall Branch of the Fairfax County (Va.) Library System, provided many of the books I used, and its staff also assisted in acquiring material from other libraries in the county and elsewhere. Research in the microfilmed *Congressional Record* was aided by the reading room staff in the Law Library at the Library of Congress.

Former Democratic senators J. William Fulbright of Arkansas, Russell B. Long of Louisiana, Mike Mansfield of Montana, and Herman Talmadge of Georgia graciously consented to recent interviews so that I could follow up on information acquired in the oral histories and elsewhere. Those interviews were helpful, and it was a pleasure to talk to the former senators again after the intervening years.

WSB-TV in Atlanta has generously permitted me to quote extensively from "Georgia Giant," a three-part television series aired in 1970 as a tribute to Senator Russell. I have quoted from transcripts of the three programs and also from the unedited tapes of the interviews. CBS has permitted extensive quotes from an interview by Harry Reasoner with Senator Russell, from the CBS "Portrait" series, which aired just a few months before Russell and Johnson locked horns over the 1964 Civil Rights Act.

At Seven Locks Press, publisher Norman Sherman, who had seen many of these events unfold as an aide to Vice President Hubert H. Humphrey, took on this book after a number of other publishers had rejected it. Thereafter, he and his staff—notably Kathleen Florio and Lisa Rubarth—were wonderfully understanding and helpful to a writer untutored in the mechanics, not to say the atmospherics, of book publishing.

Several of the books that I read deserve special mention, in particular Merle Miller's *Lyndon*. The biographies of Lyndon Johnson by Doris Kearns, Robert Caro, and Robert Dallek were important sources, and while I was completing my research, *Richard B. Russell Jr., Senator from Georgia*, by Gilbert Fite, was published. It is the only biography in print about Russell, and I was fortunate to have access to it.

To develop a general chronology of events that were important to the long Russell-Johnson relationship, I have drawn on William Manchester's two-volume *The Glory and the Dream: A Narrative History of America, 1932–1972*, and the Rowland Evans–Robert Novak book, *Lyndon B. Johnson: The Exercise of Power*, was also very useful in that regard. Stanley Karnow's *Vietnam: A History* was my road map for that unfortunate story. Information on legislation was obtained in *Congress and the Nation*, volumes I, II, and III, covering the years 1945–1972, as reported by *Congressional Quarterly*.

INTRODUCTION

On January 5, 1971, two weeks before Dick Russell began his final downward spiral, I ran into two longtime Russell aides—Bill Darden, by then a judge on the Court of Military Appeals, and Bill Woodruff, of the Senate Appropriations Committee staff—in one of the Senate cafeterias, and we had lunch together. Our discussion quickly turned to Russell's health, and they painted a melancholy picture. Each had recently visited the senator in the hospital and had found him weak, worried, and deeply depressed.

They reported that a family gathering at Christmastime and a visit by President Nixon had buoyed his spirits for a while, but they said he had lapsed into a black mood in which his illness was a pervasive preoccupation. I asked whether Lyndon Johnson had called. (I had heard of a coolness between the old friends, but I did not know then of a controversy over a judgeship nomination.) They said Johnson had not visited or called. We agreed that one of the former president's expansive phone calls might cheer Russell up if anything could.

Returning to the Senate Press Gallery, where I had a desk and a typewriter, I sat down and wrote a letter to Johnson at the ranch. Looking at my copy now, I am shocked to see that I began it, "Dear Lyndon." I had never, in more than twenty years of association, called him "Lyndon." (I had never called Dick Russell "Dick" or Jack Kennedy "Jack," although Kennedy and I had been at prep school together.)

I began by saying that I was "meddling in something that is none of my business" and then told Johnson, in some detail, of my luncheon talk with Darden and Woodruff, both of whom Johnson had known as a senator. "Obviously," I said in concluding, "I am writing because there might be something you can do. May I say again, however, that I am not suggesting there is anything you *ought* to do—or even that there is anything at all that *can* be done. I do feel sure that you would want to know about this."

Johnson replied cordially on January 13 and said: "It grieved me to have your report on Senator Russell. Dr. Hurst, a mutual friend of ours, who treated both of us, called the other day and gave me a somewhat bleak report.

"Senator Russell has been a tower of strength for his nation and his state, and I hate so much to see him incapacitated at his age. I will be praying for his recovery and will try to figure out anything I can do that will be helpful."

I acknowledged that letter, but Russell had died before Johnson received my reply. On February 6 Johnson wrote from Acapulco: "We were both fortunate in having the opportunity to know Richard Russell when he was in his prime and no man could have been finer than he was."

My inquiries at the time and my recent research indicate that Johnson did not call or write Russell during his final illness.

My initial exposure to Richard B. Russell came during his chairmanship of the inquiry into President Truman's firing of Gen. Douglas MacArthur in 1951. As a very junior member of the United Press (UP) staff at the Senate, I occasionally sat in on Russell's press conferences at the conclusion of each day's hearings. Like the rest of the press corps, I was impressed with the way Russell handled those hearings as the national turmoil gradually subsided.

Not long thereafter an incident occurred that I now believe was important in my later dealings with Russell. It took place one morning in the old Senate restaurant, where the senators' dining area was just a few feet and a draped curtain away from the press table in the public dining area. Several of us had drifted from the press table into the senators' sanctum to talk to Russell. After setting ground rules under which he could not be quoted by name, he talked for half an hour or so about matters of mutual interest.

The following morning, having written an article attributing some of Russell's comments to "a top-ranking Senate Democrat," I was distressed to find Russell quoted by name on the front page of the *New York Times*. Then it occurred to me that William S. White, a *Times* congressional correspondent, had joined the group at Russell's breakfast table after the ground rules had been discussed and probably had not heard the ground rules. I called Russell and explained that, under the circumstances, I would have to rewrite my story, then on the UP wire, to quote him directly. He said he understood and thanked me for calling. I thought of the call as a routine courtesy, but as my subsequent calls to him were promptly returned and our talks became more cordial, it became clear that I was now viewed as a reporter to be trusted.

I soon had occasion to deal with Russell more frequently, when I became responsible for coverage of the Senate Armed Services Committee and the Military Appropriations Subcommittee, of which he was also chairman. I began talking with him on an everyday basis, and he began referring to me and Ed Haakinson, who covered those committees for the Associated Press (AP), as his "praetorian guard."

I started dropping in at his office on Saturdays, when the wire service routine was less hectic and allowed more time for leisurely talk. After a remodeling of the Senate restaurant, which hid the senators away in a corner of the building behind a reception room, I began checking on Russell's table each morning when I arrived at the Capitol. I could usually learn from members of his staff or from the waiters and waitresses whether he was in a mood to be interrupted at breakfast. In good moods he offered me coffee.

Perhaps because he grew up as one of thirteen siblings, Russell was not noted for his generosity, and I had reason to know we were close when he gave me a couple of oranges from a basket that had been sent by one of his Florida colleagues. ("Well!" said Marge Warren, one of his devoted secretaries, "he never gives us any!")

In the late 1950s, when he autographed a picture of the two of us taken for promotion purposes by a UPI photographer, he wrote: "To my friend John Goldsmith, with admiration and devotion." He was never in my home nor I in his (until after his death), but as reporter-source relationships go, he was, indeed, my good friend.

After I left UP (by then United Press International) to work with Robert S. Allen on his column, I saw less of Russell, but we remained close. He arranged for me to see transcripts of the closed-door hearings of the Armed Services Committee after they had been stripped of classified material and before they were bound and made generally available. The transcripts sometimes contained previously unpublished comments by top officials on national security policy and weapon systems. First access to them was very helpful to me in finding material for the column.

By the time I lunched with Darden and Woodruff shortly before he died, I had been regularly covering the "good" doings of Richard B. Russell (as opposed to his "bad," civil rights activities, in which I was only occasionally involved) for nearly twenty years. I was, of course, aware that he was the leading Senate strategist in a racial cause I strongly opposed. During the last eight years of that period, I was a member, vice chairman, and chairman of a suburban Virginia school board that was conscientiously engaged in desegregating its faculties and classrooms. When Russell joked about my late-night school board meetings, as reported in his morning paper, I thought I might one day write a book about the mellowing of his racial views.

As the member of the UPI Senate staff responsible for national security matters, I wrote about many of the hearings of the Senate Preparedness Subcommittee and about many of the subcommittee's reports when Lyndon Johnson was its chair. I covered the hearings that led to the creation of the National Aeronautics and Space Administration (NASA). I also dealt regularly with Johnson when assigned to cover "dugout chatter," the short session for reporters with majority and minority leaders before each meeting of the Senate, so named by UPI newsman Warren Duffee after a pregame baseball radio show.

Working for UP and its successor, UPI, was a wonderful experience—every day of the week except payday. Competing with the stodgy AP and often winning (score sheets were regularly circulated by the two headquarters recording how many major papers used UPI on a given story and how many used AP) was like playing for the underdog in a never-ending world series. Salaries at UPI were low, however, even for the news business, and that became oppressive at times. In one such period in the 1950s, Johnson offered me a job, and I was ready to take it when I discovered that I would not be working for Johnson directly, or on his policy committee staff, but for the Democratic whip, Earle Clements. I had nothing against Clements, an able Kentucky Democrat, but working for him just didn't sound very stimulating.

Looking back, I find it hard to believe that I ever considered going to work for Lyndon Johnson, even under heavy financial pressures. Of course, I did not know at the time how arrogant, boorish, crass, devious, egotistical, and so on, he could be. (His ambition, much trumpeted now, did not concern me. I was working in the Senate environment, where all the principals had offered themselves to the voters of their respective states as fully able and more than willing to confront some of the world's most difficult problems.)

I was present for UPI at the news conference on a Saturday in 1955 at which Johnson, the Senate majority leader, raged at an AP correspondent who pressed him on a pending immigration bill. His explosive loss of temper that day was linked in some speculative reports to the heart attack he suffered later that afternoon. In 1956 I covered the Johnson favorite son headquarters at the Democratic National Convention in Chicago. In 1960 I covered the Johnson headquarters at the Los Angeles convention and was surprised by his acceptance of the vice presidential nomination there. During the campaign that followed, I rode the meandering "LBJ Special" from Washington, through the South to New Orleans, and believed that the whistle-stop train played a major role in the Kennedy-Johnson victory. In the aftermath of the Kennedy assassination, I wrote to an expatriate aunt living in London that Lyndon Johnson was thoroughly objectionable personally but very able and might emerge as a good president.

As the UPI reporter covering Goldwater in 1964, I traveled for two weeks with Johnson during the campaign. (A routine, scheduled trade-off by campaign reporters was standard in UPI after a 1948 embarrassment, when veteran White House correspondent Merriman Smith was abruptly shifted from the Truman campaign in anticipation of a Dewey victory.) During my exchange period, I flew with Johnson to meet Lady Bird in New Orleans at the end of her whistle-stop trip and heard him deliver a speech there that remains a high point in my memories of presidential campaigning. Early one morning, on a flight returning to Washington from a campaign appearance in Boise, I encountered the president in an aisle of the darkened cabin of Air Force One. I whispered that I had enjoyed the change from the already ill-fated Goldwater entourage. "Well," he said, with some asperity, "I offered you a job once."

After election day I was assigned to the Johnson White House until Congress convened in January. In 1968, soon after I became a columnist, George Reedy, a former UPI colleague and then a White House aide, helped me schedule an hour-long White House interview with Johnson. The talk was on a not-for-attribution basis, but it allowed me to write one of those pretentious columns saying: "The President is known to believe . . ." and "President Johnson has told friends . . ." A couple of days later I received an autographed photo of the interview in progress.

During Johnson's Senate days I was favored at Christmastime with pralines and/or venison sausage, and on one occasion I remember Willie Day Taylor of Johnson's staff delivering that year's gift to my suburban Virginia home. In remembrance of the 1960 whistle-stop tour, I, along with xx

other veterans of the trip, was given silver cuff links featuring a stylized picture of a train's back platform. After the successful 1964 campaign, reporters who traveled with the president received a gold tie clip picturing the Johnson campaign plane. After our correspondence at the time of Russell's death, I had no further contact with Johnson.

These are the circumstances responsible for the mind-sets I brought to the writing of this book. At first it was to be a book about Russell. I had started squirreling away material (a profile I wrote on his thirty-third anniversary in the Senate, among other things, and transcripts of a 1970 WSB Atlanta TV series called "Georgia Giant") for nearly twenty years before I got around to starting it. When I did get around to it, I discovered that a well-qualified academician had been preparing a scholarly Russell biography for several years. Under the old rubric "write about what you know," the sensible thing seemed to be a book about the friendship of these two men, who, in their interaction, may have had as great an impact on the nation's history as any pair of friends since the two revered founding fathers Thomas Jefferson and James Madison. When I started the research I quickly discovered that Dick Russell's racial views did not mellow or change at all over the course of his life. To the end, he deplored racial mixing and foresaw (accurately, as we have discovered) that racial harmony would be very hard to come by. He came to realize, however, that racial equality would eventually be the law of the land and, at the end, was trying to accommodate to that political reality.

Especially significant for a researcher studying Dick Russell and Lyndon Johnson is the influence of their mothers. Ina Dillard Russell, who was a college graduate and had been a school teacher, would bear fifteen children and raise thirteen of them, seven boys and six girls, to maturity. Her family would eventually include a clergyman, a physician, several teachers, a college professor, and three attorneys—one of whom would become governor and then senator, and one a federal appeals court judge. Because Richard B. Russell Sr. was often absent (as a judge and for a while as a practicing attorney he commuted to Atlanta), she ran the household and staff and was the family disciplinarian.

Dick Russell adored his mother, whom he called "dear" from early childhood, and when he became governor, he proudly installed her in the mansion as his official hostess. The Russell girls believed their mother favored the boys, even her sons-in-law when they married, but especially Dick. On one occasion, however, when an acquaintance said she surely must be proud of her son, she replied that she certainly was, then added in some confusion, "Which one?"

Rebekah Baines Johnson, also a college graduate, from a prominent Texas family, had ambitions to be a successful writer before she married Lyndon's father and went with him to scratch a living from the Texas hills. Raised in affluent, but abstemious, gentility, she was quickly required to abandon her accustomed lifestyle and her hopes and dreams.

Life with hard-drinking, occasionally impoverished Sam Johnson was hard. Rebekah raised five children, but, from the beginning, she saw her oldest son, Lyndon, as the offspring in whom her own hopes and dreams might one day be fulfilled. She ceaselessly groomed him to be an achiever and relentlessly prepared him for success.

Chapter One

RESUMÉS

1948

In the summer of 1948, Richard B. Russell's reelection to the Senate was seen as a sure thing. First elected in 1933, he had faced only one serious electoral challenge—in 1936, when, after a bitter campaign, he had handily defeated Eugene Talmadge, the prototypical redneck campaigner who had succeeded him as governor of Georgia when Russell moved to the Senate. As the 1948 political conventions approached, Russell was being touted in the South as a possible Democratic candidate to replace the unpopular president Harry S. Truman.

Although he was the junior senator from Georgia in terms of seniority, Russell, in fifteen years of Senate service, had become a power in his own right. He was a top-ranking member of two of the most important Senate committees, appropriations and armed services, and was influential in agricultural policy making as a leader in what was then called the "farm bloc." A New Dealer at the beginning of his Senate career (he had made a seconding speech at the 1932 Democratic National Convention for his friend Franklin Roosevelt), he had become more conservative as economic conditions improved. He was the acknowledged floor leader for senators from the states of the failed Confederacy when they joined forces to resist civil rights initiatives. Now Russell commanded a third force in other deliberations as well, and when the Senate legislated, it usually did so after Republicans or Democrats secured the support of Russell's Southerners. Often the successful alliance was between Southerners and Republicans.

Senator Russell had begun to attract national attention. In the closing days of World War II, he had led a Senate delegation on a round-the-world survey trip of deployed U.S. military forces, and the group's widely publicized report had provoked the first debates about postwar U.S. policies. In 1946 he had successfully won approval of a law making permanent a popular initiative he had been promoting on a year-by-year basis—the National School Lunch Program, which has been feeding youngsters ever since.

Georgia voters were proud that Russell was the leader of Southern forces, and they applauded his other accomplishments, national and international. Their political loyalties were engaged, however, by his continuing successes on their own behalf, notably remunerative farm programs (especially price supports for Georgia cotton) and ever-growing federal assistance in the state made possible by his membership on the appropriations and armed services committees.

He was an attractive public figure. In Georgia and in the Senate, he had established a reputation for integrity. Despite his leadership in the controversial fight against civil rights, he was viewed by allies and opponents as an upright, honorable man. That dated from his early years, and even his siblings had been impressed. His younger brother Henry, known as Jeb, recalled that when he first began thinking about a career in the clergy, brother Dick took him out on the porch for a talk. "Jeb, we don't want any hypocrites in the family," Dick Russell said.[1] Brother Fielding, ten years younger, called him Sir Richard, "because he was a great believer in the term *noblesse oblige,* and I've never known anybody who was more concerned with a man fulfilling his duties and obligations, unless it were my father."[2]

Born in 1897, Russell had been raised and educated in Georgia. Both his parents, Ina Dillard and Richard B. Russell Sr., came from old colonial families. The Russells had been impressively prosperous before the Civil War (one cousin had held more than 100 slaves), and Dick Russell's father had fled as a child before the on-marching General Sherman.[3] Substantial landowners, Richard Sr. and Ina were in comfortable circumstances in the 1890s but were sometimes pressed for cash by the demands of raising their large family.

Their fourth child and first son, young "R.B.," attended Winder public schools, received additional instruction at home from a teacher hired by his father, and graduated from two private secondary schools in Georgia. He would have liked to have attended the U.S. Naval Academy; but no appointment was available, and he entered the University of Georgia, twenty miles down the road in Athens, where his father had compiled a distinguished academic record.

The Russell home, from young Dick's teenage years, was outside the town of Winder in what had been one of his father's cotton fields. The big, white, two-story house with a large front porch was nothing at all like Tara, the luxurious antebellum plantation featured in Margaret Mitchell's novel *Gone with the Wind,* which Russell would later admire. But segregation of whites from blacks was as rigidly applied, and the Russell property was farmed by tenants, usually black, whose economic lifestyle as free share-croppers was only marginally different from that of Tara's slaves.

Though pushed by his parents, young Dick's academic record at the university did not match his father's. He maintained a gentleman's grades and graduated with a law degree in 1918. After brief service in an Athens naval reserve unit, he began a law practice in Winder. In 1920 he announced for the state legislature, where his father had served, believing that campaigning would serve to bring his name and law practice to the attention of the community. He quickly decided that he could win, however, and by dint of a personalized handshaking campaign was elected to represent Barrow County in the Georgia House of Representatives.

In 1923, as a leader in a group of young lawmakers, he was elected speaker pro tempore of the Georgia house and in 1927 was elected speaker. Three years later he was elected governor and was sworn in by his father, who was now chief justice of the Georgia Supreme Court. After reorganizing the state government, as he had promised during the gubernatorial campaign—consolidating a hodgepodge of 102 departments, bureaus, and commissions into 17—Russell won election to the U.S. Senate in 1933, filling the unexpired term of William J. Harris, who had died of a heart attack.[4]

Russell did not become the South's leader because he was the loudest or the angriest Senate opponent of civil rights initiatives. In the Senate of Theodore Bilbo and James Eastland, he acquired a very different reputation as a quieter, reasonable, and resourceful opponent of those measures. To become the youngest speaker ever to preside in the Georgia House of Representatives, he had thoroughly mastered the rules of that body, and on arrival in the U.S. Senate, he immediately began to study its rule book. Not only did he master the twists and turns of the rules, but he was the acknowledged expert on precedents that had been developed since the days of Daniel Webster and John C. Calhoun.

To protect the interests of Senate Southerners (who met periodically to define those interests), Russell relied heavily on the rule (and precedents) that assured virtually unlimited Senate debate. Rule XXII required the votes of two-thirds of the senators present to invoke cloture, the procedure that would end debate and bring a pending issue to a vote. Filibusters under Rule XXII had blocked antilynching legislation in 1938, bills prohibitng poll taxes in 1942 and 1946, and a fair employment bill in 1946. Other civil rights measures, such as bills to outlaw segregation in transportation and to overthrow state laws banning interracial marriages, could not even get Senate consideration, so deadly was the threat of filibuster.

Although Russell had only twenty-two Southerners in his caucus, he had easily won these civil rights showdowns. He had discovered that many senators from the North and West, who were publicly pledged to expanding rights for Negroes, were not seriously committed on the issue. He had been able to persuade many of them not to limit debate on civil rights bills and thus set a precedent under which a large majority could overwhelm a minority on other matters. He found that unlimited Senate debate was a principle on which an announced supporter of civil rights legislation could credibly desert and vote with the Southerners. Only recently, on two occasions in 1946, had civil rights proponents been able to muster even a majority for limiting Senate debate, far short of the necessary two-thirds.

Besides defending the principle of unlimited debate, Russell argued in his speeches that the "so-called civil rights bills" were unconstitutional and would inject federal agencies into matters such as law enforcement, voter qualifications, and hiring practices that were properly reserved to the states. He called each of the bills as it was debated an opening wedge for the whole body of civil rights legislation that was designed, he contended, to destroy completely the social system of the South. He often read from the *Daily Worker* and other Communist publications to show that the pending civil rights proposals were embraced in the party's legislative program. Of course, he said, Negroes of the South were not taken in by such Communist propaganda.

Opposing antilynching bills, he read from FBI statistics listing the number of murders perpetrated in large Northern cities. He said he was not a supporter of poll taxes, but he contended that abolishing them was the business of state governments. He thought a Fair Employment Practices Commission would unleash "thought police" in the marketplace, and he argued that telling an employer whom he could hire abridged the right to hold property, which was assured in the Constitution.[5] Time and again he complained about prejudice against the South.

Because he was the strategist, much of Russell's participation in these debates was procedural—requesting quorum calls, arranging recesses, setting times for speeches, and the like. He often asked leading questions of other Southern speakers, to give them a breather in the long hours of debate. Only on rare occasions did he reveal his own feelings about the status of Negroes in the South, but he had his own clear vision of how that status was developing.

During a poll tax filibuster in 1942, he declared that never, "since the beginning of man," where two races had been thrown together as the white and black races had been thrown together in the South, had there been as much progress "in establishing fair and just relations between those people" as had been made in the South "in the brief period of seventy-five years.

"No minority race under similar circumstances has ever enjoyed as large a measure of justice and freedom in such a brief period," he said. "We have worked hard and painstakingly, down through the years, to evolve a plan of having the Negro in our midst with the least possible friction, and we have made remarkable progress in adjusting the inevitable problems and conflicts which arise when two races live side by side."

Negroes in the South, he said, were building their own social system, "a civilization of their own within the social system and civilization of the South, but it is separate and apart and you cannot bring them together by law or edict. It is not in the interest of either the Negro or the white race that this should be done."[6]

Democratic representative Lyndon B. Johnson of Texas was a long-shot candidate for a Senate seat in that summer of 1948. His recent record as a member of the House was by no means distinguished. Elected to fill a vacancy in 1937 and a champion of Franklin Roosevelt, he had become an FDR protégé with ready access to the White House and to the young architects and administrators of the New Deal. With their help and with the blessing of the influential Rep. Sam Rayburn of Texas, whom he had come to know as a congressional clerk in the 1930s, young Lyndon had appeared to be a congressman to watch.

With a personal assist from President Roosevelt, he had succeeded in bringing electricity and federally subsidized power lines to the farmers of his district, and in 1940 he had endeared himself to a number of House candidates by running a Democratic campaign office that raised and distributed needed funds. He had helped another House mentor, Rep. Carl Vinson, chairman of the House Naval Affairs Committee, narrowly win extension of the military draft in 1941.[7] Early in World War II, after securing a navy commission, he had been awarded a Silver Star by Gen. Douglas MacArthur for participating in a bombing raid while a member of an FDR-appointed survey team in Southeast Asia.

But even as a privileged junior member of the mostly senior "Board of Education" that met—and drank—informally in late afternoons with now Speaker Rayburn, Johnson had become frustrated with his slow progress under the rigid House seniority system. Losing interest in the business of Congress, he had bought a radio station in Austin, ostensibly for his wife (with a loan from her father), and in recent years he had devoted much of his time to improving his own financial prospects.[8]

His financial situation had always been difficult. First child of Sam Ealy Johnson Jr. and Rebekah Baines Johnson, Lyndon had been born in Johnson City, Texas, in 1908. The Johnson family had come to Texas from Georgia in 1846, and both Sam Johnson Jr. and his father had served in the Texas House of Representatives. Sam Jr.'s full-time employment was sometimes uncertain, however, and the economic situation of the family was often precarious.

After graduating from the Johnson City schools in 1924, young Lyndon resisted parental pressure for college and took off for California with a group of friends. There he did odd jobs and clerked for a while in the law office of a cousin. Returning to Johnson City two years later, he worked for a while on a road gang but finally bowed to his mother's determination and enrolled at San Marcos State Teachers College.

He got a secretarial job with the college president, was active in campus politics, got an early taste of Texas politics, and eventually edited the college paper. To augment his slim bankroll, he dropped out of college in 1928 and taught Hispanic youngsters in an elementary school in Cotulla, Texas, for a year before returning to college and graduating. He was teaching in a Houston high school when he was offered a job in 1931 as secretary to a newly elected congressman, Richard Kleberg, whose family owned the giant King Ranch.

He learned about Washington by running the congressional office for Kleberg, who was often occupied with golf and other diversions. In 1933 Johnson got himself elected president of an organization of congressional employees called the "Little Congress." While in Texas on business for the congressman, he met and very quickly married Claudia Alta Taylor, who, as an infant, had been described by a nurse as being as pretty as a lady bird. The young Johnsons became friendly with Rayburn, who had served in the Texas legislature with Johnson's father; and it was Rayburn who inter-

ceded with President Roosevelt to get Johnson appointed as Texas admin-
istrator for the New Deal's newly created National Youth Administration
(NYA) in 1935.

After compiling an excellent NYA record by placing impoverished
young Texans in jobs and in colleges, Johnson seized the opportunity to run
for Congress in his own home district when the incumbent died in 1937.
It was his pro–New Deal campaign that attracted the attention of FDR, and
the president, among other favors, helped his young friend Lyndon become
a member of Vinson's House Naval Affairs Committee.

Johnson's 1948 campaign was his second try for a Senate seat. In 1941
he had launched an unsuccessful bid, again campaigning as a New Dealer
with Roosevelt's tacit support. He had been defeated on the basis of late
returns that were recorded several days after the balloting, when his
election had seemed assured.

Chapter Two

TRAINING

1949–1952

Y ears later, after he had become Senate majority leader, Lyndon Johnson would tell, on himself, a Texas tale about his election to the U.S. Senate. Seated at his large desk in the plush office he had commissioned for himself just off the Senate floor, surrounded by newsmen, Johnson talked about the parish priest in a barrio in the area south of San Antonio along the Rio Grande. As his two secretaries poured drinks for the group, Johnson told how the priest, walking along the dusty street one autumn morning, found a young boy overcome by tears.

"Pablo!" said the priest. "What's the matter? Why are you crying?"

"It's my father," the boy sobbed, "my father."

"Now Pablo," said the priest gently. "You remember we talked about this when your father went away. He has gone to the house of the Lord and is waiting to meet you there some day."

"I know," said Pablo, through the tears. "But yesterday he came back to vote for Lyndon Johnson, and he didn't even come by to say hello."

The margin of victory that sent Johnson to the Senate was finally reported as 87 votes of 998,295 votes cast, and the votes that provided the winning margin had again been reported late.[1] Johnson's opponent in the primary, retiring conservative governor Coke Stevenson, had tried to block Johnson's candidacy in the federal courts, and a GOP-controlled Senate Elections Subcommittee launched an inquiry. But attorney Abe Fortas, a Johnson friend from the New Deal years, got Supreme Court Justice Hugo Black to dissolve the court action, and the Senate inquiry collapsed when Democrats won control of the Senate on election day.

However, Johnson's slim victory margin earned him the nickname "Landslide Lyndon," and on January 2, 1949, when the Senate welcomed its new members, Johnson did not appear to be marked for rapid advancement. Indeed, after his lackluster record in his final years in the House, he was one of the less imposing figures who took the Senate oath for the first time that day.

In 1946, in a backlash against World War II wage and price controls, American voters had sent a flock of Republicans to Congress. In 1949 the pendulum swung back again, and the Senate Democratic Class of '48 had a number of standouts. Included were Clinton P. Anderson, who had resigned as President Truman's secretary of agriculture to run for the Senate in New Mexico; University of Chicago economics professor Paul H. Douglas, who had been an authentic marine hero in World War II; Russell B. Long, son of the Louisiana "Kingfish"; Rep. Estes Kefauver, who had bested the powerful Crump machine in Memphis to win in Tennessee; oil baron and former Oklahoma governor Robert S. Kerr; and the liberal former Minneapolis mayor Hubert H. Humphrey, fresh from a fiery civil rights speech that prompted a Southern walkout at the Democratic National Convention. Like Johnson, Humphrey, Kefauver, and Kerr would eventually seek their party's presidential nomination.

The Senate that greeted the Class of 1948 was a more orderly body than the Senate of the 1990s. With television still in its infancy (the political conventions of 1948 were the first to be experimentally telecast) individual senators had not, for the most part, discovered themselves as personalities in the news. They were individually less aggressive and more inclined to seek common cause than their successors in later years. Orderly procedures were assured by a bipartisan group of respected senators who have often been referred to as the Inner Club.

Members of the Inner Club were not necessarily the most senior members of the Senate, and although Republican and Democratic leaders were often members, the Inner Club operated outside of the two-party framework. Like a corporate board of directors, its members made most of the big decisions and had an important role in deciding who would make the small ones.

Because he had been a member of the House Naval Affairs Committee and then the Armed Services Committee after a 1947 reorganization, it made sense that Johnson would seek a seat on the Senate Armed Services Committee. After his political career was over, however, Johnson would tell a biographer that he sought a seat on the Armed Services Committee because he wanted to cultivate Richard B. Russell of Georgia. He knew that Russell was a senior member of the Armed Services Committee and top strategist for the Senate Southerners. He also knew that Russell was a very influential member of the Inner Club.[2]

Without belaboring what might have been, it should be noted that when Johnson asked for a seat on the Senate Armed Services Committee, Russell could have blocked the appointment. As a senior member of the Democratic Steering Committee, which recommended committee assignments, Russell was in a position to do so; and he had no qualms about vetoing prospective Armed Services Committee members. When South Carolina's Strom Thurmond (who in 1948 had accepted the States Rights —quickly dubbed Dixiecrat—presidential nomination Russell had rejected) arrived in the Senate in 1955, he applied for membership on the Armed Services Committee. Thurmond had logic on his side, since he was a major general in the Army National Guard. But Russell, now chairman of the Armed Services Committee, was not impressed, and Thurmond waited four years, through the organization of two Congresses, before he got a seat on the committee.

Nor was it preordained that Russell and Johnson would develop a close friendship. At the time, and in the years since, many observers have remarked on the dramatic differences between them: Russell, a favored son of the Georgia elite, reserved, proper, polished, always the gentleman; Johnson, a product of the Texas hardscrabble, brash, rough, crude, sometimes to the point of boorishness.

There was also a bit of history that might have kept them at arm's length. Johnson had projected himself into national politics and into the inner circle of FDR's New Deal by enthusiastically adopting Roosevelt's plan to pack the Supreme Court as the centerpiece of his successful campaign for a House seat in 1937. Russell, an old friend of FDR's who had supported the New Deal up to that time, balked at the Court plan and went to the White House to propose a compromise. When the president declined and pushed ahead, Russell opposed the bill. It was defeated; and when FDR tried to retaliate by "purging" some of its opponents, including Walter F. George, Russell's senior colleague, Russell began to slide off the New Deal bandwagon.

Observers usually do not point out, however, that the often-cited differences between Russell and Johnson were largely matters of style rather than substance. Generally ignored are the substantial similarities between the two. Both were highly intelligent: Johnson, an astute problem solver; Russell, with a wide-ranging brilliance. Both had large egos, but both were deeply dedicated to the good governance and well-being of their country; and both looked to a time when the South could be returned to the mainstream of the country's political and economic life. Both had, in a very real sense, been born to politics. Although Johnson's Texas upbringing was' far more austere than Russell's, both families were deeply rooted in the history of their states. Both men had grown up to revere fathers who had held public office, and both had talked politics at the dinner table from childhood. Both adored and were everlastingly influenced by their mothers. Indeed, both might have been described as "mama's boys."

One aspect of their upbringing that differed and that was to prove important later in their relationship concerned the matter of race. Both of their fathers had opposed the Ku Klux Klan. But Russell's childhood was in the tradition of the Old South, with black servants in the house and black tenant farmers in the fields, while Johnson seldom saw a black, and his upbringing was grounded in a populist tradition largely free of racial overtones.[3]

In January 1949, Russell was favorably disposed toward the young Texas congressman, and not only because of an acquaintanceship stemming from their membership on the two congressional armed services committees. Rep. Carl Vinson of Georgia, autocratic chairman of the House Armed Services Committee, spoke highly of Johnson, and one business encounter had attracted Russell's attention.[4] Stymied as a member of the House in efforts to get appropriations to help his constituents electrify their farms, Johnson had come with a small group of congressmen to seek Russell's support as chairman of the Senate Appropriations Subcommittee on Agriculture. Russell quickly assured the House delegation that he was all for rural electrification and that they could count on his support.[5] Russell had been favorably impressed by Johnson on that occasion, and in January 1949, Johnson was assigned to the Armed Services Committee.

The nickname "Landslide Lyndon" had produced some senatorial smiles, but the circumstances of Johnson's narrow victory in the Texas Democratic primary would cause no serious Senate reverberations. Russell and his fellow Democrats were aware that Johnson had been declared primary winner over Coke Stevenson on the basis of belatedly reported ballots from the heavily Hispanic "Valley" south of San Antonio after voting irregularities had been reported, especially in a box (precinct) in Jim Wells County. They were also aware, however, that Johnson had been counted out as the apparent winner in the 1941 senatorial primary on the basis of belatedly reported ballots. (Former governor James Allred was one of many Texans who thought Stevenson's allies, opposing Johnson in that 1941 race, had produced the votes that overturned his apparent victory.[6]) In 1949 the controversy could be easily dismissed as more Texas-style politics.

Congress was reconvening after a shorter than usual summer recess. Immediately after winning renomination, President Truman had recalled lawmakers for a special "turnip day" session that accomplished little but gave the president every opportunity to continue his criticism of the "do nothing Republican Congress." When the Republican candidate, Thomas E. Dewey, viewing his election as certain, responded with a "do nothing" campaign, Mr. Truman pulled a stunning reelection upset despite Thurmond's party-splitting Dixiecrat campaign.

Russell, after receiving 263 votes in the presidential balloting at the chaotic Democratic National Convention, had refused to lead the Dixiecrats. Years later he would recall that he was "taken a way up on the mountain" by leaders of the splinter group of Southerners who promised to raise "almost incredible sums of money" if he would head their ticket. He thought he could probably have carried South Carolina, Louisiana, Alabama, Georgia, and perhaps Texas. But he was not ready—then or ever— to bolt the party he had called the "house of our fathers."[7]

Just before election day Russell and other members of the Georgia congressional delegation had reaffirmed their loyalty to the Democratic party. Truman carried Georgia, and Russell was reelected to the Senate. (Running unopposed in the September Democratic primary, Russell had received more votes than the total received by all the candidates in the contested gubernatorial race.)

After leading a successful Southern filibuster that had blocked an anti-poll tax bill in the turnip day session, Russell was anticipating a move by civil rights proponents early in 1949 to make it easier for the Senate to shut off filibusters. Rule XXII, requiring a two-thirds vote to end debate, had itself come under attack; civil rights supporters hoped to amend that rule so that a simple majority vote could bring a filibuster to an end.

Russell called a meeting of the Southerners early in January to plan for the expected showdown and invited Johnson to attend. Well aware of Johnson's position as a new Texas senator uncommitted in the Senate's civil rights maneuvering, Russell called Johnson personally to extend the invitation and said that if Johnson did not care to attend the meeting no one else would ever know that he had been invited.[8] The thoughtful approach was the beginning of a relationship in which, as Russell was to tell an interviewer more than thirty years later, "He rather put himself under my tutorage, or he associated with me, you might say. That sounds better."[9]

From the beginning, their association extended beyond the confines of the Senate. Baseball was one of the extracurricular pleasures Russell allowed himself, and he and Johnson began attending night games at the old Griffith Stadium to check the performance of Washington's other embattled Senators.[10] Russell ate breakfast every morning in the Senate restaurant in the Capitol, and Johnson acquired that habit as well.[11] Then there was Hall's, a popular seafood restaurant, where Johnson had sometimes dined with Sam Rayburn, his mentor and patron in the House. Rayburn liked Russell, and the three of them began meeting at Hall's for dinner and talk.[12]

Johnson seemed to have a need for a close attachment to older men who could help him advance and whom he could admire. In college, at San Marcos State, it had been the college president, Dr. Cecil Evans, whom he served first as glorified gofer and later as glorified clerk. In Texas politics it had been attorney Alvin Wirtz, his financial angel; and in the House, from his early days as a congressional secretary, it had been Rayburn.

Now, at Halls, both Russell and Rayburn were at the table with him. Johnson and Russell were both skilled and joyful mimes, and the Speaker would have been an especially appreciative audience as they took off and put down a few of their self-inflated Senate colleagues.

As a bachelor, Russell was often at loose ends on weekends, and he became a fixture at the Johnsons' Sunday dinner table. He welcomed the Johnsons' friendship. After living during part of World War II with his sister Ina Stacy and her husband, he was again living alone in a Washington hotel, and he enjoyed exposure to family living.[13] Doting as he did on the nephews and nieces in his own extended family, he was glad to get to know the Johnson girls, Lynda and Luci, and he came to like, and then to admire, Mrs. Johnson, who was, he discovered, intelligent and a lady of great integrity.

"He became very much a part of our lives," Lady Bird Johnson said, explaining that he was "a visitor to our home rather often." She would, she said, make an effort to prepare dishes Russell liked—"Southern-type food, which was very natural in our household," cornbread, and dishes such as black-eyed peas and turnip greens; and Russell always said nice things about them.[14]

Lady Bird recalled that Russell became "Uncle Dick" to the Johnson girls and was at ease with them.[15] Over the years Russell, a history buff from childhood, was to have scholarly conversations on that subject with Lynda, as she grew up to become a history student herself.

"I liked Johnson," Russell was to recall years later. "I've always had a tendency to kid people that I like and associated with. . . . Johnson had the same thing, and we would pick at each other."[16]

Their barbed conversational give-and-take was to continue well into Johnson's embattled presidency. Russell kept on needling his old friend, and Johnson, he said, "rather liked it. Because I was the only man left in the world who did it . . . and he and I had kidded each other so incessantly that it had really been the basis of our association in the Senate.

"I would kid him about things, and he'd get so impatient and so upset; and he'd get so mad with some fellow he'd be about ready to cut his throat. And I'd say, 'Isn't that the same man you were telling me you thought was one of the most promising men to come into the Senate in the last several years?'. . . he didn't like to be reminded of things like that, but he took it well."[17]

There is some question whether Johnson actually attended the specific strategy session to which Russell politely invited him. Years later Russell would recall that Johnson did attend, and he would later attend other meetings of the Southern caucus, which were usually held around a large table in Russell's spacious private office.[18] It was quite clear at this point in his career that Johnson would join the Southerners in opposing initiatives such as the attempt to change the filibuster rule.

However, Russell, in keeping with the terms of his original invitation to Johnson, did not press him to join the caucus on a regular basis. Russell was quick to see that Texas, by history a Southern state, was in fact, Southwestern and becoming more Western than Southern. That reasoning, which seemed to be little more than a quibble at the time, was to prove important in years to come.

Early in 1949, Russell introduced for the first time a civil rights bill of his own, a bill he would reintroduce from time to time in somewhat different versions. As first proposed it would have set up a racial relocation committee to develop a program under which blacks and whites could move to parts of the nation where their presence would create a better racial balance.[19]

Maneuvering over the filibuster rule came to a head in March, and the attempt to change the rule was filibustered. Most of the talk focused on the principle of unlimited debate in the Senate. Russell renewed many of his arguments against several civil rights proposals, and expecting a showdown on a Fair Employment Practices Bill later in the session, he said it would be "pure state socialism" if the government could tell an employer whom to employ.[20]

On March 9, with Russell in attendance, Johnson gave his first major speech as a senator. He began by extolling unlimited debate and called the cloture procedure "perhaps the deadliest weapon in the parliamentary process." President Truman had publicly supported the drive for majority cloture, and Johnson took a swipe at the recently reelected president by saying that no cloture rule had impeded Mr. Truman when he took his case to the nation the previous summer.

Then, recognizing "the simple fact" that the debate was really about civil rights legislation, Johnson spoke as a Texan: "When we of the South rise here to speak against this resolution, to speak against the civil rights proposals, we are not speaking against the Negro race; we are not attempting to keep alive the old flames of hate and bigotry; we are instead trying to keep those flames from being rekindled. We are trying to tell the rest of the nation that this is not the way to accomplish what some may want to do for the Negro."

As Russell usually did, Johnson cited objections to each of the principal civil rights proposals—antilynching, anti–poll tax, and fair employment bills—calling the bill to establish a Fair Employment Practices Commission the "least meritorious," and arguing that it could eventually "enslave" its supposed beneficiaries. "If the law can compel me to employ a Negro and compel that Negro to work for me, it might even tell him how long and how hard he would have to work," he said.

In closing, Johnson returned to the principle of unlimited debate, declaring that "if we now shut off this freedom, we shall be cutting off the most vital safeguard which minorities possess against the tyranny of momentary majorities."[21]

When the battle ended, Russell and his Southerners had actually relaxed the rule on filibusters. With civil rights proponents unable to get the necessary votes for cloture, Senate leaders sought a compromise. Russell made concessions as to what measures could be filibustered, but he eventually negotiated a rule that required a "constitutional two-thirds"— that is, two-thirds of the entire Senate membership—to end debate, and that version was approved by the Senate. Southerners were able to say that the compromise strengthened their hand. Since cloture votes were (and are) scheduled by the leadership at times when all senators can arrange to be present, Russell knew it made no real difference.

In June of 1950, Johnson also backed Russell in securing Armed Services Committee approval of an amendment to a military draft bill that would have allowed men entering the military to elect to serve in units that included only men of their own race. That amendment was defeated in the Senate, but later that summer Johnson joined Russell and the Southern-Republican coalition in rebuffing the bill that would have assured fair employment practices by creating the Fair Employment Practices Commission (FEPC).

Although he was clearly in control of the Senate in matters relating to civil rights, Russell had already begun to have misgivings about the future. At the end of the fight over the filibuster rule, he told the Senate that he was not claiming the outright victory "which has been attributed to us." To his mother, who had wired her support, Russell replied that the victory had been "not as sweeping as some people have said."[22]

And when the FEPC bill was stymied by a filibuster the following summer, its supporters were able to persuade more than half the Senate to vote for cloture on two separate votes. After the final showdown, Russell told an old Georgia friend who sent congratulations, "We have held the bridge up until now, but it is disheartening to see how the advocates of this monstrosity increase in strength each year."[23]

In his public appearances, Russell tried to avoid the antiblack code words that inflamed the civil rights rhetoric. On one occasion, after an appearance on the television program "Meet the Press," he took pains to note that an interviewer, not he, had introduced the phrase "white supremacy," a phrase Russell claimed he never used. He explained that, although the white race had achieved more and could be viewed as superior in that sense, "this does not give any white person any rights superior to those of any other race before the law of our land."[24]

Although Johnson was supporting Russell and the Southerners in opposing legislation to help blacks, he took one step in his early weeks as a senator that reflected a sensitivity for other minority interests. When the body of Felix Longoria, a Mexican-American soldier killed in the Philippines during World War II, was refused burial in a Three Rivers, Texas, cemetery, precipitating a racial controversy, Johnson sought help from President Truman in arranging for a ceremonial burial in Arlington National Cemetery and attended the services there.[25]

In the House, as a protégé of FDR, Johnson's opposition to civil rights initiatives had been his major departure from New Deal orthodoxy; but over the years he had been edging toward the center of the political spectrum. Now the drift accelerated. Moving from the House to the Senate, he had acquired a new, larger, and much more diverse constituency. He was no longer the representative of a small, poor, largely rural, populist enclave; he was now representing all of the large and booming state. He had moved from representing marginal farmers seeking electricity for their homes and barns, to representing a variety of commercial enterprises, including some of the nation's largest oil and gas interests. A somewhat more conservative viewpoint came with that territory. The new viewpoint became apparent in Johnson's first months as a senator, when he headed a commerce subcommittee and then led a floor fight in which the Senate rejected President Truman's renomination of a liberal New Dealer, Leland Olds, to the Federal Power Commission, the federal agency that regulated oil and gas operations.

After his successful fight against the Olds nomination, Johnson joked in a note to Russell about thwarting a threat to the nation's gas producers and said: "I'm young and impressionable, so I just tried to do what that Old Master, the junior senator from Georgia, taught me to do."[26] The result of these maneuvers was to position Johnson as a conservative among Senate Democrats, amicably disposed toward the Southerners but not formally aligned with them. Having distanced himself from Senate liberals by leading the fight against Olds, a fight in which Olds was portrayed as a left-winger, Johnson was cast for the first time as the protector of Texas oil and gas interests.

Johnson's shifting views did not pass unnoticed by his friends from the New Deal days, and some of them were sharply critical—especially of Johnson's role in the fight against Olds. Tom Corcoran, a former FDR political adviser, went to the Capitol to talk to Johnson about it. So did Jim Rowe, former assistant in the FDR White House, who felt Johnson was smearing Olds with his "Commie" talk. Always supersensitive to criticism, Johnson took himself out of the old New Deal social circle, but about every six months he would arrange for an evening with the Rowes.[27]

As Russell's apprentice, Johnson was beginning to receive favorable treatment from other members of the Inner Club. His assignment to head the subcommittee that considered the Olds nomination was made by Sen. Edwin D. Johnson, a Democrat of Colorado and chairman of the Senate Commerce Committee, the other standing committee to which the new senator had been assigned with Russell's help. Ed Johnson, an Inner Clubber frequently allied with Russell, was half of one of the Senate's most influential state twosomes. Gruff, blunt, "Big" Ed Johnson teamed with his colleague, Eugene Millikin, a highly articulate, jovial, rotund Republican, to form a potent power base in the Senate and in Colorado, where, by common consent, they never campaigned against each other or interfered in each other's political initiatives. Lyndon Johnson's early alliance with his Colorado namesake, and then with Millikin, was to provide a continuing source of support in later years.

Johnson's high profile in the Olds controversy was the exception and not the norm during his first Senate session. Cautiously exploring his new surroundings, cultivating Russell and edging into other new relationships, he subdued his flamboyant urges and acted for the most part on the axiom, generally accepted as gospel at that time, that new senators, like little children, were to be seen and not heard.

To Russell it seemed clear that Johnson's Senate career had gotten off on the right foot. He was impressed with the efficiency of Johnson's Senate office and how the new senator quickly learned how to make his way in the Senate.[28] In November, after Johnson's first year in the Senate, Russell accepted the first of what would be many invitations to visit the Johnsons in Texas. They hunted in the daytime and talked politics into the night. In a thank-you note, Russell said it was a "perfect" trip and commented that on the way home in a private plane, Speaker Rayburn, also a guest, had especially enjoyed seeing his home spread in Bonham, Texas, from a vantage point of 700 feet.[29]

In the spring of 1950, Ina Dillard Russell was named "Georgia mother of the year" by a national magazine, which catalogued the various successes of her thirteen children. Russell told his mother the honor was "about the nicest thing that ever happened to a member of the Russell family."[30] For Russell it was a public validation of his own private reverence for his mother, to whom he always sent a check once a month. The Johnsons had come to appreciate Russell's love for his mother, and marking the ceremony in May, Lyndon and Lady Bird sent a congratulatory telegram.[31]

Johnson's attentions to Russell did not go unnoticed by their colleagues. Years later Alabama senator Lister Hill, who as a House member had known Johnson slightly, recalled the new Texas senator playing up to the powerful leader of the Senate's Southern bloc. "He captured Dick," said Hill, who as assistant Democratic leader, or whip, in 1947, had foreseen the party's civil rights struggles and had given up his leadership post to avoid being caught in the middle of them.[32]

On June 25, 1950, North Korean troops rolled across the border into

South Korea. By the end of the following week, Johnson, after clearing it with Russell, had introduced a resolution calling for an Armed Services Subcommittee to monitor U.S. participation in the escalating Korean War. The proposal was patterned after the World War II investigating committee that had rocketed a previously undistinguished senator named Harry Truman into a position of national prominence.

As author of the resolution, which was quickly approved by the Armed Services Committee and then by the Senate, Johnson had a proprietary interest in becoming chairman of the new subcommittee. Earlier in the year, Estes Kefauver had offered a resolution calling for an investigation into organized crime, and he had become chairman of the investigating committee. However, Sen. Millard Tydings, Democrat of Maryland, was chairman of the Armed Services Committee, and it appeared for a time that Tydings was himself interested in heading the subcommittee Johnson had proposed. Tydings, who was up for reelection that year, had incurred the wrath of the already rampaging Sen. Joseph R. McCarthy, Republican of Wisconsin. McCarthy was supporting John Marshall Butler, a handsome but otherwise lightly endowed Republican, against Tydings, and Tydings thought publicity as a war investigator might help his reelection campaign.

As was generally the case in delicate maneuvers involving Russell, there was no rancor, no controversy; but it somehow came to pass that Tydings, faced with the rigors of a difficult campaign, decided that he did not want to take on additional time-consuming duties, and Johnson was named chairman of the Senate Preparedness Subcommittee.

The subcommittee produced the first run of national headlines for Johnson as a senator. Its members visited President Truman at the White House and received his blessing. Then they began a study of the nation's industrial mobilization, focusing first on synthetic rubber and tin. A parallel study looked at military manpower needs as they affected agriculture and other segments of the national economy. From mid-1950 until early 1953, with Johnson as chairman, the Preparedness Subcommittee was to issue forty-four separate reports (some foreshadowing 1980s disclosures about spare parts and surplus materials irregularities) and claim savings for the treasury of $5 billion.[33] Those savings did not approach those of the Truman committee, however, and some writers have minimized them in discussing Johnson's Senate accomplishments. In fact, his chairmanship of this subcommittee was an important prelude to his later successes.

Each of the subcommittee's forty-four reports was unanimous. In this small and relatively unimportant arena Johnson began seeking compromise and consensus—a search that would carry over into his later performance in leadership roles. With help from Russell, who became chairman of the Armed Services Committee when Tydings was defeated by Butler in November, Johnson began to exert influence on both sides of the Senate aisle. The original members of the subcommittee, in addition to Johnson, were Democratic senators Estes Kefauver of Tennessee, Virgil Chapman of Kentucky, and Lester Hunt of Wyoming; and Republican senators Styles Bridges of New Hampshire, Leverett Saltonstall of Massachusetts, and Wayne Morse of Oregon. It was a real challenge for any chairman to bring such a group to consensus, and the early months of the war in Korea were not conducive to unanimity among diverse groupings of Republicans and Democrats on matters involving the conduct of the war.

Since most of the subcommittee's reports were critical of some phase of the war effort and, by implication, critical of the Truman administration, the three subcommittee Democrats might have posed a purely partisan problem for consensus making. Fortunately for Johnson, however, the subcommittee Democrats were not inclined to make trouble, partisan or otherwise. Kefauver was, as previously noted, preoccupied with a much publicized investigation of his own. Hunt and Chapman were generally willing to go along with the chairman.

The subcommittee Republicans were not averse to criticizing the president, of course, and their views and personalities posed a much more difficult problem for a chairman in search of compromise. Of the three Republicans only Saltonstall, a forthright Boston blue blood, was by nature usually willing to go along. Morse, already a GOP maverick who would eventually break with his party, had strong views on many subjects and was often disposed not to go along. Styles Bridges was one of a kind, the quintessential wheeler-dealer, opinionated but always ready to talk about quid pro quo and, if arranged, to deliver as agreed. Conservative in most respects (he was an enthusiastic supporter of Sen. Joseph McCarthy's unruly search for Communists in government), he nevertheless had the confidence of many moderates in both parties.

Johnson's association with all three of these Republicans was to be important beyond his search for consensus in the Preparedness Subcommittee. Saltonstall was to become chairman of the Armed Services Committee in the early Eisenhower years. With Millikin and Ohio's senator Robert A. Taft, Bridges was to remain one of the powers among Senate Republicans and a member of the Inner Club. And during most of his career,

Johnson would be dealing with a "Morse problem" of one kind or another.

More important for Johnson than achieving unanimity within his subcommittee was Russell's perception that Johnson was able to achieve it. Beyond baseball, breakfast, and good fellowship, Johnson was demonstrating that, given an opportunity and the necessary resources, he could be relied upon to do a Senate job professionally. As chairman of the new Preparedness Subcommittee, he formally submitted a copy of the subcommittee's first report to Russell, chairman of the parent Armed Services Committee. Russell replied that the report was a good job that "laid the groundwork for a real contribution to the national interest."[34]

With Russell's help, Johnson was making a comeback as a Texas lawmaker. From his first days in Washington, heading the congressional office of Rep. Richard Kleberg, Johnson had established a reputation as a workaholic who drove himself and his staff fourteen hours a day. That reputation had followed him as Texas head of FDR's National Youth Administration and into his early years in the House. Now the Washington slumbers of his final years in the House were over.

In the Senate, Johnson the dynamo was back, and his staff was again working long hours and enduring his acid criticism, leavened by occasional intervals of perceptive understanding and compassion—a combination that would characterize Johnson Senate offices over the years and later his offices as vice president and president.

Other freshman Democrats in the Class of 1948 besides Johnson and Kefauver were making headway in the Senate, notably Kerr of Oklahoma and Anderson of New Mexico, who had already attracted the favorable attention of Russell and other members of the Inner Club. One freshman who had not made headway was Humphrey of Minnesota, who had offended the elders with his loud and brash self-confidence. He had even tried to abolish the largely inconsequential but immensely honorific Subcommittee on Nonessential Federal Expenditures, which was the special province of the revered Sen. Harry F. Byrd, Democratic of Virginia.

Humphrey was unhappy and a bit frustrated. As the popular, liberal mayor of Minneapolis, he had been particularly proud of maintaining a close working relationship with conservative leaders in the community. He was surprised to find the Senate—and even the press—so Southern-oriented, though he quickly came to realize that it was the Senate Southerners who were able to get things done.[35]

Many years later, in the twilight of his eventually distinguished career, Humphrey would recall hearing Russell say to a group of Southern colleagues, in tones meant to be overheard: "Can you imagine the people of Minnesota sending that damn fool down here to represent them?"[36]

As the months went by, however, it became apparent to Johnson that Humphrey was nobody's damn fool. He began inviting Humphrey to his office for an occasional late afternoon drink to lecture him on how the Senate worked. Eventually he included Russell in some of those sessions, and Russell came to appreciate Humphrey's intelligence, though he would always question Humphrey's judgment.

Looking back on those early days, Humphrey would say that Johnson did more than any person in Congress to bring him to a friendly relationship with Senate conservatives.[37]

A president can expect to lose congressional seats in midterm elections, and in 1950, Harry Truman, embattled over controversial domestic programs and enmeshed in an unpopular war, was no exception. For Senate Democrats that off-year election had disastrous results. Democratic leader Scott Lucas of Illinois and Democratic whip Francis J. Myers of Pennsylvania were both retired by the voters. It was the first of two electoral events in the 1950s that were to play important roles in the rise to power of Lyndon Johnson.

Speculation focused immediately on Russell as the likely successor to Lucas. But Russell took the position that he could not properly promote an administration program in the Senate while opposing, as he did, major segments of that program, notably in the field of civil rights.[38] In huddles before Congress reconvened, Democratic members of the Inner Club agreed to make Ernest W. McFarland of Arizona the new Democratic leader.

McFarland had played a key foreign policy role in the days before World War II, but his best Senate days were now behind him. His senior colleague, Carl Hayden, was the important senator from Arizona. It was assumed, however, that major decisions would continue to be made in the Inner Club, and McFarland was thought to be a good man to perform the largely procedural duties of majority leader.

The job of whip would carry even less clout. It had never been a position of real power, and Francis Myers had put no gloss on it. Lyndon Johnson, however, saw it as a mark of distinction for a senator with only two years service and told Russell he would like to have the job. Oklahoma's Bob Kerr, who, like Johnson, was close to Russell, supported the Johnson bid. As they walked together to the caucus called on January 2, 1951, to elect a new Democratic party leadership, Russell gave Johnson the word.

"He didn't know he was going to be assistant leader until we were walking down the hall together going to the caucus," Russell was to recall later, "... and I told him I was going to put him in nomination for assistant leader."[39] With Russell as sponsor the caucus action was unanimous.

Johnson's responsibilities as whip were to keep track of Democratic senators and see that they got to the floor when votes were in prospect. In discharging those responsibilities he found himself relying heavily on the head of pages in the Democratic cloakroom. The cloakroom, behind the Senate chamber and out of the public eye, was where senators relaxed, smoked, chatted, and took phone calls. Strategy discussions were often held there during Senate sessions.

The head page, Robert G. "Bobby" Baker, was to advance rapidly in the Senate hierarchy as Johnson himself advanced. Eventually, after Johnson left the Senate, Baker's moonlighting activities, spurred by his overriding ambition and abetted by Kerr, would send him to jail for tax evasion, conspiracy, and fraud; that sorry comeuppance has since tended to obscure his very real skills.

Growing up in the Senate, Baker had become an eager observer of what made it function. He learned its rules, its history, and its precedents (he even went to law school at night to better his legal understanding). From his vantage point in the cloakroom, he studied the members of the Senate, got to know their habits, their likes and dislikes, often their hopes and dreams; and he remembered it all.[40]

The 1950 congressional elections also retired Millard Tydings, chairman of the Senate Armed Services Committee, and Russell succeeded him as chairman when the Senate reconvened. He reappointed Johnson as chairman of the Preparedness Subcommittee and referred a universal military training bill, which he had introduced, to that subcommittee. Johnson presided at hearings on the bill, which proposed military training or equivalent public service for all young men, and in the ensuing months they worked together to shepherd the bill to passage in the Senate.

The close personal relationship between Russell and Johnson progressed, and they were often seen together during Senate deliberations, talking at the back of the Senate chamber: two tall figures, face-to-face and standing very close together—Johnson, taller of the two, erect, his head cocked and thrust forward; Russell, hands on hips, arms akimbo, with head tossed back and chin held high, staring down through bifocals.

On April 10, 1951, President Truman fired Gen. Douglas MacArthur, the commander of United Nations forces in Korea, for insubordination. The unpopular president's discharge of the World War II hero, in a political climate already overheated by criticism of the "no win" war and by Sen. Joe McCarthy's charges of Communist infiltration in government, provoked an emotional public furor. Forty years later, it is hard to understand how the firing coalesced public attitudes—anti-Truman, anticommunist, and antiwar. One symptom, noted by Johnson biographer Robert Dallek, is that 7.5 million people turned out in the streets of New York to greet the dismissed General MacArthur, almost twice the number that had greeted the victorious General Eisenhower in 1945.

The public outcry included demands for a congressional investigation. In the Senate, Russell's Armed Services Committee voted to conduct an inquiry, and so did the Committee on Foreign Relations. After some wrangling, committee negotiators finally agreed that the two committees would sit together for a MacArthur inquiry with Russell as chairman.

From long personal experience Russell knew MacArthur to be a brilliant man and, as a speaker, something of a spellbinder.[41] Since national security issues were to be discussed, after some partisan squabbling Russell was able to arrange that the joint committee conduct its hearings behind closed doors. That decision was not a popular one at the outset, especially with the press. However, by positioning transcription facilities and security clearance experts in a nearby committee office, Russell made sure that the general's testimony would be available to the press outside the hearing room, in pages of security-cleared transcript, an hour or less after it was given.

Under that format, press and public got a full but dispassionate verbatim report of MacArthur's views on how the Korean War might be won. Then, as Russell called other military and foreign policy leaders to testify, the public got very different verbatim testimony. Witness after witness disputed MacArthur on strategy and upheld the historic principle of civilian control of the military. Many of the top military leaders in Washington had long been disenchanted with MacArthur's arrogance, and their comments were devastating.

Johnson assigned the staff of his Preparedness Subcommittee to Russell for the hearings, and staff members became a night shift, reviewing and summarizing each day's testimony and preparing statements and questions for the day to follow.[42] Russell and Johnson took the lead in close questioning of MacArthur and subsequent witnesses, and their inquiries disclosed that MacArthur had little understanding of the nation's defense and foreign policies beyond the narrow confines of the Korean peninsula. When the hearings ended in late June, they had included forty-two days of testimony, amounting to more than two million words from virtually all of the government's top national security officials, civilian as well as military. Although much of the testimony disputed MacArthur, all shades of opinion were aired.

Weeks before the hearings ended, Russell began to worry about drafting a final report on the general's dismissal in the partisan atmosphere that had characterized many of the hearings. On his desk calendar he scrawled a note that a formal report "can only serve as a textbook for political arguments."[43] At first it appeared that the committee would issue three conflicting reports, one by conservative Republicans siding with MacArthur, one by liberal Democrats berating him, and a third by moderates less aggressively critical.

To head off one possible aftermath of the hearings, Russell finally read a statement into the record stressing that the diverse views expressed in the long hearings should not be interpreted, by friend or especially by foe, as a sign of U.S. weakness or lack of resolve. It was, he said, a "general statement of principles . . . refuting any idea we are disunited."[44] In the end, the joint committee decided not to issue any formal report. During the long days of testimony all shades of conflicting opinion had been aired. Dissenting, a few of the GOP conservatives issued what they called a minority report, but the furor had gradually subsided and the crisis had been defused.

Russell's adroit handling of the MacArthur hearings projected a new picture of Russell for a liberal segment of the press and public and further enhanced his growing national reputation. To many liberals, Russell had been known as a rather evil genius, a sincere but hopelessly misguided believer in states' rights, who led Senate Southerners in frustrating all attempts to pass civil rights legislation. Against that was now contrasted the image of a sensible, if conservative, Senate strategist who was capable of containing and deflating a highly emotional surge of public outrage.

With the approach of the 1952 presidential elections, Russell came under heavy pressures to formally announce as a candidate for the Democratic nomination. The pressures were diverse. Politicians and press throughout the South were urging him to run for a variety of regional reasons, and when he did announce and enter the Florida primary, his motives were widely misunderstood. It was assumed that a man as intelligent as Russell would realize that a candidate with his civil rights record could not be nominated in a Democratic National Convention. Therefore, the further assumption was that Russell's candidacy was aimed at injecting a conservative element into the convention and its platform, an element that might even lead to another Southern walkout.

Russell's objectives, as outlined in private discussions with Johnson and a few others, were quite different.[45] The organized crime investigation that Tennessee Democrat Kefauver had launched, coming at a time when television was becoming more widely accessible, provided the first series of congressional hearings to be a smash hit in the nation's living rooms. The flickering picture of Kefauver, angrily drawing Fifth Amendment pleas from top Mafiosi in major cities, made him a national figure, a new and appealing Mr. Right. When Kefauver announced as a Democratic presidential candidate committed to a liberal platform (angering other Southern Democrats), Russell was pressed by Johnson among others to enter the Florida Democratic primary to present an authentic Southern alternative to the Tennessean.

Russell and Johnson were sure that the nomination of Kefauver or a candidate with similar views would precipitate another walkout of Southern delegations at the convention. Having rejected a third-party candidacy himself in 1948, Russell was determined to avoid another party split that would further distance the South from the mainstream of American politics. For his part, Johnson wanted no Southern walkout that would force him, as a party leader, to choose a side and alienate either Northern or Southern Democrats. With Russell as an avowed candidate, they were reasonably confident that other Southerners would keep out of the presidential race and Southern convention delegations could be held together within the Democratic party. On that basis, Russell entered the Florida presidential primary.

To emphasize that his was not a wholly Southern strategy, Russell campaigned extensively outside the South. He was generally well received, and some of his associates believed that he deluded himself for a while into thinking he had a real chance at the nomination.[46] Russell's sister Ina, who served as hostess for Russell at the convention, shared that view.[47] Johnson, providing enthusiastic support, went to the convention in Chicago and set up a Russell campaign headquarters that featured, as a hostess, movieland's busty Jane Russell, said to be a cousin of Russell's.

Early in June, a little more than a month before the convention was to convene, Russell went to the White House to talk to President Truman about a revolt at a camp for Korean War prisoners on an offshore island called Koje Do.[48] Before Koje Do was mentioned, however, Russell was surprised when Mr. Truman said: "Dick, I do wish you lived in Indiana or Missouri. You would be elected president hands down. We have differed on a great many issues, but we have always understood each other. You are a great Democrat, and I respect you. You have always stood by the party organization."

At that point in the preconvention maneuvering the president had not supported any prospective nominee, and Russell replied diplomatically that they had both managed to stay with the Democratic party, despite their differences. He added that he hoped they could agree in Chicago on a party platform that would keep the party together. Russell did not say more, with the subject of the meeting still to be discussed, and Truman responded that the party was big enough for all of its conflicting elements. The discussion turned to Koje Do.

At the end of the meeting, however, Truman again said he wished he were in a position to help Russell. Russell replied that he would be glad to have the president's backing. He said he believed he could win the nomination and the election with a little more support.

"I would give my right eye to see you president," Truman said, "but you know that the left-wing groups in Chicago, New York, St. Louis, and Kansas City must be kept in the Democratic party if we are to win, and they will not vote for you. We must keep these groups in the party."[49]

Walter F. George, Russell's senior Senate colleague from Georgia, placed Russell's name before the convention delegates assembled in the Chicago stockyards arena. George, whose Senate seat had once been contested by Russell's father, was an orator of the old school. He was quite ready to supply the traditional oratorical flourish for such occasions. He offered the convention "a president who believes in equal opportunity for all, equal educational opportunity, equal economic opportunity, equal political opportunity, a man who is temperamentally fit, a man who is physically fit, a man who is mentally fit for the presidency of the United States, a man who believes in the common brotherhood of man and a man who believes in the common fatherhood of God, the next Chief Executive of the United States, Richard Brevard Russell."[50]

When the votes were counted, Russell received 261 votes from twenty-two state delegations and the Panama Canal Zone. The nomination went to Illinois governor Adlai Stevenson, and at the end, Russell urged his delegates to support the party nominee. Thanks to some skillful jockeying by convention chairman Sam Rayburn, there was no walkout.[51]

Shortly after Stevenson was nominated, a group of party leaders headed by Democratic National Chairman Frank McKinney called on Russell and asked him to run for vice president. He declined, saying that he could not follow any president blindly and stressing that he preferred to stay in the Senate. Russell suggested Alabama senator John J. Sparkman, who had been one of his convention strategists. After a huddle of convention leaders, Sparkman was offered the nomination, accepted, and was nominated the following day.[52]

Recalling the circumstances many years later, Russell contended that he was "trapped" into an all-out campaign for the nomination because he realized, after entering the Florida primary, that he could not honorably withdraw. "I did hold the South together," he said. "I didn't get Tennessee, which went for Kefauver, and eight or ten votes in Alabama which went for him; and Senator Fulbright was a favorite son in Arkansas; but with those exceptions I got practically all the votes in the Southern states."[53]

The convention also produced an incident that was to be a lifelong embarrassment for Russell. It arose from his attempt to develop a position on labor-management relations that would not offend all of organized labor. In his races in Georgia, Russell had always run with labor support, especially from the railroad unions; and in the New Deal days he had voted for the prolabor Wagner Act. In 1948, however, Russell had voted for the Taft-Hartley Act, which was bitterly opposed by the union hierarchy. In his preconvention speeches, Russell had stated that, as president, he would propose a revision of the Taft-Hartley law. He commented that Robert A. Taft himself had proposed a score of amendments to the law only two years after it was first approved.

Russell did not, however, favor outright repeal of that law, and he made it clear that he would retain the law's national emergency provision unless a substitute could be enacted that would protect the national interest during crippling nationwide strikes. The national emergency provision allowed a president to ask a federal court to order strikers back to work and punish their union if they refused. Russell saw it as one of labor's main targets in the drive to repeal Taft-Hartley.

Not until Russell and his advisers arrived in Chicago was it finally decided that Russell would call for a meeting of the best minds in business and labor to draft a new law that would "supplant" Taft-Hartley. It was Lyndon Johnson who suggested that Russell outline his proposal in an interview for which radio time had already been purchased. But an overzealous aide (whom Russell would later suspect was planted in his campaign by supporters of Adlai Stevenson) immediately leaked word to the press that Russell was going to urge "repeal" of the Taft-Hartley law.

Russell awakened the following morning to discover that newspapers all over the nation were quoting informed sources in the Russell campaign saying that he was preparing a statement advocating repeal. Despite his best efforts to set the record straight, Russell's apparent advocacy of outright Taft-Hartley repeal was interpreted by many at the convention and thereafter just as he had anticipated—as an unprincipled, last-minute bid for support in an already lost cause. Russell never forgot it.[54]

Other aspects of the unsuccessful campaign had a lasting effect on Russell. Friends and associates felt that he was deeply hurt by the events leading to his rejection. He had indeed known, rationally, that he could not be nominated. Before campaigning in the North, however, he had not heard political leaders (up to and including the president of the United States) tell him to his face that he was obviously the best-qualified candidate, but that they could not support a Southerner with his views. That knowledge came as a visceral blow. For the first time a prediction by his mother during his early days away from home had been proven wrong: In her letters, his mother had told him to remember that he was Dick Russell, and he could accomplish anything he set out to do.[55] This time he had not been able to do that, and he couldn't believe that it was his fault.

Late in the summer Russell paid a visit to the Johnson ranch, and Lady Bird Johnson sensed a change. Looking back years later on Russell's 1952 defeat, she recalled that, although she had not attended the convention, she had a feeling that it was a "benchmark" in Russell's life. "It was the time when he put his chips in and tried, and not receiving the nomination probably caused him to retreat into the ivory tower," she said.[56]

In the autumn, before the election, Russell had become concerned about his health. Complaining of pain in his left shoulder, a cough, headaches, and occasional stomach distress, he went to Rochester, Minnesota, for a complete physical examination at the Mayo Clinic. In due course, Dr. James C. Cain reported that all tests were within normal limits and that Russell's general health was "excellent."[57] Many examinations were to follow over the years, at many locations, without such a wholly favorable report.

Chapter Three

JOURNEYMAN

1953–1956

D wight Eisenhower was an easy winner in the 1952 elections, and a young Republican named Barry Goldwater won the Arizona Senate seat held by Ernest W. McFarland, who became the second Democratic leader in a row to be defeated in his first test at the home state polls. Not a position of real power at the time, the party leadership was becoming something of a hazard for a senator up for reelection. Nevertheless, Lyndon Johnson, up in 1954 and very much aware of his narrow victory in 1948, wanted the leadership post.

The day after the 1952 election, Johnson spoke in San Antonio at a regional meeting of officials from rural electric cooperatives. Addressing the results of the previous day—the election of Eisenhower and a closely divided Senate—Johnson said the nation had elected a new leader, and the role of Senate Democrats should be to work with him toward solving the nation's problems. He used a Texas analogy: Any jackass can kick down a barn, but it takes a skillful carpenter to build one. He said congressional Democrats should be builders.

Listening to postelection radio commentary in Winder, Russell heard a short account of Johnson's speech, and he liked what he heard. He strongly agreed with the position Johnson had taken. He called Johnson at the ranch and suggested that Johnson be a candidate for Democratic leader at the party caucus in January. Johnson, who was already eyeing the leadership post, began telephoning other Democratic senators, including those just elected for the first time, to ask for their votes. He arranged for a few senators, including Russell, to issue public endorsements of his candidacy.[1]

Word of Johnson's bid for party leadership, with Russell as an early advocate, was bad news for the Senate's Democratic liberals, who began casting about for an opponent. Humphrey, the obvious choice, was clearly too controversial. What was needed was a quieter Northerner or Westerner who could hope to get a majority in the January Democratic caucus. After a number of calls and huddles, the liberals settled on Sen. James E. Murray of Montana, an elderly veteran with good liberal credentials.

Soon after his return to Washington, Johnson called Humphrey to his office to see if he could get Humphrey's support and perhaps assure unanimous backing in the caucus. Humphrey heard Johnson out and then told him he was already pledged to Murray. According to Humphrey's account, Johnson angrily castigated the liberals in general and Humphrey in particular and, one by one, named senators counted for Murray by Humphrey who had already pledged their votes to Johnson. He bluntly refused to talk to Humphrey about assuring better liberal representation on Senate committees.

Nominating Johnson for Democratic leader at the caucus on January 2, 1953, Russell spoke of Johnson's experience as whip and his proven ability in that post. He stressed Johnson's courage and his tolerance and concluded that Johnson "possesses the qualities we need as leader."[2] As Johnson had predicted, only a few of the liberals spoke up for Murray, and eventually it was Humphrey who moved that Johnson be selected by acclamation.

After the caucus, Johnson went to Humphrey's office and said he was now ready to talk about representation on committees. He would discuss it with Humphrey, he said, but he didn't want Humphrey bringing in a lot of his liberal associates. Johnson then agreed to a number of requests made by Humphrey on the liberals' behalf, among them Paul Douglas of Illinois to go to the Finance Committee, Herbert Lehman of New York to the Judiciary Committee, and Humphrey himself to the Foreign Relations Committee. Johnson also pledged that liberals would be better represented on Democratic steering and policy committees.[3]

The caucus victory made Johnson the nominal leader of forty-eight Senate Democrats. There were forty-seven Republicans and Wayne Morse of Oregon, who had declared himself an Independent but said he would vote with the GOP on organizational matters. Vice President Nixon's tie-breaking vote gave Republicans a victory in the organization show-down, and "Mr. Republican," Robert A. Taft, became majority leader. Johnson became minority leader.

Having mollified the liberals, Johnson took steps to consolidate his position as minority leader and make the post amount to something in the Senate power structure. The question of which senators would serve on the most coveted committees had traditionally been decided in party councils (and in the Inner Club) with slavish attention to seniority. Senior senators had first call on vacancies on such top committees as appropriations, armed services, foreign relations, and finance. Former House members and governors then received priority.

Johnson thought it would make better sense if each Democrat was guaranteed a seat on at least one major committee. That would require other Democrats, especially Southerners with towering seniority, to surrender some preference in the pecking order. Johnson went to Russell for help. Russell knew the plan would disadvantage Southerners, but he was well aware that his own Senate fortunes had been helped by early committee advantages.

Russell had arrived in the Senate in January 1933 as a young governor with a reputation as an articulate Southern liberal. At the time, Senate Democratic leader Joseph T. Robinson of Arkansas was having trouble placating a recently arrived, former liberal Southern governor, Huey Long of Louisiana. When Russell requested a seat on the Senate Appropriations Committee and resisted any other assignment, Robinson decided to head off a confrontation and comply. A few months later Russell was named chairman of the Agriculture Appropriations Subcommittee, a post that would make him a continuing power in farm legislation, because the committee chairman, Carter Glass of Virginia, was at war with Ellison D. "Cotton Ed" Smith of South Carolina.

Russell would later recall: "I got on the Appropriations Committee merely because of Huey Long's impact on the leadership, and I got to be chairman, in my first year, of a subcommittee on agriculture, which was a great rarity, on account of a feud between Carter Glass and Ed Smith."[4] He knew that a leg up in committee could help a new senator's career tremendously. He agreed to support Johnson's plan in the Democratic Steering Committee.

Approval of the plan by the steering committee put the skills and talents of every Democrat to good use at once, while new Republican senators waited in line to serve on important committees. Johnson's plan meant that Stuart Symington of Missouri, who had been a secretary of the air force, went immediately to the Armed Services Committee, and Mike Mansfield of Montana began at once what would be distinguished service on the Foreign Relations Committee. The plan also meant that all the freshmen and other junior Democrats were indebted to their newly elected minority leader for enhancing their Senate roles and, consequently, their visibility back home.

Johnson also gave a new look to the Senate Democratic Policy Committee, which had done little but record Democratic senators' votes since its formation in 1947. As chairman, Johnson augmented the committee's staff, assigning George Reedy, a former newsman who had been working for the Preparedness Subcommittee, as staff director and hiring Gerald Siegal, a bright young attorney, as counsel. Working with the new staff, which often sought advice from outside experts, the Policy Committee became a forum where members could discuss and refine positions to be taken by Johnson and the Democrats in the narrowly divided Senate.

While the Democrats were still basically divided, the new leader was able to forge a sort of uneasy unity, working through Humphrey with the liberals and through Russell with the Southerners. On most matters he could present a united front in dealing with Taft and other GOP leaders. It was leadership that his predecessors, Lucas and McFarland, had rarely been able to achieve.

Much has been written about the Johnson "treatment" by writers trying to explain how, in years to come, he was able to compile a legislative record unmatched by any other Senate leader in recent years. Arm twisting and pressure are the tactics that have come to be associated with Johnson's successes; but that is a misreading, or at least a deceptively incomplete reading, of the way he operated. Because he rarely excelled in delivering prepared speeches and often came through poorly on television, it has never been widely understood that Johnson was one of the most persuasive one-on-one talkers of his time. For all his good ol' boy mannerisms, he could charm, cozy up to, and finally convince almost anyone.

This is not to say that Johnson never used pressure tactics. He preferred persuasion, however, and used threats only after he was convinced that an individual could not be less aggressively persuaded. And it should be noted that being persuaded by Johnson could itself be a stressful experience. He was intense and his discourse often coarse. His body language was sometimes body belligerence. He leaned his head and shoulders into a dissenter—in the 1990s vernacular, he was "in your face"—and the aftereffects could be as unsettling as overt threats of committee purgatory or perks withheld.

No one knew this better than Hubert Humphrey. In 1977, after

witnessing and experiencing the "treatment" for nearly twenty years, he
described Johnson as really "a born political lover." It was, Humphrey
said, "really not true" that Johnson was heavy-handed in dealing with his
colleagues. "He was sort of like a cowboy making love. He wasn't one of
those Fifth Avenue, Madison Avenue penthouse lovers. He was from the
ranch . . . he knew how to massage the senators. He knew just which ones
he could push aside . . . which ones he could threaten, and above all he knew
which ones he'd have to spend time with and nourish along. . . ."[5]

In an earlier interview, Humphrey recalled Johnson's instructions:
"'You've got to study every member of this body to know how they're
really going to ultimately act.'" He said Johnson told him a strategist must
consider senators' "'background, family, attitudes, even moods before you
even ask them to vote.'"[6]

To assist in such exhaustive appraisals Johnson kept accumulating
every bit of information he could find about senators in both parties. In
addition to his own efforts in this regard, he relied on his own staff and on
Senate staff members, especially the ever-observant and forever-retentive
Bobby Baker, who was promoted to assistant secretary to the minority by
the new minority leader.

Taft's doctrine for Senate Republicans had held that the duty of an
opposition party was to oppose the initiatives of a Democratic president.
Johnson and Russell, with help from Humphrey in restraining combative
liberals, quickly launched the Democrats on a very different course. As
Johnson had indicated in San Antonio after the election, the strategy was
to avoid outright opposition to the popular new president's proposals and
instead modify them to meet Democratic specifications.

The strategy, which would continue through most of the Eisenhower
presidency, sometimes put Johnson at odds with impatient Democrats
anxious to draw clear party lines. But Senate Republicans were, in fact, as
divided as Senate Democrats; they formed groupings of old-line, Taft
conservatives on the one hand and moderates more closely attuned to
Eisenhower's policies on the other. This was especially true in matters
related to foreign policy initiatives, where conservative Republicans were
anxious to repudiate policies of FDR and Truman, initiatives with which
General Eisenhower had sometimes been associated. Often Johnson was
able to send Democrats riding to the president's assistance to rescue his
proposals from the assaults of GOP conservatives and approve them—
after appropriate modification.

President Eisenhower appreciated the help provided by Johnson and Russell in the Senate, and by Sam Rayburn, Johnson's old mentor, who was steering House Democrats on a similar cooperative course. Frequently the Democratic leaders went to the White House late in the afternoon to have a private drink with the Republican president and discuss legislative strategy.[7]

Johnson's first session as Democratic leader provided no major legislative battles, but he impressed senators in both parties with his ability to resolve minor differences, reach consensus, and move Senate business along. He was particularly effective in helping to secure the passage of a National Defense Education Act, a foot in the door for federal aid to schools.

The Johnsons' close relationship with Russell continued, and he was often in their home, usually invited, Lady Bird would later recall, "on the spur of the moment."[8] As a bachelor he was much sought after, she said, but seldom accepted formal invitations. Russell had made the rounds of the Washington social circuit in his early Senate days, but he now declined most invitations of all sorts, including those honoring diplomats and other dignitaries, making exceptions for individuals he regarded as really important, such as Winston Churchill and Joe DiMaggio.[9]

Lady Bird Johnson learned that Russell, during those early Senate years, had been engaged to be married, and she believed the engagement was broken off because of a disagreement over the young woman's Catholicism. (Pat Collins, a Justice Department attorney, was a friend of Russell's sister Ina. She and Russell would remain lifelong friends after they ended their engagement. Years later Ina would recall that Pat's Catholicism had indeed caused problems. Dick Russell had wanted brother Jeb, at the time a Protestant clergyman, to perform the ceremony; and there was the usual question of whether children of the marriage would be educated as Catholics. Ina thought the engagement had simply dragged on to a point where the right moment for a wedding had passed them by.[10])

At the end of the congressional session in July, a number of senators took the floor to commend Democratic leader Johnson for his first year's work. After reading their words of praise in the *Congressional Record*, Russell, who had not been present for the colloquy, wrote to Johnson, noting that the comments had come from "senators of every shade of thought.

"I knew you would do a good job," said Russell, "but I am frank to say that I did not believe any man could have achieved as much harmony within the Democratic Party and contributed as much to the operations of the Senate as a whole as you have done during the first session of the 83rd Congress."[11]

Replying, Johnson said none of the statements made on the Senate floor "means quite as much as your note, coming from a man whom I regard as one of the great statesmen of the day. Whatever I accomplished during this session could not have been accomplished without your help, your advice and your sympathetic understanding. . . ."[12]

Shortly after Russell returned to Georgia for the recess, he was shaken by the death of his mother. Even after they left the Georgia governor's mansion, where she had been his official hostess, and he went off to Washington, she had remained his first lady. When he was in Washington or traveling around the world, he wrote her regularly. For Russell, she represented all that a woman could achieve. Like his failed bid for his party's presidential nomination a year earlier, her death was something he knew, rationally, had to happen. Viscerally, it was another deep disappointment he found hard to accept.

Johnson hated funerals and, as a rule, would never attend them. He sensed how deeply Russell would be affected by this loss, however, and he was on hand in Winder when Ina Dillard Russell was buried in the small family cemetery behind the Russell home. Russell wrote Johnson that attending the funeral was the act of "a true friend." Replying, Johnson called their friendship "strengthening and inspiring" and said he was "always available to the limit of my powers when you are in need."[13]

Reconvening in January 1954, the Senate was beset by problems at home and abroad, and concern about Communism figured in both. Fighting in Korea had ended the previous year, but the influence of Communist China and its Moscow ally still appeared to be increasing in Asia. In Washington, the influence of Sen. Joseph R. McCarthy and his allegations of Communist penetration in the government had reached a new peak, and his gutter tactics in the anti-Communist campaign had provoked increasing concern.

When the paper-thin Republican majority had organized the Eighty-third Congress, McCarthy had become chairman of the Senate Government Operations Committee and its Permanent Investigations Subcommittee. His hunt for Communists had intensified and attracted widespread public support, but some of its overtones—his injudicious scattergun procedures and a madcap and grossly unsenatorial romp through Europe by McCarthy investigators Roy Cohn and G. David

Schine—had appalled many of the Senate's liberal Democrats. More importantly, an earlier attack on a Methodist bishop by another McCarthy aide had alarmed some of Russell's influential Southerners.

Some moderate Republicans were privately worried about McCarthy, too. In November he had abandoned an uneasy accommodation with President Eisenhower's White House, and some of his soft-on-Communism salvos were now falling on administration targets, especially John Foster Dulles, the secretary of state. After Taft's death the Republican leadership had passed to Sen. William F. Knowland, Republican of California; but Knowland also supported McCarthy's campaign and was not disposed to restrain it.

Johnson was well aware of the increasing concerns about what was now being called "McCarthyism," and he knew the time might come when McCarthy would have to be curbed by Senate action. When McCarthy made one of his snide attacks against Carl Hayden, Arizona's universally respected senior senator and an influential member of the Inner Club, Johnson decided that action would have to be taken. For the moment, however, with McCarthy attacking (and antagonizing) GOP leaders, Johnson was content to take the view that McCarthy was a Republican problem.

Johnson warned Humphrey, however, that he and his liberal associates should keep clear of McCarthy. As Humphrey recalled it, Johnson said: "'He just eats people like you.'"[14]

Fighting in Indochina, previously an item inside the morning paper if included at all, was beginning to make front-page headlines. French forces there were losing in their attempt to reassert control over their prewar colonies. Troops led by Ho Chi Minh, the China-trained leader of North Vietnam, were rolling back French troops, and Paris was asking for U.S. help against the new Communist encroachment.

Secretary of State Dulles, opposed to Communist inroads anywhere in the world, was inclined to help the French. Adm. Arthur W. Radford, chairman of the Joint Chiefs of Staff, agreed and said U.S. naval and air support could be provided to French forces from carriers in the Tonkin Gulf. President Eisenhower was unwilling to act without assurances of congressional support, and on April 4 Johnson and Russell, with other congressional leaders from both parties, met with administration representatives to discuss the situation.

Russell viewed the administration's financial aid to the French effort in Vietnam as money "down a rathole," and at the meeting, both Russell and Johnson opposed going unilaterally to the aid of the French.[15] Russell's notes on the meeting suggest he felt the United States could become involved in "another Korea," eventually lose if it acted alone, and "dissipate men and assets." He apparently asked, pointedly, whether British air units would be involved, in view of British economic interests in the area.[16]

At an unannounced meeting of the Democratic Policy Committee, Johnson stated that the president had asked him for an assessment of Democratic reaction if U.S. troops were sent to help the French. Walter George, not a member of the Policy Committee but the highly respected chairman of the Foreign Relations Committee, had been primed by Johnson and gave a devil's advocate rationale for committing U.S. troops. In the words of one attendee, "the meeting almost literally exploded" with violent objections to the use of U.S. forces of any kind, and Johnson advised the president that any such action would incur angry reaction from Senate Democrats.[17]

On May 5, another long White House meeting was held on the situation in Vietnam. French forces were now surrounded at Dienbienphu, and congressional leaders were urgently asked to support a U.S. carrier air strike to assist them. Russell and Johnson again opposed intervention, and Russell's notes on the meeting end with this scrawled comment: "If B [Britain] not willing to fight . . . Indochina . . . I am not willing to commit U.S. forces . . . Malaya and Burma."[18]

Planning for a carrier strike, already underway, was scrubbed. The following night, at a Jefferson–Jackson Day Dinner, Johnson asked applauding Democrats rhetorically: "What is American policy in Indochina?" He attacked Secretary of State Dulles, who had walked out on a Geneva conference a week earlier in opposition to the conference formula for partitioning Indochina. The French were overrun at Dienbienphu the following day, concluding a series of events that Russell and Johnson would have many occasions to look back on in years ahead.[19]

Ten days after the fall of Dienbienphu, Indochina was pushed off the front pages when the Supreme Court handed down its historic ruling that segregated schools were unconstitutional. The decision in *Brown v. Board of Education* struck at a keystone of the Southern way of living, and Russell quickly joined the chorus of Southern spokesmen who bitterly criticized it.

The ruling was no surprise, in the sense that a Supreme Court decision had been expected in the case involving schools in Topeka, Kansas. The surprise was that Earl Warren, the former California governor appointed to head the high court by President Eisenhower only seven months previously, had managed to secure agreement of all his colleagues and had spoken for the Court in a unanimous decision.

Johnson accepted the Court's action as a fait accompli and said he hoped the South, in time, could accommodate it.[20] Russell, however, felt that Warren had drawn the Court into overstepping its powers and invading a realm reserved to Congress by the Constitution. Sharply differing with the ruling, he also took a dim view of the judicial capacity of the new chief justice. It was an opinion Russell would find hard to restrain when they had occasion to work together ten years later.

Russell's reaction to the Court decision went beyond its constitutional implications. He could foresee its consequences throughout the South. Unlike some of his Southern colleagues, Russell had no illusions about the adverse economic effects of the historic racial patterns in the Southern states. He knew (and would eventually say publicly) that slavery had hurt the South by tying the economies of Southern states to an outmoded, serf-reliant agriculture while the rest of the country was enjoying the fruits of mechanization and industrialization. He thought the South was still feeling the aftermath of the Civil War and often commented that the South, having lost that war, was much more willing to forget it than was the North, which had won.

He believed Negroes (never "niggers") should have equal economic opportunity. But he had resisted civil rights bills because they appeared to open the way to an integrated social order in the United States, which he believed would lead to a general national decline. His resistance had been successful up to now, but the unanimous ruling on schools made it clear that the courts would now take a hand in shaping that social order.

It was equally clear that the Senate, his own battleground, was changing, too. The 1947 report of the President's Civil Rights Commission and Truman's subsequent message had given civil rights activists a whole new constituency. His own Southern bloc was shrinking. Many senators from states outside the South were now very serious about the issue, and it was getting harder and harder to find senators who would give lip service to civil rights legislation and then vote to block it.

The downfall of Joseph R. McCarthy had been foreshadowed in February when the senator, his temper out of control in a hearing at which he was presiding, berated Brig. Gen. Ralph W. Zwicker, commandant of the Army Training Center at Camp Kilmer, New Jersey. McCarthy complained that Zwicker had failed to block the promotion of a dentist who, McCarthy said, was a member of the Communist party.

The browbeating of Zwicker, a much-decorated veteran of the World War II Battle of the Bulge, angered the secretary of the army, Robert T. Stevens. But McCarthy ran roughshod over the secretary's complaints when they met at a private luncheon with GOP subcommittee members that was designed to produce a compromise, and the meeting was immediately immortalized as the "Chicken Lunch." President Eisenhower took a hand in the matter at that point and came mildly to the support of Zwicker and Stevens. McCarthy then further angered the White House by renewing his attack on Zwicker in a strongly worded statement.

Early in March, a usually mild-mannered New Englander from Vermont, Republican senator Ralph Flanders, ridiculed McCarthy's anti-Communist campaign in a speech on the Senate floor; and the following evening the distinguished television commentator Edward R. Murrow aired an attack on McCarthy, using film clips of McCarthy's witness bashing and vulgarity, on his popular program, "See It Now." Reaction to these events showed a swell of public opinion against McCarthy.

The roof fell in on McCarthy a few days later when the army released a chronology of repeated efforts by McCarthy, counsel Roy Cohn, and other subcommittee aides to secure favorable treatment for David Schine, Cohn's former sidekick, who had been drafted into the army in November. Beginning before Schine's induction, the chronology listed unsuccessful efforts to secure a commission for Schine, efforts to get him preferred assignments, and pressure to get him passes and other special treatment.[21]

The question of who in the Senate would look into the army chronology was resolved when McCarthy agreed to step down as chairman—and as a member—of the Investigations Subcommittee. McCarthy, however, was given the right to cross-examine witnesses at hearings, and so was the army. In late April the subcommittee, temporarily chaired by Sen. Karl Mundt, Republican of South Dakota, began the televised, much publicized Army-McCarthy hearings.

For fifty-six days, millions of Americans watched as the subcommittee pursued, in detail, an army bill of particulars addressing the Cohn-Schine chronology and a McCarthy bill of particulars designed to show that the army tried to blackmail the subcommittee into muting its criticism. McCarthy, despite his nonmember status, dominated the proceedings with points of order, abusive questions, and other antics he had customarily employed. Finally, Flanders offered a resolution to strip McCarthy of his chairmanships, but neither Knowland nor Johnson was disposed to act quickly on the Flanders resolution.

McCarthy's behavior had been especially distasteful to senators such as Russell and some of the other senior Southerners for whom decorum was essential to successful Senate operations. But it was clear to Russell and Johnson that McCarthy's behavior must not become a partisan issue for Senate Democrats.

Now well into his second year as Democratic leader, Johnson was comfortable in his new role. Using Russell and Humphrey as his lieutenants he was able to exert influence in both parties. Russell, as a senior member of the Inner Club, dealt easily with Styles Bridges, Gene Millikin, and the other senior Republicans. As Humphrey saw it: "Dick Russell would outmaneuver the Republicans five times a day, but he was always getting them when he needed them."[22]

Russell sometimes dealt with Republican leaders in Johnson's behalf, but he did not solicit the votes of individual Republicans or Democrats. As a venerated member of the Senate, that was not his style. Democratic senator Russell B. Long of Louisiana, who would later serve as party whip, recalled that on difficult questions Russell was always asked how he was going to vote. When he had decided, he responded candidly and explained his decision, sometimes adding that his rationale would not be effective for the constituents of the senator who had inquired.[23] Of course, Johnson and his party aides made good use of Russell's intentions on any issue, once he had made them known.

Johnson had dealt circumspectly with Taft, the almost legendary Republican stalwart, and he had an easier time after Taft's death with Knowland as GOP leader. Humphrey said, "Knowland was no match for him at all. . . . I mean, [Johnson] was clever, fast and furious when he needed to be, and kind and placid when he needed to be. There is no comparison. They [were] not in the same league."[24]

Humphrey recalled that Johnson would call him on the phone when preparing for a vote: "I expect you to get the following senators. . . . Now go after them . . . they're your kind of guys and they're all wobbly . . . and don't give me any of that 'I don't know' stuff. . . . The most important thing around here is to know how to count. If you don't know how to count, you can't be a leader."[25]

Johnson's own vote-getting tactics were often complex and sometimes reminiscent of supermarket tie-in sales. He might get a commitment from Senator X to vote "aye" if Senator Y would vote that way. He would get Senator Y's vote by saying that X was voting "aye" and then feel free to urge others to vote with X and Y.

When Lyndon Johnson spoke in the Senate just before the vote was taken on the motion to censure Joe McCarthy, it was his first public statement favoring the disciplinary action. In view of McCarthy's sustained attack on Truman and his associates, Johnson was still being scrupulously careful to avoid any appearance that the censure move was a partisan Democratic reprisal, and he was careful to say that senators must vote their own convictions on the issue.

However, informal minutes, now available, reveal that Johnson's energized Democratic Policy Committee had held at least four meetings before the censure on just how to proceed against McCarthy, calling in other interested Democratic senators to solicit their views. The course agreed upon was developed by Johnson and strongly endorsed by Russell. It led inexorably to the vote of condemnation.

Ralph Flanders had quickly discovered that his proposal to strip McCarthy of his chairmanships would not fly. Other Republican committee chairmen were wary of any such precedent for disciplining chairmen, and so were the Southerners, many of whom would again be chairmen when and if the Democrats resumed control of the Senate. After checking the precedents, Flanders offered instead a resolution to censure McCarthy for his conduct.

When McCarthy supporters noted that Flanders's short censure resolution cited no specifics, Flanders produced a bill of particulars citing thirty-three instances of misconduct. Arkansas's Democratic senator J. William Fulbright, once labeled "half-bright" by McCarthy, added six others, and Sen. Wayne Morse chipped in with seven.

Johnson had received a letter marked "personal" from Jim Rowe, his old friend from New Deal days, about McCarthy and the Flanders resolution. Rowe, then a prominent Washington attorney, said that if Johnson had other ambitions (he did not specify presidential ambitions) a vote against the Flanders resolution would "destroy the possibility of achieving those ambitions for a long period." Johnson would be a "sectional" majority leader, Rowe said. "You would be Dick Russell all over again."[26]

Preparing for the McCarthy showdown, Johnson had consulted privately with Sen. John L. McClellan, Fulbright's Arkansas colleague. McClellan, as top-ranking Democrat on the Investigations Subcommittee, had been an eyewitness to much of McCarthy's abusive behavior. McCarthy had been careful to avoid any slur against McClellan, who had not publicly criticized McCarthy's conduct. However, McClellan told Johnson in confidence that he thought there should be disciplinary action and that it should be taken as the result of a committee report, "like an indictment."[27]

That was exactly what Johnson wanted to hear—it was the course of action he had been planning—but he did not want it to be a Democratic initiative. He was able to persuade Knowland, as Republican leader, to propose creation of an evenly divided six-member committee to consider the Flanders resolution and report to the Senate.

On July 29, 1954, the day before Flanders formally offered his censure motion and renewed his attack on McCarthy, Johnson called a meeting of the Democratic Policy Committee to which he invited a number of other senators, including Fulbright and several Democratic liberals. He said Knowland planned to call up the Flanders resolution for Senate consideration and asked whether Democrats should take a party stand. In a long discussion, Fulbright said he just wanted to see action taken. Another invited guest, Sen. Henry M. (Scoop) Jackson of Washington, who had been a McCarthy target as a member of McCarthy's subcommittee, cautioned against any action that would be considered partisan. Russell stressed that Democratic Policy Committee action would just cause Republicans to "draw closer to McCarthy." Several others agreed, and there was no dissent. The committee decided to take no formal party stand on the assumption that such an action would rally Republicans around McCarthy.

Four days later Johnson again summoned the Policy Committee. Again guests were invited, but not as many attended. McClellan, absent at the previous session, was on hand, but Fulbright was not. At the outset, Johnson noted that Knowland had now proposed creation of a six-member committee. McClellan said he was quite ready to vote on the Flanders censure resolution, but he suggested that "a man should have an opportunity to appear before a committee before censure is considered," and he added that McCarthy's popularity, approaching a low ebb, could be restored by pressing for an immediate censure vote. In the ensuing discussion, Russell said, "The one sure way to get a vote of censure is to get a report upon which you can predicate it."[28] Again there was general agreement, and the session lasted less than an hour.

Many of McCarthy's critics in and out of Congress—including Fulbright—bitterly attacked the creation of a special committee. They saw the committee concept as a graveyard where the censure resolution could be interred, as had many other proposals that threatened to create a major controversy. But after three days of debate, the Flanders resolution was referred to a new committee by a vote of 75 to 12. Vice President Richard

Nixon would formally name the members, but the two party leaders would select them.

After conferring with Johnson, Knowland selected Arthur V. Watkins of Utah, a former judge, as chairman, to serve with Frank Carlson of Kansas and Francis Case of South Dakota. On August 5 Johnson summoned the Policy Committee again to talk about the Democratic members. He said he had been unable to engineer a bipartisan arrangement that would have placed Russell's colleague, Walter George, and Colorado Republican Gene Millikin on the panel. That would have lent enormous prestige to the proceedings. (LBJ did not tell the committee that Russell had also declined, apparently believing, with George, that McCarthyites were still strong and vocal in conservative Georgia.)[29] Johnson said he proposed to name Ed Johnson of Colorado, John Stennis of Mississippi, and Sam Ervin of North Carolina as the committee Democrats. All were highly respected, and both Stennis and Ervin were former judges. There was a brief discussion about whether McCarthy, a Roman Catholic, might complain that there were no Catholic committee members. Johnson said he had asked Mike Mansfield, John F. Kennedy, and John O. Pastore, all of whom were Catholics, and none was willing to serve. A statement announcing Johnson's recommendation of his three members, as proposed, was approved by the committee, and Vice President Nixon announced the committee membership that afternoon.

The new committee began its hearings late in August with testimony from McCarthy himself. Ground rules allowed McCarthy or his counsel, the distinguished criminal lawyer Edward Bennett Williams—but not both—to speak on any issue. Like the Army-McCarthy sessions, the censure hearings were held in the marble-pillared caucus room, but no television was permitted.

Chairman Watkins ran a tight ship. At one point early in the proceedings, Williams questioned the impartiality of Democratic committee member Ed Johnson and produced a clipping that quoted Johnson as saying there wasn't a Democrat in the Senate who didn't loathe McCarthy. Ed Johnson calmly replied that he was sure he could act without prejudice, and the GOP members dismissed the matter as immaterial. McCarthy tried to interrupt, but Watkins quickly reminded him that Williams had already spoken on the matter. McCarthy tried to interrupt again, and Watkins coldly ruled him out of order and declared there would be no further interruptions.

With its authority firmly established, the committee took testimony for two weeks. The listed charges against McCarthy's conduct had been lumped into five general categories, and in its voluminous final report the committee recommended that McCarthy be censured on two of them: abuse of General Zwicker and contempt of a Senate committee.

The Senate began debate on November 8, and the following day Johnson called his Policy Committee together again for a discussion of how the Senate sessions should proceed—the hours, use of Saturday sessions, and the like. Before the final vote on December 2, the count based on abuse of General Zwicker was dropped (some Democrats were prepared to vote against it), and a new count was added based on McCarthy's comment during the censure debate that the Watkins Committee had been a "handmaiden" of the Communist party.

The final Senate vote was 67 to 22, and all the Democrats present— forty-four of them—voted to "condemn" McCarthy's conduct. Two absent Democrats were recorded for censure by pairing—a procedure in which their uncast votes were offset by the votes of absent Republicans. Sen. John F. Kennedy of Massachusetts, hospitalized with his recurrent back problem, was not recorded. No Democrat supported McCarthy. It was a Johnson tour de force. Humphrey later called it "one of [Johnson's] greatest strategic victories."[30]

Despite President Eisenhower's personal popularity, Democrats regained control of the Senate in the 1954 congressional elections, and, when Congress convened in January, Lyndon Johnson became majority leader. He had no doubts about how to proceed. It would be more of the same. The Democrats' margin over the Republicans was razor thin, and Eisenhower's popularity was still high. Johnson saw no reason to abandon the strategy of cooperating with the Republican president and modifying his legislative proposals to suit Democratic tastes.

Other factors supported Johnson's strategy. With a moderate Republican president submitting legislation, fewer proposals provoked the wrath of the Southern Democrats. As differences among Democrats became less frequent, it became obvious that, except for civil rights, the basis for the old coalition of Republicans and Southern Democrats was eroding. Those two groups seldom had occasion to join forces as they had done in the past to defeat liberal initiatives of Roosevelt and Truman. With the Democrats more frequently united, division in the GOP between Taft conservatives and Eisenhower moderates became more apparent.

As majority leader, Johnson, with his Policy Committee, now had the key role in deciding what matters the Senate would consider. The Policy Committee, with Russell as its frequent emissary to senior Republicans, had largely taken over the functions of the Inner Club, since many of the powerful members of the two were the same. Johnson could usually do as he liked with Republican leader Bill Knowland, who occasionally surrendered his leadership role to oppose White House initiatives.

Under these conditions, Johnson was able to function as the Senate's coach, captain, quarterback, and chief cheerleader. First to arrive at the Capitol in the morning and last to leave at night, he spent his days talking, face-to-face and on the telephone, with senators—requesting, persuading, and threatening when he deemed it necessary. On the floor, he was the man in charge—arranging for an appropriate senator to offer a key amendment (or offering it himself for that senator); delaying if necessary or forcing an end to debate; demanding a quorum call, then a vote; and finally, using signals he had devised to guide the clerk, controlling the pace of the roll call. A circular motion with the forefinger meant speed it up; palm down meant slow it down to allow for the arrival of absentees.

He often secured quick action by asking for approval of procedures by unanimous consent, which he could usually obtain during routine, sparsely attended Senate sessions. He had a stable of senators who were ready to talk at any time on their favorite subjects, and when delay was necessary, he would arrange for one of them to take over. One of his standard tactics for shutting off lengthy debate was to negotiate with participants on how much more time would be needed and then to nail down a time limit by unanimous consent.

Johnson's tactics for speeding Senate action brought both praise and criticism. Under his leadership the Senate was undeniably productive. Critics in and out of the Senate complained, however, that constructive debate, for which the Senate had been famous over the years, had all but disappeared.

Russell was literally behind Johnson as Democratic leader. By custom, Johnson occupied the front row seat on the center aisle, to the presiding officer's right in the Senate chamber. He arranged for Dick Russell to occupy the second row seat directly behind him. From that vantage point Russell, recognized as the premier expert on Senate rules, was able to provide quiet advice on procedure as well as policy.

At the beginning of the new session, Johnson, with Russell's help on the Democratic Steering Committee, had again followed the rule of assuring each Democrat at least one important committee assignment without regard to seniority. Once again, each newly elected Democrat began life in the Senate indebted to the party leader.

Riding herd on all operations in the chamber, Johnson was able to upset an old rule of thumb: that the first year of a Senate session, with most bills still pending in committees, would not be very productive. By midsummer of 1955, the Senate had passed its version of President Eisenhower's highway construction bill, an extension of the reciprocal trade act, foreign aid appropriations higher than the president had requested, and, as centerpiece, a bill raising the federal minimum wage to one dollar an hour.

Passage of the minimum wage bill late one afternoon after a short quorum call and by voice vote (without a formal roll call) caught Democratic senator Spessard Holland of Florida, a principal opponent of the bill, at ease in the Senate dining room. When Holland, arriving on the floor too late, protested angrily, Johnson replied: "If you fellows aren't on the job around here, I've got legislation to pass."[31]

One of the year's lesser accomplishments, the 1955 Housing Act, demonstrated Johnson's mastery of the Senate and its subtleties. The housing bill, as sent to Congress by President Eisenhower, included a number of features, notably federal support for home mortgages, which had widespread appeal. It also included authorization for a small number of federally supported public housing units. Public housing was one of those issues that provoked automatic opposition from Senate conservatives, especially Southern Democrats. The president's bill had been processed by a friendly Banking and Currency Committee, which upped his proposed 35,000 public housing units to an authorized 750,000 units in approving the measure.

When the bill reached the Senate floor, Sen. Homer Capehart, former phonograph maker and top banking committee Republican, immediately offered an amendment cutting the 750,000 units back to 35,000, confident that Johnson could not orchestrate harmony among his discordant Democrats on this divisive issue. But Johnson, with help from Russell and the Policy Committee, quietly developed a plan.

Only as the roll was being called on the Capehart amendment did it become clear that Russell's Southerners had been persuaded to vote against the amendment on grounds that it still authorized public housing—35,000 units. Then, when the bill itself came up for approval, the conservative Southerners voted against it because it included the big public housing provision. On that final vote, however, their "nay" votes were swallowed up in the heavy vote favoring the home mortgage provisions and the bill's other popular features.

Southerners were able to explain to their constituents that they had voted consistently against public housing. In the subsequent conference to reconcile Senate and House versions of the bill, the public housing total was reduced to 135,000 units, but it all added up to another Johnson triumph.

The frantic pace took a heavy toll on Johnson. He was worn down by early summer and looked it. At a luncheon of the Texas congressional delegation late in June, Speaker Rayburn chewed Johnson out, as only Rayburn could, about the hours Johnson was keeping and bluntly told his younger friend to ease up a bit.[32]

On the first Saturday in July, after spending several hours at the Capitol, Johnson boarded his limousine (a leadership prerogative) for a drive into the Virginia hunt country, where he was to spend a restful weekend. During the drive he began to feel stomach pains and, on arrival, told his hostess he would lie down for a while. Fortunately, Sen. Clinton Anderson of New Mexico, another guest, heard Johnson complain of a heaviness in his arms and legs, and pain, now in his chest. Anderson, from personal experience, was sure Johnson was having a heart attack and insisted that a doctor be called at once.

Anderson's diagnosis confirmed, Johnson was taken by ambulance to the Bethesda Naval Hospital. There his problem was further diagnosed as a moderately severe coronary occlusion. Newspapers across the nation, which had been praising Johnson's Senate leadership—a few casting him as a possible presidential candidate—now reported his serious condition. The president and political leaders in both parties expressed concern.

After the first critical hours, however, Johnson's treatment went smoothly. Five days after the heart attack, Russell and all the members of the Democratic Policy Committee signed a "Dear Lyndon" get-well letter voicing "a common prayer that you will soon recover and be able to return to your post."[33] A week later President Eisenhower visited Johnson in the hospital and subsequently arranged that he get a foreign policy briefing from Vice President Nixon. Clearly Johnson was making good progress. Not so the U.S. Senate, which limped, without Johnson, to a belated adjournment early in August.

Convalescence at the ranch in Texas was not easy for Johnson. Restless, frustrated by being unable to fend for himself, he had bouts of depression and occasionally wondered whether he should return to the political arena, where, it sometimes seemed to him, his best efforts were unappreciated. He believed that a life was divided into three phases: preparing for it, living it, and then enjoying it.[34] After the heart attack, it now appeared that he would never reach phase three.

It was the irascible Rep. Carl Vinson of Georgia who would comment, after the Johnsons left the White House, that Lyndon's best decision ever had been to marry Claudia Alta Taylor after a whirlwind courtship in 1934.[35] She had long since accommodated herself to his lifestyle, his personal demands, his unannounced guests, and had become inured to his volatile temperament and changing moods. Slowly, constantly buoyed by Lady Bird's patience and understanding, Johnson began to recover his strength and self-confidence.

In September, as he continued to improve, he got the news that President Eisenhower had suffered a heart attack. Johnson was concerned and repeatedly sought information on Eisenhower's condition from White House aides. He also did some thinking about his own White House prospects, with the president's future now uncertain.

In the fall Johnson's doctors approved his making one political speech. He selected a small Texas town, Lake Whitney, for his return to the political wars; and, with Johnson up for reelection the following year, Democrats poured in from all over the state. Johnson, however, devoted a large part of a rip-roaring speech to the national political scene, stressing party loyalty, praising the record of the congressional session just concluded, and outlining his own thirteen-point legislative program for the session ahead.

Russell had been traveling in Europe, but he wrote Johnson early in November that he was "delighted to know that you are experiencing a complete recovery."[36] Johnson—a compulsive gift giver—did not forget his friend's birthday, and Russell, responding with a thank-you as Johnson was preparing for a December visit to Winder, said he was glad to hear that Johnson had "fully regained all of your old strength, pep and vigor."[37]

Johnson was vigorously back in harness when Congress convened in January 1956. Circumstances suggested that it would be a difficult Senate session for the Democratic leader. Three Democratic senators were openly angling for their party's presidential nomination, and Johnson himself had given it much thought. Estes Kefauver's bid was the most publicized, but Stuart Symington and Bob Kerr were also actively campaigning, and, unlike Kefauver, both were important Johnson allies.

It was now clear that President Eisenhower would again be the Republican candidate. Russell spoke highly of Johnson's abilities but said he did not expect Johnson to run. Shelving presidential politics for the time being, Johnson went back to building a legislative record that would include passage of a set of amendments to the Social Security Act, which, in retrospect, ranks among his top Senate achievements.

In showdowns such as the vote on the Capehart amendment, it was clear that Russell now had his Southerners jumping through hoops to add to Johnson's string of successes and enhance the leader's reputation. At the time—and since—critics have concluded that Johnson was callously exploiting his friendship with Russell. Only a few observers close to the events discerned that Russell had an agenda of his own in building the image of the confident Texan who could both lead and compromise.

Whether or not he ever really believed that he could be elected president himself, Russell had always hoped for a happy day when some Democrat with a Southern heritage would win the White House. Then, he believed, Southern states—civil rights controversies notwithstanding— could be returned to the mainstream of American economic and political activity, and those troublesome controversies might be more easily and gradually resolved. Russell believed his friend Johnson might prove to be the Democrat who could play that role, but 1956 did not appear to be time.

The 1956 congressional session was a particularly trying time for the Senate Southerners. In many Southern communities the 1954 Supreme Court desegregation decision was being judicially administered—Southerners complained that it was being "enforced"—for state and local governments. Lower federal courts were ordering school districts to end segregation in their schools. Protests from local officials and other constituents poured into the offices of Southern lawmakers.

Russell called a meeting of the Senate's Southern caucus, which set up a subcommittee to draft a statement reflecting the angry concerns of the Southern states. Two drafts were produced, and Russell took a hand in writing the final version of what became known as the Southern Manifesto, for signature by members of the Senate from the states of the failed Confederacy. In the final paragraphs, written by Russell, the manifesto pledged signers to use "all lawful means" to reverse the *Brown* decision, which, it said, was "contrary to the Constitution." The manifesto also appealed to all Southerners "not to be provoked by the agitators and troublemakers invading our states, and to scrupulously refrain from disorder and lawless acts."

Significantly, Russell and Johnson agreed that Johnson should not sign the manifesto, although almost all of the Southerners did so. (Candidate Kefauver and his Tennessee colleague, Albert Gore, did not sign, but Bill

Fulbright, who had sometimes parted company with his more conservative Southern colleagues, did.) Russell and Johnson reasoned that, as leader of all the Democrats, Johnson should not sign.[38] Both realized that, by not signing, Johnson would strengthen his position as a Westerner rather than a senator from the Old South, a stance that would be essential if and when he ran for national office.

Russell kept his idea of Johnson as a possible president pretty much to himself. Some of his Southern colleagues were aware of it, however, and on at least one occasion during this period he alluded to it. Russell and Johnson were both members of a congressional delegation to a meeting of NATO parliamentarians in Paris. The occasional NATO meetings provided a forum in which members of the NATO parliaments could discuss problems of the alliance. As Senate majority leader, Johnson was a major participant at this meeting.

After the final session at the Intercontinental Hotel, Russell quietly exchanged favorable comments on Johnson's performance with staffer George Reedy. While their views differed on many subjects, Reedy had remained close to Russell from the time of his assignment as an aide during the MacArthur hearings. Both Reedy and Russell thought Johnson had represented the United States well in the international gathering. Their exchange ended with Russell saying: "George, we'll make this man president yet!"[39]

One issue on which the Johnson-Russell axis did not support President Eisenhower was farm policy. Throughout the Eisenhower presidency (albeit with mixed results), both Russell and Johnson would oppose initiatives advanced by the president and his agriculture secretary, Ezra Taft Benson, on the grounds that their policies shortchanged the farmer and undervalued the farmer's role as an important producer in the American economy.

Both Russell and Johnson felt they had credentials that entitled them to speak for the farmer. In the midst of the Depression, with Johnson at the helm, Congressman Kleberg's office had moved quickly to help Texas farmers take advantage of the assistance offered by newly created New Deal farm agencies. As a freshman congressman, Johnson's major accomplishment had been to get electric power to the farms in his district by promoting the construction of a power dam and by securing President Roosevelt's help in authorizing farm power lines provided by the Rural Electrification Administration (REA).

As chairman of the Appropriations Subcommittee on Agriculture almost from the start of his Senate service, Russell had long been an important player in farm legislation. He had served for a while on the Agriculture Committee and was viewed as a leader of the farm bloc. He had developed an interest in agricultural research as well as farm prices, and had obtained funds to finance experiments in the uses of various Georgia crops, including peanuts, and for an innovative process for removing gums from the pulp of the Georgia pine to make it suitable for paper production.

Farm issues tended to cut across party lines, and Johnson was generally able to muster substantial Democratic support for Russell's efforts to enact fixed, high support prices for basic farm commodities (including cotton, of course)—support prices set at 90 percent of parity, the commodity-by-commodity standard computed to give farmers a fair, proportional share of the national income. Russell's efforts ran counter to Benson-Eisenhower initiatives, which generally involved flexible price supports to lower the cost of supporting basic crops and to reduce stockpiles of government-financed surpluses.

Events and Texas politics were backing Johnson, not so quietly, into the 1956 presidential race. By time-honored tradition, the state's national politicians—members of the Senate and House—had kept out of home-state politicking, which was the province of the governor. In 1952, however, Democratic governor Allan Shivers had led a march of Texas Democrats in support of Republican candidate Eisenhower, thereby incurring the wrath of party loyalists, including Speaker Rayburn. In 1956, Rayburn, without Johnson's concurrence, publicly endorsed Johnson as Texas's favorite-son candidate for the Democratic nomination and as head of the state's convention delegation. In the bitter campaign that ensued, the "Shivercats," painted as corrupt party-wreckers by Rayburn-Johnson loyalists, lost in the precincts by a margin of three to one.[40]

No one can say just when Lyndon Johnson began to think of himself as a possible, viable presidential candidate. He had enthusiastically supported Russell's bid for the nomination in 1952, and he surely knew from many talks thereafter that both Russell and Rayburn hoped he would be a candidate someday. Later, Russell would say that Johnson himself never revealed any presidential aspirations until the mid-1950s.[41]

Johnson's favorite-son effort in 1956 received a great deal of press. Although it was initially aimed at controlling the Texas convention delegation and preventing another bolt led by Shivers, there is some evidence that, like many others who knew they had no real chance (including Russell in 1952), Johnson caught the presidential virus for a day or two and thought he might inherit the nomination if Adlai Stevenson's drive for a second chance at the presidency failed and the convention became deadlocked. Several senators, including Russell, had made preconvention statements suggesting Johnson as a compromise candidate if that should occur.[42]

Russell thought Eisenhower would be reelected; but after Johnson became a favorite son, he called Johnson the Democrats' "best hope" and said before the national convention that Johnson was the one Democrat who might win.[43] After his 1952 disappointment, Russell did not plan to attend the convention, and he headed for Winder when Congress adjourned. He was recalled to Washington by President Eisenhower, however, on the day before the convention was to open, for an important White House foreign policy session. A plane was sent to Chicago, again the convention city, to bring Rayburn, Johnson, and other Democratic leaders back to the capital to attend the session.

After the White House meeting, Johnson urged Russell to return to Chicago with him. He said he thought there might be a happy chance he could make a serious try for the nomination. Overriding Russell's strong objections, he persuaded Russell to change his plans.

In assessing Johnson's chances for the nomination, attorney James Rowe, who had joined the Policy Committee staff after Johnson's heart attack, had drafted a memo warning that Johnson should not do what Dick Russell had done. Rowe argued that Russell, by making his unsuccessful bid as the candidate of the South in 1952, had sacrificed his influence as a national leader and had become a parochial "embittered Southerner." Discussing convention strategy, Johnson shocked Rowe by showing the memo to Russell, who read it and, according to Johnson, agreed with Rowe's advice.

Kefauver had dropped out and the other senators' campaigns had faded by the time the convention began, and the choice appeared to have narrowed down to a contest between Adlai Stevenson and Averell Harriman, who was strongly supported by former President Truman. Both Stevenson and Harriman visited Johnson in his hotel suite to seek the support of the Texas delegation. For a few hours early in the convention week, it appeared that the convention might indeed become deadlocked. "Love That Lyndon" signs and buttons blossomed in hotel lobbies and on the convention floor.

Jim Rowe told Johnson at one point that he could play a pivotal convention role by swinging the Texas delegation to Stevenson. But Johnson vacillated, unwilling to release his Texas delegates, and Stevenson forces took command by securing the necessary support from Michigan and other Northern states. The Johnson boomlet came to nothing, and Stevenson was nominated on the first ballot.[44]

When it was clear that Stevenson had the nomination in hand, Russell urged Johnson to seek the vice presidential nomination. Rowe was dispatched to tell Stevenson that Johnson was available, but within the hour Rowe was sent again to say that Johnson had changed his mind. When Stevenson threw the vice presidential choice open to the convention, John F. Kennedy of Massachusetts, lightly regarded in Washington as something of a playboy, showed surprising strength. By narrowly losing to Kefauver, who had a residue of committed delegates, Kennedy served notice that he would be playing a major role in national politics.

Sending birthday greetings to Russell just before election day, Johnson wrote that "without your judgment, your wisdom, and your friendship Lyndon Johnson would be in pretty bad shape."[45] Eisenhower's reelection came as no surprise to either of them. While Johnson had gone through the motions, to maintain his role as nominal leader of the Texas Democrats, neither he nor Russell had done much during the campaign to prevent the Eisenhower victory.

Chapter Four

FOREMAN

1957–1960

Preparing for the opening of Congress in 1957, Dick Russell and Lyndon Johnson were confronted with the same major problem, but they saw it from different perspectives. The problem was civil rights legislation, and for both the problem was urgent.

In 1956 President Eisenhower had sent Congress a civil rights bill that had provoked a minor crisis when it was approved by the House and sent to the Senate in the closing days of the congressional session. The bill was routinely referred to the Senate Judiciary Committee, where it was expected to remain until Congress adjourned in a few days. But an unusual coalition of moderate Republicans and liberal Democrats mounted a drive to discharge the committee and bring the bill to the Senate floor at once. By dint of adroit parliamentary maneuvering and with most senators anxious to quit and go home, Russell and Johnson were able to avoid a vote on a discharge motion. But it was clear that the tactic had only postponed a civil rights showdown.

When President Eisenhower resubmitted his bill in 1957, Russell saw it as another troublesome example of the legislation that he, as leader of the Southerners, had been able to sidetrack over the years. He knew that the fight would be more difficult this time, because attitudes in the Senate and in the nation were changing as communities accommodated social change in the wake of the Supreme Court's *Brown v. Board of Education* decision.

For Johnson, as leader of all Senate Democrats, the civil rights bill presented a more painful dilemma. As a Texan, he had always opposed civil rights bills and had managed to stall them without alienating liberal Democrats. But if he wanted to continue as a national party leader and a presidential possibility, he could not continue to block every civil rights measure that came along. He would have to find some accommodation.

Although Johnson had supported the South and opposed civil rights initiatives in Congress since his arrival in the House in 1937, he had come to understand the rising tide of black unrest. Discussing the plight of the Negro a few months before he began his 1948 campaign for the Senate, he predicted to an aide, "he's not gonna take this shit we've been passing out to him."[1]

In other respects, leader Johnson was positioned well when the 1957 Senate session began. President Eisenhower's reelection had not had a positive, coattail effect for other Republican candidates. Democrats had actually increased their narrow margin in the Senate, and Johnson knew that Eisenhower, as a lame duck president, would have declining influence in both houses of Congress.

With Eisenhower unable to run again (according to the constitutional amendment limiting presidents to two terms), the 1960 Democratic nomination would be a prize worth seeking. No doubt some senators would seek it (Johnson thought he might even seek it himself), but that could be dealt with later. Republicans in the Senate were still divided. All in all, Johnson thought the political climate was favorable for new legislative successes.

His own thirteen-point program now forgotten, Johnson was again content to follow the president's lead for a while. That was still the course Russell recommended. Assessing Johnson's Senate accomplishments many years later, Russell would say Johnson "had the good fortune of being (Democratic) leader for eight years when a Republican was in the White House" so that he was not, as party leader, required to conform to wishes of a president from his own party. Russell recalled that he constantly urged Johnson not to oppose Eisenhower initiatives just because they came from a Republican: "I said, 'What you don't like about it, we'll refine it.'"[2]

Working to refine presidential initiatives, Johnson was able to secure passage of the International Atomic Energy Act, an outgrowth of President Eisenhower's "Atoms for Peace" program; a reciprocal trade law extension; and a Pentagon reorganization that clearly established the authority of the defense secretary over the secretaries of the army, navy, and air force.

Russell was not always allied with Johnson, especially on foreign policy issues. In the wake of the 1956 Suez crisis and the subsequent fighting in the Middle East, President Eisenhower had asked for authority to use troops to protect the territorial integrity of nations that requested aid against enemies controlled by international Communism. The resulting

Middle East resolution in support of the "Eisenhower Doctrine" was, in essence, a warning to Egypt and other Soviet-supported Arab states to keep hands off their neighbors, especially Israel.

Russell thought the Senate was being asked to "buy a pig in a poke." He supported Sen. Wayne Morse in a proposal that would have required the president to give notice to Congress before taking action or, in an emergency, immediately submit reasons for his action to Congress for its consideration. Johnson supported the president, and the resolution as finally approved did not restrict the president's authority.[3]

In February, Russell, as chairman of the Senate Armed Services Committee, added to Johnson's stature by naming him to the five-member special subcommittee that monitored, in secrecy, the activities and budget of the Central Intelligence Agency. Responding to Russell's letter appointing him, Johnson said he was "delighted" to accept the new responsibility.[4]

Anticipating the civil rights showdown, Johnson enlisted Russell's help in handing out some political IOUs that could be called in when circumstances required it. The major transaction of this sort came a week before debate began on the president's civil rights bill. At issue was a bill to authorize construction of a high dam in Hells Canyon on the Snake River to produce cheap public power for Oregon, Idaho, and other Western states. Defeated in the Senate in 1956, the bill had been the center of a public power controversy that spilled over into congressional election contests that summer. In the public power tradition, Democrats in the West favored the government-built high dam in Hells Canyon. Most Republicans backed the Idaho Power Company's plan for three small dams the power company would build and control in the same watershed. Wayne Morse of Oregon had keyed his successful bid for reelection to the Hells Canyon dam, and a young Idaho Democrat named Frank Church had taken the Senate seat of Republican Herman Welker in a campaign that included a promise to secure passage of the Hells Canyon bill.

Johnson had pulled no strings for the high dam forces in 1956. Most of the Southerners had voted against it, and the bill was rather easily defeated 51 to 41. In 1957, however, Johnson went to work. During the 1957 roll call, forty of Johnson's Democrats voted for the Hells Canyon bill, including Russell and four other Southerners who had voted against the high dam the previous year. The bill was passed 45 to 38.[5]

In mid-June, the House, as expected, passed the administration's civil rights bill without substantial change. The bill allowed the attorney general to seek court orders on his own initiative to protect civil rights such as those mandated in the *Brown* decision; included a provision designed to assure blacks the right to vote; created a civil rights division in the Justice Department; and created a Civil Rights Commission to study civil rights problems and issue reports.

This time the coalition put together in the Senate by GOP leader William Knowland prevented the House bill from being referred to the Senate Judiciary Committee. The vote to circumvent the committee was 45 to 39. As in the early days of the McCarthy censure debate, Johnson had taken no public position on the civil rights bill. He voted with the Russell forces to refer it to the Judiciary Committee, but he did not use his leadership resources (especially the head-counting skills of Bobby Baker) to assure its referral. The 45 to 39 vote was proof, if proof was needed, that the 1957 civil rights bill would command a Senate majority on a final showdown. As always, the unanswered question was whether a successful filibuster would be mounted against the bill.

Before the House-passed bill was technically before the Senate, Russell decided to make a speech carefully outlining its contents. When the bill was actually being considered by the Senate, he said, any analysis of its provisions would be "clouded by cries of Southern filibuster which will ring throughout the land."[6]

Russell, who usually welcomed questions in the give-and-take of Senate debate, began his speech in an unusual manner, by asking that he not be interrupted. Then he launched an intense, angry critique that also seemed to be out of character for the usually mild-mannered Russell. The bill, he declared, had been misrepresented. It was, he said, as much a "force bill" as the hated measures imposed on the Southern states during the post–Civil War Reconstruction period.

Focusing on Title III, the section designed to permit the attorney general to secure federal court orders to end civil rights abuses, Russell declared that the provision had been "cunningly designed" to give the attorney general unprecedented powers to enforce such orders, "including the armed forces if necessary, to force a commingling of white and Negro children, in the state-supported schools of the South.

"I unhesitatingly assert that Part III of this bill is deliberately drawn to enable the use of military forces to destroy the system of separation of races in the Southern states, at the point of a bayonet, if it should become necessary to take that step," he said.

No such charge had been leveled against the bill when President Eisenhower submitted it or during House consideration of the bill. Russell commented caustically that, based on his analysis of what the president had said at a news conference, "I doubt very much whether full implications of the bill have ever been fully explained to President Eisenhower."

The predebate speech produced a major controversy. It took several days for legal experts—and then the press—to discover, as Russell had, that the enforcement process for Title III was keyed to an all but forgotten Reconstruction-era statute that could indeed involve the use of federal troops. Asked about Title III at a news conference, President Eisenhower appeared uncertain and told a questioner he would be glad to discuss it with Senator Russell.

Russell, who had known Eisenhower from the time that Eisenhower had been a young military aide in Washington, went to meet with the president at the White House. Born and raised in Texas and matured in the U.S. Army (which had been desegregated by a Truman order less than ten years previously), Eisenhower was no civil rights advocate. He had never used the presidency's "bully pulpit" to rally support for the *Brown* decision, and he had commented afterward that the appointment of Chief Justice Warren was one of the worst mistakes he had ever made. He had been pressed to submit a civil rights bill by his politically attuned attorney general, Herbert Brownell.

Russell did not, then or ever, disclose exactly what President Eisenhower said in their discussion of Title III. Recalling the talk years later, Russell said only that: "It was one of the most interesting conferences I ever held with a president. He just sat there and poured out his soul about that bill and the Supreme Court and several other things. I was amazed, and then I realized that he had known me for a long time."[7] The gist of what the president said, however, was that Eisenhower was determined to guarantee the right to vote for all Americans.

That suited Johnson. From the beginning he had seen the voting rights section as the bill's key provision. He knew it was viewed as less objectionable—or at least less intrusive—by Russell and some of the Southerners than many of the other civil rights remedies being discussed in the wake of the *Brown* decision. Johnson thought it would be hard for anyone to resist the argument that all Americans should have a right to vote.

When the controversy over Title III arose, Johnson thought it might be just the lever he needed. The possible use of troops, spawned from a Reconstruction statute, had infuriated Southerners. The way that it was proposed, hidden away in cross-references so that only a very good lawyer like Russell could find it, suggested that Congress was being hoodwinked.

As Johnson saw it, Title III must go, as a sop to Russell's angry Southerners. Then perhaps the voting rights provision could survive. Like a circus ringmaster, Johnson decided to throw meat into the cage and try to rescue the lion tamer while the big cats were having their fill.

Johnson discussed dropping Title III with Russell, who quickly said that Southerners could not vote for a federal voting rights bill. But Russell said such a bill, without other objectionable features, might not provoke a Southern filibuster. That was enough for Johnson.

Sen. Clinton P. Anderson of New Mexico, a supporter of the bill who nonetheless wanted to avoid a "march through Georgia" atmosphere in the Senate, told Johnson he thought Title III should be deleted.[8] Johnson asked Anderson to sponsor a motion to delete it, but Anderson, as a supporter of the bill, was reluctant to take the lead. Johnson then suggested that Anderson get a Republican backer of the bill to join in the motion to delete, and Anderson offered the motion jointly with Sen. George D. Aiken of Vermont, a GOP liberal and one of the best-liked men in the Senate.

Just before the vote, Republican leader Knowland tried to carry the day by stating, after a last-minute White House visit, that President Eisenhower really did support Title III; but the vote was not even close. Title III was deleted by a vote of 52 to 38, with only 13 Democratic votes against deleting.

Russell's Southerners did not filibuster, as they might have, against formally taking up the civil rights bill, and debate on Title III was to the point. Johnson injected occasional pep talks, complimenting members on the "historic" nature of the debate and noting at one point that the Senate, supposedly "handcuffed" on the civil rights issue, was laying "a basis for meaningful Senate action."[9] He welcomed the deletion of Title III.

The voting rights provision caused a major problem, however. As drafted, it allowed trials resulting from court orders in cases involving voting rights abuses to be held without a jury. During House consideration of the bill, an unsuccessful attempt had been made to add a jury trial amendment, but the attempt had failed. Johnson's plan was to add a jury trial amendment in the Senate. He thought no one, not even the Southerners, could object to trial by a jury of their peers. But that was precisely the trouble. Civil rights advocates angrily opposed jury trials on grounds that Southern juries would never convict a white offender, no matter how guilty, in cases involving denial of voting rights.

During the Title III debate, Johnson had been getting advice from a team of lawyers that included some of his old New Deal friends: FDR advisers Jim Rowe, Tommy Corcoran, and Ben Cohen among them. As debate dragged on, Johnson kept asking his experts to come up with a compromise, but there seemed to be no resolution to the jury trial dispute, with both sides deeply and emotionally entrenched in principle. Liberal Democrats, often distrustful of Johnson's maneuvering, were restless; and at one point, Johnson arranged that they win a small battle by adding an amendment to include an improved jury selection process. Some senators were even suggesting that the civil rights bill itself be dropped, when a Johnson aide came upon a scholarly article on the subject of contempt proceedings by Prof. Carl Auerbach of the University of Minnesota Law School.

Auerbach argued that there was a difference between criminal and civil contempt cases.[10] In the latter, he said, contempt of a judge's order was always enforced summarily without a jury, since an offender could go free at any time by obeying the order. In criminal cases, however, in which defendants could be jailed, they should be entitled to a jury trial.

It was an abstruse legal concept, but Johnson saw it as a solution to the deadlock. He turned to another of his legal advisers, Dean Acheson, who had been secretary of state in the Truman administration, and asked Acheson to draft an amendment to the voting rights provision embracing Auerbach's concept—juries in criminal, but not in civil, contempt cases. To sponsor the amendment, Johnson drafted Wyoming trustbuster Joseph C. O'Mahoney; Estes Kefauver, the non-Southern Tennessean; and Frank Church, clearly a beneficiary of the Hells Canyon maneuvering.

The battle was not over. Some civil rights advocates still contended that the jury trial amendment would gut the bill. Johnson got help, however, from an unexpected source. Some labor union officials, generally friendly to civil rights causes but always fiercely opposed to arbitrary court injunctions, worked the Capitol corridors in support of jury trials. Russell commented at one point that union officials should favor the amendment "lest they be the first to fall into the toils" of juryless proceedings as provided in the bill.[11]

Johnson and his aides and legal advisers talked to civil rights advocates, and Johnson called in all the debts outstanding, including those of the Western supporters of the public power dam in Hells Canyon. The compromise jury trial amendment, with the improved jury selection process, was approved and incorporated into the civil rights bill. The margin was not overwhelming—51 to 42—but the Senate, Johnson said, was operating "in its finest deliberative traditions."[12]

In periodic meetings with the Southern caucus during the debate, Russell had kept his colleagues advised of Johnson's willingness to remove the most objectionable features from the civil rights bill. It had not been necessary to talk prematurely about a filibuster. Like an experienced, well-trained military unit, the Southerners were ready to go to battle stations at the sound of an alarm.

Russell had conveyed to his Southern colleagues Johnson's arguments against a filibuster, which, to a large degree, matched Russell's own thinking: politically, the bill without Title III and with the jury trials amendment could be tolerated (not supported, of course) in the South. Southern senators could tell their constituents that they had exposed the devious attempt to revive Reconstruction injustices and had eliminated that provision. And then they had added jury trials so that no Southerner could be jailed as a "criminal" at the whim of a federal judge.

Further, the South's old alliance with conservative Republicans had been weakened, and a filibuster might fail—might be shut down by a two-thirds vote. When that happened, Russell said, the next target would be the filibuster rule itself. When civil rights forces could command a two-thirds margin in the Senate, they could drastically change Rule XXII, which had been the South's first line of defense against civil rights initiatives over the years.

After the approval of the jury trial amendment, Russell met with the Southern group and said he was by no means certain that votes were available to sustain a filibuster. He recommended that no attempt to filibuster be made. Russell said each Southern senator could speak on the bill as long as he liked, but he did not propose to lead a concerted effort that might weaken the position of the South in the long run. The group agreed not to filibuster.

But Sen. Strom Thurmond of South Carolina was dissatisfied. He went to Russell and argued that the bill should be filibustered. Thurmond asked that another meeting of the Southerners be called to reconsider, and Russell refused.

The Senate, by a vote of 72 to 18, finally passed its first civil rights bill in more than seventy years; and Johnson, whose efforts to refine the bill had by now made his support quite evident, voted for the first time to approve a civil rights bill. To publicize his dissent, Thurmond later spoke on the Senate floor for a record-breaking twenty-four hours and eighteen minutes against the final version of the bill.[13]

Both Johnson and Russell came under immediate criticism. Despite the

Senate's historic action, Johnson was accused by die-hard civil rights advocates of selling out the president with his maneuvering and dashing their own high hopes. He was also attacked for supporting the bill by some Texans who shared the views of a Houston critic who sent him an unsigned, two-word telegram: "NIGGER LOVER."[14]

Russell was accused of abandoning his long-held stance of unequivocal opposition to civil rights initiatives. One Georgia congressman, Rep. James Davis, joined critics in the South in questioning Russell's conduct as Southern strategist. Russell steadfastly contended that, at the end, he could not be sure of the votes to mount a successful filibuster.

Johnson's motives—and Russell's—have been debated over the years. From the present perspective it seems clear that Johnson's opposition to civil rights had, since childhood, been perfunctory and had eventually been altered by other considerations, including his ambition as a national politician, his sense of what the Democrat-controlled Senate ought to do, and his sensitivity to the rights of other minorities, such as the Spanish-American children he had taught in Cotulla as a young man.

Russell himself may not have known in August 1957 how much his long-standing, reasoned opposition to all civil rights initiatives was being tempered by his hope that Johnson might succeed in national politics and even become a president attuned to the Southern culture. Those considerations were not at odds with one another, and Russell's position in the Southern caucus was not unsound. Without Title III and with the addition of the jury trial amendment, Southerners would have had great difficulty lining up support to sustain a filibuster.

Southern senators differed about the motives and tactics of Russell and Johnson. More than twenty years later, Thurmond would tell an interviewer that Johnson had convinced Russell that he, Johnson, ought to be president and had told Russell that he had to pass a civil rights bill. "I think Russell didn't fight it as hard as he ordinarily would have if that had not been the case," Thurmond said. "He was trying to help Lyndon get elected president, and I thought I saw through the situation."[15]

Sen. Herman Talmadge, who had unseated Walter George in 1956 to become Russell's Georgia colleague, said Johnson had helped Southerners remove some of the bill's "most objectionable features," and thereafter the bill's supporters had sufficient votes to halt a filibuster and pass the bill. Russell, Talmadge said, "recognized when they got the overwhelming majority of the votes that we couldn't defeat the bill."[16]

Louisiana's senator Allen J. Ellender thought Johnson's political ambition extended far beyond the Senate at that time, and Johnson was "looking at stars far away" when he changed his position on civil rights.[17] Asked years later about Johnson's motives, whether he was driven by expediency or felt the time had come for a civil rights bill, Alabama's Lister Hill said, "It might have been both, to be fair about it." In Hill's opinion, there was no doubt at that time about Johnson's presidential ambitions.[18]

Senate passage of the amended bill did not end the civil rights controversy. The bill contrived by Johnson and passed by the Senate was quite different from the bill submitted by President Eisenhower and passed by the House. Some of the House bill's supporters talked of making radical changes in a Senate-House conference and even predicted a presidential veto. Saner heads finally prevailed, however; and with some minor fine-tuning to the jury trial amendment, Johnson's bill was sent to the White House and signed by President Eisenhower.

Even as a voting rights law, the civil rights bill didn't amount to much. More voting rights safeguards would have to be added later to assure blacks the right to vote. But Johnson's bill was a first, and as such, it was a wedge for future action. Johnson realized that, and on the day after the bill passed the Senate, he wrote Russell: "There is only one word that adequately describes Dick Russell—superb. The country recognizes your skill and brilliance. I hope that in the days to come it will also realize that your statesmanship did more to heal old wounds than any other thing."[19]

Four days after the bill was finally approved, Arkansas governor Orval Faubus, up for reelection in 1958, began a series of moves that would reopen and rub salt in all the old wounds. Faubus called out the Arkansas National Guard and ordered it to prevent nine black teenagers from registering at Little Rock's hitherto all white Central High School as ordered by a federal court. Faubus said he wanted to maintain "peace and order" and prevent what he foresaw as violence and bloodshed.

In the end, the governor's claim became a self-fulfilling prophecy, and President Eisenhower had to send federal troops to restore order in Little Rock. Russell quietly advised Faubus on court tactics during the dispute and, at one point during the maneuvering, seriously considered going to Little Rock.[20] Johnson, at the urging of Jim Rowe and others, kept well clear of the Little Rock controversy.[21] (Faubus was overwhelmingly reelected in 1958 and for several terms thereafter).

In early October Americans were shocked to learn that Russia had placed *Sputnik*, a basketball-size satellite, in orbit in what was then called "outer space." Having matched the United States in nuclear technology in far less time than U.S. experts had predicted, the Russians had now jumped ahead in space. Less than a month later another Soviet satellite was successfully launched; this one, carrying a dog as passenger, was quickly dubbed "Muttnik."

These Russian accomplishments in civilian space technology had frightening implications for military missilery, and many Americans were deeply concerned. The United States had been involved in a modest space effort, parallel with development of military missiles; but a successful U.S. satellite was not yet in sight. The Eisenhower White House greatly underestimated the public reaction to the sputniks and was slow to respond.

With Congress in recess, there was no immediate response by its leaders; but Johnson was alerted by his staff to the public mood and sensed a need for action. With Russell he attended a Pentagon briefing on missile and space programs; and from the presentations of the armed services, both senators concluded that, although some progress was being made on missiles, other aspects of space technology were receiving little attention.

Russell was being urged to head a MacArthur-like inquiry; but after they discussed the situation, Russell announced that Johnson's Preparedness Subcommittee, largely inactive since the end of the Korean War, would conduct an investigation of the U.S. space effort and the implications of the sputniks. Johnson beefed up the subcommittee staff and persuaded an old friend, New York attorney Edwin Weisl, to head the staff for the inquiry.

With Russell's blessing and Weisl's help, Johnson went all out in planning the space hearings. Dr. Edward Teller, known to the nation as the father of the hydrogen bomb, was recruited to be the first witness. Jim Rowe was dispatched to Boston to persuade top academic scientists Vannevar Bush and George Kistiakowsky to testify. The sessions were scheduled to be held in a small, low-ceilinged hearing room, formerly a cafeteria, which would appear in the eye of the television camera to be packed at all times.

It was a situation, rare in Washington, in which a congressional leader had grabbed the ball on a much-publicized issue and was running with it well ahead of the president. (Eisenhower had been quoted as saying that Lyndon Johnson could keep his head in the stars, but he, Eisenhower, would keep his feet on the ground.)

Johnson presided as Teller and the witnesses who followed set forth their vision of a day when the nation that dominated civilian and military operations in space would dominate the world itself. (Johnson would carry that message to the Democratic caucus in his own state of the union address when Congress reconvened in January. Thereafter he would support and present to the United Nations a U.S. Resolution on Outer Space.)

The Johnson-led Senate was swelling its legislative output. A public works program was passed, as was an education bill that drew criticism because it was narrowly drawn, to Johnson's specifications, to avoid the old thrusts of opposition to federal aid to schools. Legislation making Alaska a state was sent to the president. And later, Johnson proposed that civilian activities in space go forward under a new National Aeronautics and Space Administration (NASA). With the Eisenhower White House finally on board, a bill to create the new space agency was approved, and Johnson became chairman of a new standing committee of the Senate to ride herd on NASA, which further increased his Senate influence.

By 1958 the "Warren Court," as the Supreme Court was now called, was under heavy fire. Beginning with *Brown v. Board of Education* and continuing in a number of antisubversion cases, the Court had incurred the wrath of many conservatives. A number of bills to curb the Court's powers had been introduced in the House and Senate. The broadest was offered by Rep. Howard Smith, a Virginia Democrat and powerful chairman of the House Rules Committee.

Several of the restrictive bills were approved by the Senate Judiciary Committee, which was headed by the ultra-conservative Democratic senator James O. Eastland of Mississippi; and it became evident that one or more of them would be cleared for consideration on the Senate floor by the still conservatively oriented Democratic Policy Committee. After extensive preparations, and with the Congress in its preadjournment rush, Johnson decided to face the music.

As a starter, he called up a bill reversing a Court decision that dealt only with the District of Columbia; and after several hours of debate, he corralled the votes to defeat it, 41 to 39. Then, to swell the momentum, Johnson called up a bill to curb the Supreme Court's appellate powers, and it was defeated, 49 to 41.

Finally he turned to the Smith bill, which would have inverted the judicial system by giving certain state laws precedence over conflicting federal statutes. The bill became engulfed in a controversy over a civil rights amendment. By the time Johnson had quelled that controversy, the Senate was in a night session—always dangerous—with senators slipping away to keep engagements in town or slipping into Capitol hideaways to have a drink or two, and sometimes a drink too many.

Johnson's first effort to kill the bill failed on a vote of 39 to 46. After some maneuvering, Johnson tried again and failed 40 to 47. Then, from the desk behind him, Johnson heard the quiet but urgent voice of Russell, who had spoken eloquently in favor of the Smith bill for the benefit of his home state constituents. "Lyndon," he said, "You'd better adjourn this place, or they're going to pass that God-damned bill."[22]

Johnson took the hint and moved that the Senate quit for the night. Proponents of the bill tried to keep the Senate in session; but Johnson, as a leader usually can on procedural matters, easily got the votes to adjourn for the night. When the Senate met the following day, Johnson offered his colleagues a new alternative. Rather than try again to kill the Smith bill, he moved that the Senate send it back to the Senate Judiciary Committee. Three senators who had supported the bill the night before were somehow absent, and one Republican senator, Wallace Bennett of Utah, switched sides. The Smith bill was returned to the Judiciary Committee, where, with a final congressional adjournment at hand, everyone knew it would die in a few days.

It was not a happy time for Russell. One day, in an uncharacteristic display of temper, he reacted explosively to a press report that the Pentagon had financed a study of how the United States might surrender if it ever lost a war. Though no one in Congress was in a better position to inquire about the report, Russell did not take the time to investigate. He took the floor with an angry attack on whatever Pentagon official was responsible. Russell's friends were astonished at his impetuous, intemperate display, occasioned by an obscure, ill-advised think-tank study.

A sixty-year-old bachelor living alone in a hotel, Russell was perhaps entitled to an occasional angry loss of perspective. More and more frequently now he was turning down invitations for "social" occasions and he had quite happily adjusted to a slower pace.

He was self-sufficient, and living alone did not usually pose problems. From early childhood he had been a voracious reader. He read adventure stories, but history soon became a consuming passion; and, as a boy, he read widely about the war between the states. The Napoleonic wars also captured his imagination. He had named a rooster Napoleon and, swinging a stick as his baton, he marched through the fields showing no mercy to the weeds and bushes in his path. A childhood photo caught him, barefooted and bare-legged, wearing a broad-brimmed hat to shade his eyes. Cradling an open book in his lap, his expression suggests that he had been startled by the photographer and abruptly returned to the world of reality. As a senator, he generally kept the big table in his Senate office piled with books of all sorts. History was still a favorite, but Westerns and other novels were in the mix.

He had always been interested in sports but, after prep school, mostly as a spectator. The golfer Bobby Jones had tried to get Russell interested in golf when he was governor, but he never really got the bug. A real baseball fan, however, he was always able to cite statistics and name the home towns of the major leaguers. The University of Georgia football team had his attention on autumn Saturdays, and later, when Senate offices were furnished with WATs lines, he would arrange to listen via WATs to local radio broadcasts of Georgia games.

The invitations he accepted now were usually to quiet dinners with Senate friends such as the Johnsons and the Bill Fulbrights. John Stennis, the Mississippi Democrat who was the senior member of his Armed Services Committee, and Milton Young, a Republican from North Dakota who was often his ally in battles over farm policies, had also become especially close in the clublike Senate.

And unbeknownst to most of those friends, he had a steady lady. Russell had first met Harriet Orr sometime in the early 1940s. A Washington secretary, she had a job in the Defense Department, and Russell sometimes called her "Miss Secretary." Russell had been dating both Harriet and Pat Collins in the 1940s, before he and Pat became engaged, and after the engagement ended, he continued to see them both. After Pat married Sal Andretta, a Justice Department official, Russell and Harriet had frequent dinners together on weekends, took occasional drives in the country, and went to a movie now and then. She had grown up in Charlotte, North Carolina, and Russell had come to know the entire family— Harriet's mother, Mrs. Susie Orr, and a sister and brother. Eventually, Harriet would visit in Winder on a couple of occasions, and, traveling between Washington and Winder, Russell would break his trip in Cherry Grove, North Carolina, where the Orrs had a summer home.[23]

When Congress finally adjourned in August of 1958, it appeared to Johnson that prospects for the following year's session were good. Pollsters and pundits were predicting that Democrats would gain congressional seats. The president would have decreasing influence as a lame duck, and the Democratic leadership could continue to roll.

There was no hint that most of Johnson's accomplishments as Senate leader were behind him. But, as frequently happened when he was riding a successful tide, Johnson was beset by doubts—or professed to be. In late August, he wrote Russell that "one thing is completely apparent. It is that, except for you, I couldn't have lasted a month.

"I look upon you as the closest friend I have because you have been a part of every decision I have made and because you have sponsored me time and time again without counting the cost. I want to thank you for your counsel and your confidence without which I could not have made [it] through the session.

"I doubt seriously whether I should continue through the next session," Johnson said. He was going to Texas to let things settle down, he said, and "then I want to have a long talk."[24] If they did talk in this context, the conversation went unrecorded, but it is clear that Johnson's attack of indecision was shortlived.

At about that time, Russell received some bad news of a personal nature. After a serious childhood case of pneumonia and years of respiratory difficulties—annual bouts of flu, another siege of pneumonia in 1956, and further difficulties the following year—his lung trouble was diagnosed late in 1958 at the Walter Reed Army Medical Center as emphysema. For years a chain smoker, with a habit that had reached a couple of packs of cigarettes a day, he decided to heed the doctors' advice and—after several stops and restarts—finally give up smoking.

Dissatisfaction with the Johnson leadership and the Johnson-Russell tactics, long simmering among the Senate's liberal Democrats, boiled over in February 1959, when William Proxmire of Wisconsin attacked Johnson's "one man rule" in a Senate speech and called for more frequent caucus meetings of all Democrats to set party policy. First elected in 1957 to serve out a term after the death of Joseph R. McCarthy, Proxmire had just been reelected in his own right.

As the pollsters had predicted, the November elections had greatly strengthened the Democrats in both the House and Senate. The Democratic side of the Senate chamber's middle aisle could barely accommodate the desks of the sixty-five senators in Johnson's majority, which included fifteen new members. President Eisenhower, still personally popular, had lost more political clout.

The congressional session had begun auspiciously for Johnson. Before the usual session-starting battle over the rules, Russell had advised his friend that Southerners would tolerate (not filibuster against) a return to the pre-1949 antifilibuster formula: cutting off debate by a vote of two-thirds of the senators voting rather than two-thirds of the entire Senate. With that pledge in hand, Johnson was able to fight off a liberal drive for a cut-off by majority vote and secure approval of the slightly eased rule. With Russell's help, Johnson had pulled another rabbit out of his hat, avoiding what had promised to be a major, time-consuming controversy.

Just when Johnson seemed to be on a roll again, Proxmire launched his attack. Encountering Proxmire in the cloakroom, Russell said his attack on Johnson reminded him of a brave bull who charged down the track into a locomotive: "That was the bravest bull I ever saw, but I can't say a lot for his judgment."[25]

Compounding the Proxmire attack, an analysis of the roll calls on modification of the antifilibuster rule revealed a down side for Johnson. Six of the Senate's fifteen new Democrats had supported the tougher proposal and had voted against the milder Johnson-Russell modification when it was finally approved.

It was not that some of the new senators were predisposed against Johnson, but they were different. It can be argued, in retrospect, that the 1958 congressional elections produced the first batch of the sort of senators who would become the standard after the 1960s. They would have liked to be team players, but they were primarily interested in their own images. Their politics was closely tied to media exposure, especially on television. In their view, a degree of independence was good in and of itself. In addition, for all Democrats the very existence of a large majority tended to ease the pressure for party unity.

Senate Republicans, though their numbers were reduced, were rallying under a new leader. Sen. Everett M. Dirksen of Illinois had been elected to succeed Knowland when Knowland left the Senate to run for governor of California. Dirksen was Knowland's opposite. No ideologue (he could reverse his position on an issue without a qualm), he was nevertheless a shrewd partisan whose mellifluous oratory (some reporters called him "the Wizard of Ooze") masked a keen sense of how the Senate operated. He would not be Johnson's patsy.

And, of course, there were the Democratic senators who were already maneuvering to win the presidential nomination and run against Vice President Richard M. Nixon, who the experts were predicting would be the Republican candidate in 1960. John F. Kennedy, easily reelected to the Senate in 1958, was building a nationwide campaign organization. Hubert Humphrey, Stuart Symington, and Johnson himself were also mentioned prominently as the election year approached.

Against this backdrop, Johnson adopted a new script. No waiting for the president's initiatives this time. Bills would be passed, lots of them. There were predictions of a legislative harvest by Easter unlike anything since FDR's initial "one hundred days." The new tactic would require support of Senate Southerners, and Johnson commented at one point that his major concern was "keeping Dick Russell from walking across the aisle and embracing Everett Dirksen."[26]

Not only did the new tactic run directly counter to the course long counseled by Russell; it conflicted with a basic tenet of Russell's political philosophy. Russell was a legislative minimalist. He had often said that no bill was better than passing a bad bill, and he had always avoided assessments of Congress (which Johnson loved) based on the number of bills passed. He had occasionally suggested that the Senate and House should legislate in the first year of a new Congress and then confine their activities in the second year to approving the necessary appropriations, so that the bureaucracy could accommodate the prior year's legislation. He believed it took time to convert legislative grants of authority into sensible, understandable rules and regulations that the public could accept and respect.

Johnson was well aware of Russell's concerns, but he forged ahead, prodding his aides and urging committee chairs to clear bills for floor consideration. President Eisenhower was shocked by the scope—and especially the costs—of Johnson's legislative agenda. Beginning his final two years in the White House, the Texas-bred old soldier now bowed less frequently to the moderate advisers from Eastern states whose political skills had helped put him in the White House. He was angry, and he had a four-letter word for Johnson's legislative program: veto. He vetoed a housing bill twice and, under the veto threat, was able to water down an airport construction bill. Johnson's pre-Easter blitz died aborning, and there would be no more miracles.

With the enlarged Democratic majority, Johnson had known from the start of the congressional session that there would have to be another civil rights bill. In the early days of the session he had introduced his own bill, featuring a conciliation service to mediate, but not adjudicate, in civil rights disputes. He had planned to get the civil rights issue out of the way in 1959 before the 1960 presidential maneuvering began in earnest. But Johnson's bill satisfied no one; it was too much too soon for Russell's Southerners and far too little too late for civil rights advocates who regarded the 1957 bill as less than half a loaf. When the Easter blitz fizzled and the pace of Senate action slowed, action on civil rights had to be deferred, and Johnson scheduled civil rights as the first order of business for 1960.

Clearly the 1960 civil rights struggle was going to be far different from Johnson's miracle in 1957. This time no immediate accommodation was possible with Russell and the Southerners. Strom Thurmond's one-man filibuster in 1957, in effect putting down his Southern colleagues, made it impossible for any Southerner to appear to compromise on the civil rights issue this time. A filibuster was inevitable.

With no committee-approved civil rights bill at hand and none expected from James O. Eastland's Senate Judiciary Committee, debate began in mid-February on a minor bill, already approved by the House. Senators were invited to offer their civil rights initiatives as amendments. By the end of the month it was clear that a well-organized filibuster by the Southerners was in progress.

It was a real filibuster, unlike the gentlemanly, business-hours filibusters of recent years. Debate, or a semblance thereof, went round the clock. Civil rights supporters retired in the evening on cots set up in nearby Capitol hideaways and committee rooms. Southerners, except for a platoon of Russell-designated speakers, went home to get a good night's sleep. When one of the Southern speakers suggested that a quorum was not present in the nearly empty Senate chamber, the quorum bells rang. Civil rights supporters rolled off their cots and on to the floor to keep the Senate in session. Most of the Southerners slept soundly as a quorum was finally obtained and another Southern speaker, from the platoon on duty, took up the talkathon.

Early in March civil rights proponents offered a motion to halt the filibuster. Johnson, on a political tightrope, opposed it, saying the Senate should not close off debate until it had decided what it wanted to include in the bill. Needing a two-thirds vote, the cloture motion fell twenty-two votes short and failed to get even a majority. The debate went on. On March 24 the House passed a somewhat watered-down version of a five-part, administration-sponsored civil rights bill, and it became the focus of the Senate filibuster.

Johnson's nose counts indicated that the filibuster could not be broken on the bill that was before the Senate. Finally, after a huddle with Attorney General William P. Rogers, Johnson agreed to delete the bill's broadest provisions, targeting discrimination in schools and employment. Little remained but a provision allowing court-appointed referees to register voters in some civil rights cases. As debate on the bill continued, a series of liberal amendments were defeated, and not much was left to offend Russell and his allies. (The controversial Title III, deleted from the 1957 act, was rejected twice.) In addition to the voting referees, the bill eventually included provisions extending federal jurisdiction to cases involving racially inspired bombings of public facilities. Early in April, after nearly two months of deliberation, the watered-down bill passed the Senate 71 to 18. It was signed by President Eisenhower early in May.

On the surface and in the press, the fight had been a bitter one; but after the cots had been put away and a more orderly process restored, it was clear that amid the confrontation, Russell and Johnson had again managed to accommodate each other's interests. Johnson, now under liberal fire as Senate Democratic leader, could point to another civil rights bill—weak, but the second in three years after an eighty-year hiatus—to maintain his position as a national Democrat and a possible national candidate. Russell and his Southerners had fought the good and much-publicized fight, defanging another vicious "force" bill.

Of course, the battle left Russell's views and strategy unchanged. After the filibuster had emasculated the bill, he wrote a constituent: "I would be willing to make any sacrifice, personal or otherwise, to enable the people of my state to avoid . . . the terrible dangers of mongrelization."[27]

Beginning early in 1959, Sam Rayburn, Jim Rowe, and former Johnson aide John Connally had been pressing Johnson to commit himself to campaigning for the presidential nomination. Their urgings found Johnson, in Rowe's word, "ambivalent" about making the race that Rayburn and Russell had long envisioned for him. Ambivalence was not a posture usually associated with Johnson, but throughout his career he would experience episodes of uncertainty and even self-doubt. In 1941, for example, he had temporized about making his first try for the Senate until his friends started talking about John Connally as a possible candidate.

Late in 1959 Russell had corresponded with Texas governor Price Daniel, who was urging Russell to take the lead in enlisting Southern state delegations to support Johnson for president at the 1960 Democratic convention. Russell, who had publicly stated that he viewed Johnson as the strongest potential candidate, told Daniel that any overt effort on his part to mobilize the South behind Johnson would make it impossible to get necessary support from other states. He cited his own 1952 experience and concluded that a major effort by him would do "a great deal more harm than good."[28]

In 1960, Johnson's ambivalence to a presidential bid was complicated by what would today be called a midlife crisis. As is often the case in these matters, a woman was involved, and the relationship was more than the flirtations Johnson had sometimes indulged in; but the heart of the problem was a nagging uncertainty about what to do with the rest of his life. The pressures to offer himself as president did not ease that uncertainty.

Finally, under Connally's direction and with Johnson's tacit acquiescence, a Johnson for President headquarters was opened in a Washington hotel and began issuing highly inflated estimates of Johnson's delegate strength. By this time, Kennedy had already won presidential primaries in seven states. It was becoming clear that any other candidate, to be successful, would have to stop Kennedy from taking the nomination on the first convention ballot.

To strengthen his own position and weaken Kennedy's, Johnson persuaded Rayburn to adopt a timetable under which Congress would recess for the two political conventions and return to Washington in August. The scenario envisioned Democratic candidate Johnson pushing liberal bills to passage after the Democratic National Convention and triumphantly fulfilling the pledges of the party's convention platform.

Not until May 5 did Johnson finally make it official, announcing that he would be a candidate at the convention in Los Angeles. In retrospect it is clear that his announcement came far too late. It is also clear that an earlier announcement could not have won him the nomination. An earlier start might have given him a better organization, but it would not have changed the central thrust of Johnson's campaign, and the thrust was fatally flawed. Johnson thought the support of senators and representatives could be translated into votes of convention delegations; and, as he planned, many of his Senate colleagues, including Russell, enthusiastically endorsed his candidacy. Master of the operations and nuances in one political arena—the U.S. Senate—he failed to understand the many forces at work in the political conventions of that era. In the end he sat in his Los Angeles hotel suite, surrounded by supporters, reporters, and campaign aides, and watched on television as the state-by-state roll call gave Kennedy an easy victory.

A few days before the Senate recessed for the two conventions, Sen. Herman Talmadge, Russell's Georgia colleague, had slipped into a vacant seat next to Johnson in the Senate chamber. Talmadge said quietly that he wasn't planning to attend the convention. He said Johnson would have the unanimous support of the Georgia delegation, but Talmadge predicted that Kennedy would win the presidential nomination on the first ballot. "If

Kennedy's as smart as I think he is," Talmadge said, "he's going to offer you the vice presidency, and I hope you won't accept it." Recalling the conversation years later, Talmadge said Johnson quickly replied, "Good God, Herman, you know I've got no idea of doing any such foolish thing."[29]

In the final hours before the convention roll call for the presidential nomination, Johnson had bitterly attacked Kennedy. Speaking at meetings of state delegations he used some of the intensely personal anti-Kennedy themes that had been developed earlier by some of his campaign aides. He criticized Kennedy for missing hundreds of Senate roll calls while out campaigning. Then, in the half-shout he often used for emphasis, Johnson said he had not been born with a silver spoon in his mouth. Nor had his father ever wanted the Germans to win World War II.[30]

In the wake of comments of that sort it is not surprising that Johnson's name was not among those prominently discussed as convention delegates speculated on Kennedy's vice presidential choice. Talmadge's prediction appeared to be far off the mark, but on the morning after winning the presidential nomination, Kennedy visited Johnson in his hotel suite and offered him the second spot on his ticket.

Uncertain and ambivalent about his try for the presidential nomination, Johnson received conflicting advice on whether to accept the vice presidential nomination. Rep. Hale Boggs of Louisiana, who had been active in the convention on Johnson's behalf, urged him to accept. So did staffers George Reedy and Bobby Baker. But Bob Kerr threatened to shoot him if he accepted, and Sam Rayburn was said to be bitterly opposed to the idea. Rayburn called Russell in Winder (Russell had again decided to skip the convention) and reported that Russell was also opposed.

Evidence has accumulated in recent years, in statements reported by Rep. Tip O'Neill of Massachusetts and others, that Rayburn and Johnson had privately concluded before the convention began that Johnson should—and would—accept the vice presidential nomination if a bona fide offer was made by Kennedy himself. Both Rayburn and Johnson were deeply suspicious of the Kennedy convention entourage, however, and both were determined to avoid any intimation that LBJ was actively seeking the vice presidency.[31]

O'Neill reports that in a discussion in Los Angeles before Kennedy was nominated but after his victory appeared certain, Rayburn surprised him by agreeing with Democratic congressman Wright Patman of Texas that if Kennedy wanted Johnson for vice president, "Lyndon has an obligation to accept it." Rayburn then offered to "talk to Lyndon" and gave O'Neill a phone number where Kennedy could reach him. O'Neill quickly gave Kennedy the gist of that conversation and the phone number. After the convention, O'Neill says Rayburn remarked to him: "I guess that we both played a part in Los Angeles that will never make it into the history books."[32]

In any event, when Kennedy actually made the offer, Johnson told him that he could not accept unless Rayburn could be persuaded to withdraw his objection. He also warned that Kennedy's liberal supporters would be "madder than hell" at the idea of Johnson on the ticket and that Kennedy would have to "straighten them out." As later publicized, it was the idea of a Nixon presidency that cleared the way for Johnson to accept.[33] Knowing of the Speaker's antipathy to Nixon, Hale Boggs used that prospect as an argument in seeking to persuade Rayburn. Kennedy himself, when he met with the Speaker, said he needed Johnson on the ticket to win the White House. Rayburn exacted a promise that Kennedy would make full use of Johnson as vice president and said he would go along.

At the time and since, many writers have asked how Johnson could walk away from his powerful position as Senate majority leader to seek the powerless vice presidency. They tend to forget that Johnson, as noted above, was enmeshed in a congressional session in which his leadership had been bitterly challenged by fellow Democrats and which had produced few of the legislative successes of prior years. And Johnson knew that whoever won the presidency, Nixon or Kennedy, the Senate leader would be dealing with a far more assertive chief executive than President Eisenhower. Indeed, if Kennedy won, the leader would have to carry water for another Democrat, which, as Russell noted, Johnson had never had to do.

Following the convention developments in Winder by radio and television, Russell was distressed to hear that Johnson was about to accept the vice presidential nomination and run on a platform that he viewed as one of the worst he had ever seen. He reached his nephew Robert (known as Bobby), a Georgia convention delegate, in a Los Angeles hotel and sent him to urge Johnson—too late as it turned out—not to accept.[34]

Kennedy's liberal supporters were, as Johnson had predicted, madder than hell and tried to change Kennedy's mind by threatening a fight against Johnson on the convention floor. Kennedy was not swayed, however, and the furor subsided. Johnson was nominated by acclamation. From Winder, Russell courteously declined Kennedy's invitation to come to Los Angeles for the convention's final hoopla, wiring "Congratulations on your masterful campaign which brought such a sweeping victory."[35]

After he returned to the ranch, Johnson called Russell in Winder and, in Russell's words, "recounted the convention and taking (the) vice presidency." According to Russell's notes, Johnson said Kennedy wanted him on the ticket, "Rayburn finally came over," and he would have been "left out" of party affairs had he declined Kennedy's offer.[36] Russell responded courteously but remained unconvinced. He wrote a friend that his reaction to Johnson's acceptance of the number-two spot was "one of disappointment."[37]

The postconvention congressional session—quickly dubbed the "rump session"—was a disaster. Nothing was accomplished in the partisan atmosphere charged with campaign controversy. Kennedy took over a Capitol office near Johnson's, and Republicans twitted Johnson by referring to Kennedy as the leader's leader.

Johnson had hoped for passage of bills on health care for the aged, aid to education, another housing bill, and a boost in the minimum wage—all strongly supported in the Democratic platform approved at the convention. None of those bills reached the White House. A minimum wage bill passed the Senate, but Senate-House conferees had been unable to reconcile Senate and House versions of the bill when Congress finally adjourned on September 1.

The margin by which John F. Kennedy was elected president over Richard M. Nixon was so narrow that every event and every individual could be looked upon as decisive. There can be no doubt, however, that Kennedy would have been defeated without Johnson. When the campaign began, the entire South was lost to Kennedy, and, while Johnson boasted of campaigning "from Austin to Boston," his pivotal contribution was to win back part of the South.

A vitally important week of the campaign came in mid-October, when Johnson's whistle-stop train made its leisurely way through eight Southern states en route from Washington to New Orleans. Campaigning by rail has been a part of most presidential races, but the six-car "LBJ Special" was probably the last whistle-stop train to have a noticeable effect on an election outcome.

The trip got its theme at an early stop in Culpepper, Virginia, when Johnson shouted to a crowd gathered around the rear car's observation platform: "What has Dick Nixon ever done for Culpepper?" Its operating scheme was simple. The car in front of the observation car, with its rear speaking platform, was a parlor car, and, while Johnson was addressing the crowd in Culpepper from the rear platform, a group of important officeholders and other prominent Democrats from the train's next whistle-stop were welcomed by campaign aides as they climbed into the parlor car. As the train left Culpepper these dignitaries were escorted into the rear car to meet Lyndon, Lady Bird, and their campaign entourage. When the train reached the next stop, before Johnson began what he called "the speakin'," the local Democrats appeared happily on the rear platform with the Johnsons and then climbed down into their hometown crowd while dignitaries from the next stop were being welcomed in the parlor car.

A total of 1,247 Democratic leaders, mostly from small communities, were entertained on board during the train's 3,800-mile trip. In the smallest railroad towns the train did not stop, but it slowed so that track-siders could see Johnson on the platform and hear "The Yellow Rose of Texas" blaring from the train's speaker system. Occasionally Johnson left the train to make appearances in larger cities, and in New Orleans a crowd estimated at 100,000 turned out for a torchlight parade featuring a preview of Mardi Gras floats.

As he often did during national campaigns, Russell took off for Europe. He liked traveling abroad. He had made his first trip to Europe on a shoestring in 1927, staying in homes and pensions and visiting the places he had read about since childhood. As a senator, he had traveled extensively with committees and survey groups; but he particularly enjoyed traveling with a single staff member, showing the flag as chairman of the Armed Services Committee at U.S. military installations and then traveling for pleasure in Germany, France, and England. He liked it all.

He read and privately joked about reports in the Georgia press that his travels in presidential election years kept him insulated from the campaign rhetoric. Nursing his acute displeasure with the liberal party platform and its strong plank on civil rights, Russell had not formally endorsed the Kennedy-Johnson ticket. As he wrote a constituent in late September, "I cannot bring myself to endorse in public speeches a socialistic platform that I believe to be destructive." Recalling that he had campaigned for Al Smith in 1928, he said Kennedy's religion had nothing to do with his position.[38]

Nevertheless, Russell had done his bit to support his good friend. Two of Russell's Senate staff members worked as advance men in the Johnson campaign, and when Johnson left the "LBJ Special" to speak at Mercer University in Georgia, Russell provided a letter for the rally describing Johnson as "the ablest legislator who has served in the Congress in the past half century," well qualified to hold any position he might seek.[39] More importantly, Russell's nephew Bobby was one of the LBJ advisers in the

parlor car when Georgia politicians boarded the "LBJ Special." Most of the
state's prominent Democrats knew that Bobby Russell was a favorite of his
Uncle Dick's and that the Senator had high hopes for Bobby in Georgia
politics.

A chance encounter in the final days of the campaign helped the
Kennedy-Johnson ticket. In Texas to nail down his home state's twenty-five
electoral votes, Johnson went to Dallas for a rally on November 4. Entering the Adolphus Hotel, Johnson and Lady Bird found themselves surrounded by several hundred people who had attended a posh Nixon rally
a few hours earlier. As the Johnsons headed for the elevators the upscale
crowd became hostile and abusive. The state's only Republican congressman, Rep. Bruce Alger, crowded close to Lady Bird swinging a placard
reading "LBJ Sold Out to Yankee Socialists." It took nearly thirty minutes
for Johnson to shepherd Lady Bird protectively through the shouting,
swearing mob.

Russell would later say that he finally acceded to Johnson's telephone
pleas and participated at the end of Johnson's campaign for vice president.
Members of Russell's staff recall that, with some difficulty, Bobby Russell
reached his uncle in Europe by telephone and described the now-publicized
Adolphus Hotel incident in some detail. Russell was especially angered that
Lady Bird had been endangered by a mob of unruly, rich, and profane
Republicans. He cut short his trip and returned to join the campaign,
traveling on Johnson's chartered plane in the final days and speaking for
the ticket in Texas.[40] Russell's decision to campaign actively for the
Kennedy-Johnson ticket was important front page news in Atlanta newspapers, and it was also influential in nearby portions of South Carolina
where those papers had wide circulation. Russell's campaigning was
another small event that took on a larger significance when analysts began
looking at the very narrow Kennedy-Johnson victory.

Over the years, Johnson had showered Russell with small gifts—
gadgets, neckties, even a wristwatch with an alarm like the one he wore,
which sometimes buzzed unexpectedly, disturbing the decorum of Senate
deliberations. After Christmas, Russell wrote the newly elected vice
president to say that he greatly appreciated the Christian Dior handkerchief, "although I will have to buy a new suit to go with it."[41]

Chapter Five

SHOP STEWARD

1961–1963

It was another Texan, John Nance Garner, who characterized the vice presidency, in language Lyndon Johnson might have used, as "not worth a bucket of warm spit." Johnson had seen vice presidents become invisible—beginning with Garner himself—and he did not intend to disappear. He thought he could add substance to the shadow as he had done in the jobs of Senate Democratic whip and Democratic leader.

Before Congress convened in 1961, Johnson, still the Senate majority leader, called a meeting of close Senate friends in a downtown Washington hotel where reporters and other undesirables were not likely to intrude. Present were Mike Mansfield, who was to succeed Johnson as leader, Dick Russell, Hubert Humphrey, Bob Kerr, Florida senator George A. Smathers, and aide Bobby Baker.

Johnson told the group in confidence that after he became vice president he wanted to continue to chair the Senate Democratic Caucus. "He had the illusion," Humphrey would say later, "that he could be, in a sense, as vice president, the majority leader." Mansfield had no objections. He was planning, in any event, to present a much lower profile as Democratic leader than Johnson had.

Humphrey, however, thought "it was perfectly obvious this wasn't going to work," and the others generally agreed. They said there was no precedent for such an arrangement and predicted that it would encounter strong objections, since the Constitution prescribes only that a vice president preside in sessions of the Senate and vote in case of a tie.

Johnson persisted, however, and, as Humphrey noted wryly, Johnson was "not an easy man to tell that you can't do something."[1] On January 3, as Democratic leader, having not yet resigned his Senate seat, Johnson presided at the caucus of Democratic senators. At that meeting, after Mansfield had been elected majority leader and Humphrey had been elected whip, Mansfield offered a motion that Johnson, as vice president, continue to serve as chairman of the caucus, known formally as the Democratic Conference.

The reaction was precisely as his friends had predicted, and it deeply disturbed Johnson. He had expected that liberals, who feared that Vice President Johnson would try to run things, would offer critical comments and constitutional objections. But so did Southerners Olin D. Johnston of South Carolina and A. Willis Robertson of Virginia. Even Johnson's longtime ally, Clint Anderson, pressed the constitutional argument of separation of powers.[2]

Again, Johnson did not relent. Mansfield's motion finally went to a vote and, mathematically speaking, was approved 46 to 17. But with senators—"no" and "aye" voters alike—filing out of the conference room with grim expressions and angry whispers, it was clear, as Humphrey had known from the beginning, that it wasn't going to work. It was left to Russell, Humphrey recalled, to convince Johnson that his plan for a regency was dead.[3]

Vice President Johnson retained only one of the many powers and perks he had acquired during his twelve-year run in the Senate. With Mansfield's happy acquiescence, Johnson retained the so-called Taj Mahal, the rococo suite of offices he had commissioned for himself just outside the Senate chamber. Mansfield moved to a smaller, equally accessible suite around the corner.

While President-elect Kennedy was mulling over his cabinet choices, Russell had been appalled to read in speculative news stories that Kennedy was thinking about nominating his younger brother Bobby to be attorney general. Russell sent word to Kennedy that appointing a man who had never practiced law to be the nation's chief law officer made no sense.

By Christmastime, Russell was able to tell Georgia supporters that Kennedy had assured him personally that there was no truth to the press reports. Jack was not going to appoint Bobby.[4] In early December, Russell had met with the president-elect to talk about his cabinet. He wanted Kennedy to appoint his friend and farm adviser D. W. Brooks as secretary of agriculture, but Kennedy said the post had been promised to Orville Freeman.

"Of his own volition," Russell wrote in a memo describing the session, Kennedy then commented that appointment of Bobby as attorney general had been discussed, "but he did not feel he should appoint him to that post. He stated that he knew there would be a great deal of litigation involving racial relations, and he did not feel he wanted the name Kennedy to be a curse word in the Southern states."[5]

Russell had agreed that such an appointment would not be "wise," and when the Robert Kennedy appointment was announced, Russell was furious—about the appointment and about being misinformed. Over drinks in the Taj Mahal, Johnson told Bobby Baker: "Dick Russell is absolutely shittin' a squealin' worm. He thinks it's a disgrace for a kid who's never practiced law to be appointed as the highest lawyer in the land. Personally I agree with him. Russell and a lot of others fear that the Justice Department might become too politicized with the president's brother headin' it. They might have a point."[6]

But as vice president–elect, Johnson understood that he now had a new set of loyalties, and after the presidential campaign, he also was much better acquainted with Jack Kennedy. He told Baker: "I don't think Jack Kennedy's gonna let a little fart like Bobby lead him around by the nose. If I learned anything in the last year it's that Jack Kennedy's a lot tougher, and maybe a lot smarter, than I thought he was."

Johnson said Kennedy had told him his father had insisted on Bobby being attorney general. Johnson said the president had asked him to quiet the fears of the Southerners. It was, Johnson said, the first thing the new president had asked him to do. He told Baker to "lead all our Southern friends in here by their ying-yangs and let me work on 'em."[7]

Johnson told each of the Southerners that Senate confirmation of Bobby Kennedy had become Johnson's first test as vice president—a test that would determine whether Johnson would be in a favored position to help his Southern friends with matters of perks and patronage in the Kennedy administration. With Russell, as Baker recalled it, Johnson came down hard: "Now, what good will it do me if Dick Russell—the best friend I've got in the whole world—gets up and snorts and fusses and embarrasses me and the president and the president's brother and his mamma and daddy?"[8]

Unconvinced, Russell put the question of Bobby Kennedy's nomination before a meeting of the Southern caucus. Two years later, after the attorney general's civil rights stance had angered many Southerners, Russell told a constituent about the meeting and said the "Southern group" talked about opposing Bobby Kennedy's nomination when it reached the Senate floor. However, "those who had worked with him on the McClellan committee (a 1960 investigation of labor racketeering) felt they could keep him within bounds," Russell said. He added: "They have found out much better."[9]

Johnson's major service to the new president in this matter was to persuade Russell and other Democratic opponents of the Robert Kennedy nomination not to insist on a roll call vote in the Senate. Johnson argued that Democratic votes recorded against Bobby would embarrass the president and would also put the naysayers at odds with John F. Kennedy at the outset of his new administration. The nomination was approved by a voice vote, and the voice of Richard B. Russell was heard loudly among the "nays."[10]

Soon after taking office, Johnson had tried to greatly expand his role as vice president. He had approved and sent to the White House a staff draft of an executive order, to be signed by President Kennedy, that would have made Johnson, in effect, a deputy president, giving him "general supervision" over space and defense programs, a large part of the federal bureaucracy. The draft disappeared and never surfaced again.[11]

But Kennedy did assign Johnson two responsibilities in the new administration. In light of Johnson's background in the space program, the president assigned him to chair the Space Council, until then a largely inactive panel that was supposed to make policy and resolve interagency disputes in the space program. The appointment required an amendment to the space act Johnson had spearheaded. Kennedy also assigned Johnson to head the White House Committee on Equal Employment, a position Vice President Nixon had held in the Eisenhower administration.

Though they were not major responsibilities, Johnson took them seriously, and, especially as chairman of the equal employment committee, he began to have a new insight into important national problems. Like most vice presidents, he was asked to undertake missions abroad. While he was not always happy with these overseas assignments, they exposed him to new people with executive responsibility in high places.

Ironically, Johnson's quiet operations in support of the nomination of Robert F. Kennedy to be attorney general would be one of the few services Johnson would perform for the new president behind the Senate scenes, where he had been the acknowledged master. For a while it appeared that, as vice president, Johnson would function as Kennedy's fixer at the Capitol. That it didn't work out that way was probably the fault of both, and it can be argued that no vice president, constitutionally an arm of the executive branch, can ever exert much power in a legislative body such as the Senate.

There seems to be no doubt that Jack Kennedy and Lyndon Johnson had a good personal relationship. There is general agreement that their mutual respect came to be enhanced by a mutual affection. However, the president's sentiments were not shared by the bright young intellectuals on his White House staff, and that soured the relations between the White House and the Taj Mahal.

A little sign on Harry Truman's desk reminded visitors that "The Buck Stops Here." Unfortunately, in the byzantine maneuvering of the modern White House, many a buck is stopped, diverted, or simply disappears before it gets to the president's desk. Kennedy had a White House full of bright, sophisticated, and supremely confident aides who viewed the vice president as "Uncle Cornpone" and felt they were quite capable of dealing with Congress and other administration problems. As in other administrations, the vice president was seldom asked to act.

Johnson railed against the bright young men—"the Harvards"—who made no effort to conceal their contempt for him. And first among the "Harvards," though nominally not in the White House, was Robert F. Kennedy. As he told Bobby Baker, Johnson regarded Bobby as a "little fart." Bobby viewed Lyndon as uneducated and crude. Some of the bad blood dated from the nominating convention in Los Angeles, where Bobby, minutes after Jack selected Lyndon as his running mate, appeared in Johnson's hotel suite to argue against Johnson's candidacy. Bobby had been out of touch with Jack, did not know about phone calls that had intervened, and was not personally at fault; but the incident was not forgotten by Johnson.[12]

Nor did Johnson forget the rebuff he had suffered at the hands of a wide spectrum of Senate Democrats—those who had spoken and voted against his continuing as chairman of the Democratic Conference. He was not about to put himself in a position to be rebuffed again. The net result was that he was seldom asked to help with Kennedy's legislative initiatives, and he did not volunteer to do so.

Within administration councils, Kennedy ordered that Johnson be included in policy-making sessions, but in the meetings that were dominated by zealous White House aides, Johnson had little to offer. Aide George Reedy reported that Johnson participated "as a spectator" in meetings of the National Security Council and sometimes arranged to present his views privately to the president after the meetings.[13]

Had he been more assertive, Johnson might have raised tough questions about plans for the Bay of Pigs operation in the early months of the Kennedy administration. When it was underway, he might have persuaded the new president not to contribute further to that debacle on a Cuban beachhead by canceling a planned air strike at the last minute. Johnson did not do so. Nineteen months later, during the Cuban missile crisis, he was described as a listener who seldom spoke during the week of nearly continuous meetings of the ad hoc Executive Committee of the National Security Council, which debated alternatives and finally settled on the quarantine that was successfully imposed.[14]

In a White House meeting a few hours before President Kennedy disclosed the presence of Soviet missiles in Cuba and announced the quarantine, Russell argued for a full-scale invasion to rid Cuba of the missiles and Fidel Castro's Communist regime at the same time. Russell said the real danger to the United States lay in the more than forty Russian missiles already in place in Cuba that could reach 40 percent of U.S. cities and cause millions of casualties. "The quarantine will not remove this danger," he said in a note written after the meeting. "I therefore advocated knocking out those sites and destroying missiles with bombs and rockets before the quarantine was announced and thus prevent them from being fired by the Russian crews—" he said. Since the president, in speeches, and Congress, in a resolution, had warned that placing offensive weapons in Cuba would be considered an act of war, Russell wrote, attacking the missiles would have been "retaliation" and not a sneak attack.[15]

To his surprise, Russell was supported in that view by Bill Fulbright, and, at the time, U.S. armed forces had been quietly moved to bases in the southeast from which they could have launched such an attack. It was too late to reconsider the quarantine, however. As House Republican leader Charlie Halleck of Indiana noted sourly, the congressional leaders were only being informed, not consulted, by President Kennedy.[16]

It was a not a happy time for Johnson, but he surprised his friends and staff by accepting his subordinate position without public complaint. Over drinks with Russell or Bobby Baker, he might deplore the new administration's inept congressional liaison (as he did after the Senate rejected the president's Medicare proposal), but he made no public criticism. He remembered Vice President Garner's angry split with FDR, which was another aspect of the Garner vice presidency that Johnson did not intend to emulate.

His restraint won him no praise. On the contrary, White House aides and other Kennedy admirers enlivened Georgetown dinner parties with a sardonic put-down: "What ever happened to Lyndon?" The social and cultural successes of the Kennedy White House were a special trial for Johnson. He ridiculed, and at the same time resented, the radiance of Camelot, which surrounded the new president, his family, and his friends. No fan of Irish politicians, whom he regarded as a bunch of self-serving ward bosses, he resented Kennedy's much-publicized "Irish mafia."[17]

Speaker Rayburn might have been the one to shake up the Kennedy staff and insist that Johnson, the proven strategist, be given a more active role in pressing administration initiatives in the Senate. In the early days of the new administration, however, Rayburn was deeply involved in the toughest fight of his own long congressional career—narrowly winning a battle to liberalize the House Rules Committee; and that summer, the Speaker began to experience symptoms of the illness that would send him home to Texas, where he died of cancer in November.

Bobby Baker has pointed out that Johnson might well have served Kennedy as emissary in another arena where his services were never requested—the worrisome field of race relations.[18] Beginning with the Freedom Riders in the spring of 1961, the Kennedy administration would face a series of controversies with officials in Southern states arising from racial conflict; but Johnson—the masterful one-on-one persuader who talked like a good ol' boy but had demonstrated an ability to compromise on civil rights issues—was never called upon to keep the racial controversies from escalating into confrontations.

Nor was Johnson employed as a civil rights facilitator in the Senate, where Russell and his band of Southerners, amid increasing public pressure for action on civil rights, were frustrating or moderating the administration's civil rights initiatives. Early in the spring of 1962, a mild Southern filibuster blocked an attempt by Senate liberals to pass a bill outlawing poll taxes. Southerners argued that the Constitution reserved to the states the setting of standards for voting. Under the auspices of a Southerner, Spessard Holland of Florida, the Senate then approved a constitutional amendment declaring that no citizen's right to vote for federal candidates could be abridged or denied by failure to pay a poll tax. (Approved later in the year by the House, and after ratification by thirty-eight states, it became the Twenty-fourth Amendment in 1964.)

Early in the summer, after Eastland's Judiciary Committee had failed to act, Democratic leader Mansfield and Republican leader Dirksen bypassed the committee and offered an administration bill dealing with literacy tests as an amendment to a minor measure that had already passed the House. The bill would have provided that anyone with a sixth grade education could not be ruled ineligible to vote by failing a literacy test. Southerners filibustered using the same argument: that the Constitution lets the states determine who has the right to vote. The two party leaders made two attempts to close off the debate and force a final vote on the bill. Needing a two-thirds vote of the senators voting, neither cloture attempt won a Senate majority.

In their talks, Johnson had plenty of chances to tell Russell of his frustration as the Kennedy administration's number-two executive. Johnson was bored, restless, and unhappy. His mood was beyond ambivalence; it was a dark dissatisfaction with his life and a bleak uncertainty as to its prospects. The same despondency had emerged in Texas after his heart attack in 1955 and, briefly, during his campaign for the vice presidency. In these periods he drank more than usual (which was quite a lot), was irascible in dealings with his staff, and mourned that his best efforts went unappreciated. He would sometimes say he was going to throw in the cards, go back to the ranch, and forget public life.

Russell was aware that, in his dark mood, Johnson the person was beginning to do serious damage to the reputation of Johnson the public figure. As a senator and as Democratic leader, Johnson's behavior and salty rhetoric had been no more flamboyant than those of some of his contemporaries and predecessors and had not startled the Capitol press corps. As vice president, however, his deportment, especially on travels abroad, was on display for a different group of reporters, who took pleasure in reporting on it. Accounts of his outrageous demands on U.S. embassy staffs, of Texas war whoops in the real Taj Mahal in India, and of instructions to diplomats issued while seated on the commode appeared rather frequently and obscured important successes.[19]

One important vice presidential mission was undertaken in August 1961. Communist East Germany had blockaded West Berlin by closing all the entry routes and raising the Berlin Wall. Kennedy called Johnson to the White House and asked him to go to West Berlin at once to show the flag and underscore U.S. determination to remain there as an occupying power. To meet Johnson in the U.S. zone, Kennedy ordered a regiment of U.S. troops from West Germany to move via Soviet-controlled roads across East Germany to Berlin and into the blockaded city.

Clearly the plan had risks—for the nation and for the vice president— but Johnson acted at once. After a short meeting in Bonn with West German president Konrad Adenauer, Johnson was received in West Berlin by cheering crowds. The next day he toured the city, and speaking from the steps of the Rathaus to a crowd estimated by police at 380,000, he pledged that the freedom of the city would be maintained. Then he greeted the 1,500 U.S. troops who had made their way successfully into the beleaguered city to support Johnson's pledge. The mission was judged an unqualified success.

Even the visit to Washington, at Johnson's invitation, of an impoverished Pakistani camel driver named Bashir Ahmed, which inspired many jokes at Georgetown dinner tables, was clearly a great success when viewed from the perspective of U.S. missions overseas.

Russell and Johnson were often together during this period of Johnson's vice presidential discontent. Their personal relationship was still close, perhaps closer than ever with Rayburn now gone. When they were not together Johnson was often on the telephone with inquiries for his old friend. One of the major social events hosted by the Johnsons was a dinner honoring Russell to which cabinet members and other Washington dignitaries were invited. Johnson took the occasion to tell his distinguished guests that if it were given to him to choose a president of the United States, he would select Richard B. Russell.[20]

It was an unusual social occasion for Russell, who usually saw the Johnsons informally at their new home, "The Elms," in northwest Washington. However, there were also dinner cruises down the Potomac with the Johnsons on one of the White House yachts, the *Sequoia*; and on a couple of occasions, the Johnsons arranged lady escorts for Russell on outings that included visits to Maryland race tracks.[21]

Amid all the personal togetherness the fundamental relationship was changing. Ten years later Russell would say that it was during Johnson's vice presidency that their political philosophies began to diverge. When "he changed his mind on some matters . . . I didn't change mine. . . ."[22]

In part, the divergence came about because their perspectives had changed. No longer colleagues, they now had different jobs with different viewpoints. As vice president, Johnson took seriously his job as chairman of the White House Committee on Equal Employment; and although his activities in that regard did not always satisfy Bobby Kennedy, they did not endear him to Russell, whose role in the Senate and views on racial matters were unchanged.

President Kennedy was careful to touch base with Russell on Russell's areas of Senate expertise. At the end of the new president's first year in office, Kennedy called Russell in Georgia to talk about farm problems.

Russell agreed that acreage controls on grain producers had proved to be unsuccessful—"When acreage was reduced 10 percent they increased fertilization about 20 percent"—and suggested that controls on pounds and bushels would be necessary.[23]

It was said of Russell—and correctly, then and later—that the United States Senate was his life, but it should be remembered that he had the resources to enjoy himself alone. Unlike Johnson, he did not constantly need the adrenaline of social interplay or political give-and-take to occupy himself.

After years of living in Washington hotels, he had acquired a small cooperative apartment in the Foggy Bottom area of Washington. Members of his staff helped with the heavy burdens of bachelorhood, such as checking on laundry and buying groceries. Like the office, the apartment was full of books, and he was still often holed up in one place or the other—and quite content.

Russell's habit of burying himself in a book sometimes annoyed Johnson. Later, as president, Johnson would complain sarcastically that Russell was "home reading Plato" on an occasion when he needed to get some advice from his friend.[24]

It was not a home life of unbroken solitude for Russell, however. He continued to enjoy a comfortable relationship with Harriet Orr. By the 1960s, there was a well-established routine. On most Saturday mornings, one of Russell's aides was dispatched to buy a good steak, prime beef, at the Eastern Market near the Capitol, with money provided by the senator. In the evening, Russell would take the steak to Harriet Orr's apartment in northwest Washington, where she would prepare their dinner. On Sundays, they would sometimes go for a drive. They made occasional forays to nearby Civil War battlefields, the war having long been a major interest of Russell's.[25]

Russell's sister Ina, who saw them occasionally, said Russell and Orr were happy and content together—each sometimes preoccupied for an hour or more, he with a book, she with cooking or other chores. On a couple of occasions, Russell arranged for young men from his office to escort Harriet's niece, Margaret, to dinner with them at one of his favorite restaurants when Margaret was in Washington visiting her aunt.[26]

Shortly after Johnson was elected, Russell had spoken to him sternly, saying that votes from the South had made him vice president and that his Southern friends were "looking squarely to him" to protect their interests in that new role.[27] Early in 1963 the vice president came under fire from critics who said he was doing just that. In the biennial rules battle, Senate liberals argued that, in a new Senate, new rules could be adopted by majority vote. They cited a nonbinding, advisory opinion first offered by Vice President Nixon in 1959. Johnson ruled against them and was immediately accused of supporting his Southern friends and thereby killing hopes for Kennedy administration civil rights initiatives. Johnson had acted under precedents that had long held that the Senate, with at least two-thirds of its members remaining at the start of each Congress, was a continuing body for internal operations that did not involve interaction with the House. As usual, a Russell-led filibuster eventually frustrated the liberal effort.

After having engineered passage of the first two civil rights bills in eighty years, Johnson was stung by the criticism, but he made no public comment. He told some Democrats privately, however, that a real, round-the-clock effort could have defeated the filibuster this time. He noted that the Southerners were aging and that several of them, including their leader, Russell, were in poor health.[28]

Johnson was right about Russell's health. The lung problems that had begun in childhood and had been diagnosed as emphysema in 1958 continued. Bouts with flu frequently landed him in the hospital. In 1960 he had been given a series of shots to control hay-fever-like distress caused by allergies, and he was taking medication of various types—so many that he had to keep memos to assure that each was taken on time. Calling on one occasion to inquire about Russell's health, the vice president was advised that Russell was napping and could not take the call. In what seemed to be a flight of alcohol-induced hyperbole, Johnson said he would be glad to "hold his handkerchief" to stem the cough of his old friend if any such service was needed.[29]

All the Johnsons maintained close ties with Russell, and after he had shepherded a military pay bill though the Senate, Lynda Bird called Russell's office to speak to him. In his absence, she left a message for "Uncle Dick." She had been teasing him about the pay bill, she said, but she greatly appreciated his efforts. Her fiancé (Marine Lt. Charles Robb) would need the raise in pay to support her, she said.[30]

Russell, despite the victory on the Senate rules, was increasingly concerned about the future of his struggle against civil rights legislation. Outwardly, his position appeared secure. From a narrow Southern viewpoint, little had changed despite the actions by Congress and the Supreme

Court. Encouraged and emboldened by the Southern Manifesto, communities in the South had resisted school desegregation so successfully that only about 2 percent of black children in the region were attending integrated schools. And despite new voting safeguards contained in the civil rights bills of 1957 and 1960, which had spurred a number of voter registration drives in the South, there had been only minimal increases in the number of blacks registered to vote. In the Senate, moreover, the filibuster was still an unfailingly lethal weapon—cloture had never been voted on a civil rights bill.

Russell's was not a narrow Southern viewpoint, however; as an able politician, he was sensitive to trends. He knew the Southerners needed allies to sustain their filibusters, and since the high court's desegregation decision he had seen a series of civil rights dramas, played out on Southern stages, attract sympathetic attention in the media nationwide—especially on network television, where a white Alabama policeman could beat a black protester with a club in living rooms across the nation.

First there had been Central High School in Little Rock, in which he had been indirectly involved. Then there was the 381-day bus boycott in Montgomery, directed by a charismatic young Georgia constituent of Russell's, a clergyman named Martin Luther King Jr., who had studied the writings and tactics of Mahatma Gandhi. Then came lunch counter sit-ins, starting in Greensboro, North Carolina, and spreading across the upper South; they were especially significant for Russell because they largely involved educated young blacks—college and high school students.

The year 1961 brought the violent and bloody road show featuring the "Freedom Riders," with particularly distasteful scenes played in Anniston, Birmingham, and Montgomery, Alabama. The following year, Mississippi governor Ross Barnett tried to prevent James Meredith from entering the University of Mississippi and forced President Kennedy to use troops there. Finally, in the spring of 1963, Martin Luther King and the Southern Christian Leadership Conference confronted authorities in Birmingham. Televised scenarios showed Police Commissioner Eugene T. "Bull" Connor sending his forces against young civil rights demonstrators, using snarling dogs and high-pressure fire hoses. In the end it was the Birmingham authorities who backed off and made concessions.

Russell was keenly aware that the national mood, the sense of fairness with respect to civil rights, was hardening as a result of these events. He knew that attitudes in Congress, sooner or later, would reflect the new national mood.

In recent years Lyndon Johnson has been credited with securing approval of President Kennedy's ambitious legislative program. Actually, Kennedy had secured approval of a number of bills on his own by mid-1963—bills that defined his heralded New Frontier. In 1961, successful legislative efforts produced the Peace Corps, the Alliance for Progress, the Area Redevelopment Act, and another increase in the minimum wage. Legislation in 1962 included the Manpower Development and Training Act, a reciprocal trade act, and the constitutional amendment outlawing poll taxes. Approval of the Nuclear Test Ban Treaty in 1963 was a major achievement. (Russell, favorably inclined but deeply distrustful of the Russians, had finally voted against it). In 1963, Kennedy appeared to have passage of a major innovative tax bill within his grasp.

What was needed, as Kennedy's reelection year approached amid the rising tide of sympathy for enlarging the rights of blacks, was another civil rights bill. In a departure from its normal procedures, the Kennedy White House asked Johnson for suggestions. Johnson responded with recommendations on how to draft the bill and how to present it. Before the bill was introduced, he said, an educational campaign should be conducted in the South by administration leaders, including Kennedy and Johnson. When introduced, he said, the bill should be tough, including many of the features advocated by civil rights leaders. Johnson assigned a member of his staff to work with the White House on drafting provisions of the administration bill. In the end, however, Johnson's suggestion for an education campaign in the South was ignored, and White House aides were unwilling to accept even minor drafting changes that Johnson's staff thought necessary if the administration bill was to win Congressional approval.[31]

On June 19, Kennedy's bill was introduced. It was the most comprehensive civil rights bill submitted by a president up to that time. Its central feature was a ban on discrimination in "public accommodations"—a provision to assure all citizens the equal right to use public facilities such as restaurants, theaters, hotels, and the like. Whites-only discrimination in places of that sort had been one of the earliest targets of black protest in the Southern states. Two other major targets of the civil rights movement were not addressed in the bill, however: action against discrimination in employment, and Title III, the still unenacted remnant of the 1957 bill that would allow the U.S. attorney general to act in the federal courts on his own initiative against violations of civil rights.

The civil rights dramas continued to unfold. Amid widespread publicity, Alabama governor George Wallace finally backed down in his effort to prevent blacks from enrolling in the University of Alabama. In August 1963, more than 200,000 civil rights supporters from across the nation, nearly half of them white, answered Martin Luther King's invitation to a March on Washington for Jobs and Freedom. They had heard King forcefully and dramatically outline his integration dream.

After Congress adjourned, CBS correspondent Harry Reasoner visited Russell in Winder to do a profile of the senator for television.[32] They began their talk in rocking chairs on the porch of the old Russell home and then walked through the woods to the small family cemetery in back, where the senator's parents rested under a marble obelisk bearing tributes to them that he had written. The conversation covered a wide range of subjects: marriage—Russell would not willingly be a bachelor again; two-term limits for senators—Russell was against that; the Senate itself, which Russell called "the keystone in the arch of constitutional government."

With a new civil rights fight looming the following year, however, much of their conversation focused on civil rights, the South, and the Negro. "Have you sometimes felt, particularly in the last ten years," said Reasoner, "that you are fighting a rearguard action for a tradition that's going down to defeat?"

"Well, I could not be frank and say that there are not times when I have a feeling of overwhelming frustration—and that I know that some of the legislation that I have opposed, and will oppose, will eventually be enacted," Russell replied. "But I think it will serve a very useful purpose to slow down that legislation. I think it will probably contribute as much to the peace and tranquility and progress of the country as the passage of legislation in other fields.

"I am well aware that we're living in a social revolution, but I don't want it to be used to destroy our constitutional system. At times it seems that the American people are almost hysterical and that they will resort to any palliative that is offered to correct immediately what we all admit are social injustices and economic injustices. But I believe that they can be—those things can be cured without destroying this great American system of ours."

Reasoner asked whether, in relations with Negroes, "you would expect the things they want to happen immediately, to happen eventually?" Russell replied that he certainly hoped their economic goals would be achieved eventually; but he deplored a lack of perspective, which, he said, often caused Americans to overlook the twenty million white citizens whose situation—economically and educationally—was worse than that of the Negroes. "I think we must attack this business of economic disadvantage on a much broader front than the racial front, because it isn't confined to the Negro race," he said.

"Do you think that there are dangers in the current, almost explosive, drive for social equality?" Reasoner asked.

"Yes, I do," Russell replied, "and I think that it's gotten somewhat out of hand." He complained that the president, who should support all the nation's laws, had encouraged the wave of demonstrations. "I know the president didn't realize just what was developing here," he said, "but it could well be that he has turned the genie out of the bottle now, and he will have great difficulty getting it back in."

Reasoner asked if the South, as Russell knew it, was dying. Russell preferred to say that it was "changing its way of life," and he said he did not have what Reasoner called a "good old days complex." "I don't think we can exchange it. I don't think that we should," Russell said, "but I do hope that we can profit by the best values that were in the old life."

Reasoner said some critics of the Old South contended that "it depended to a very great extent on an unfair system, to the Negro and to the poor Southern whites." Was that so? Russell thought the system was not "nearly as unfair as some of our economy is today. We've never had a instance in human history of which I have any knowledge where the man at the bottom of the heap could get exact justice in the courts or elsewhere. I think he could get it almost as nearly then as he can now.

"Of course, the slaves had no freedom of movement, and they were liberated and it was a good thing for the country. It [slavery] was a drag on the South, on the Southern economy; it tied us to an outmoded way of agricultural life and denied any hope for industrial development. I think that it's better as it is now, though I would like to see the Negro population a little more fairly distributed throughout the nation."

Russell said forty Georgia counties had more Negroes than whites, "some of them five times as many. That presents an entirely different problem, when you come to what you call your forced association bills, than what it does to some man looking down from the Olympian heights of the Metropolitan Club or the Union League Club in New York City."

"Is it a soluble problem?" Reasoner asked.

"Well, it's got to be solved." Russell said. "We've got to solve it. It's a question of how. I don't think it's going to be overnight, and I think it's going to cause as good deal of travail, suffering, and perhaps agony; but it's one we've got to solve."

Russell said he thought most Southerners were aware that the problem must be solved. "A few of them may not admit it. The big difference is as to how we solve it and the rate of the solution. Some people want to solve it overnight. Others think that there is something to taking human nature into account, something that hasn't changed very greatly through all the ages, and you must proceed to get people accustomed to these things by degrees."

There were two reasons why President and Mrs. Kennedy and Vice President and Mrs. Johnson were in Dallas together on Friday, November 22, 1963. The first was to raise campaign funds by tapping Texas bankrolls. Some of that had been done in Fort Worth at a breakfast that morning, before they flew to Dallas. The second was to present a show of unity, however superficial, in the badly split Texas Democratic Party, where liberals and conservatives were still in constant conflict. That was the goal of the events planned in Dallas: a motorcade where the warring parties would be on display together, and a rally where they would all appear together on the platform.

Crowds in Houston and Fort Worth the day before had been large and friendly; and from his car in the motorcade in Dallas, Johnson could see the president with his wife and Texas governor John Connally in the White House limousine, waving to another big crowd as they passed the book depository building and headed for the underpass. Then the three sharp reports were heard—fireworks, perhaps, or backfires from the police motorcycles?

In the press "pool car" about 100 yards behind the president's limousine, Merriman Smith, the UPI White House correspondent, was riding in the front seat. He thought the first report might be a firecracker but knew the second and third were unmistakably gunfire. When the president's car faltered and then sped away from the motorcade, the pool car followed. Smitty grabbed the radio-telephone and dictated a bulletin that shots had been fired. A few minutes later, from Parkland Hospital, he dictated a bulletin that the president had been shot and seriously, perhaps fatally, wounded.

In Johnson's limousine, close behind the president's, the vice president had just heard the shots when he found himself buried on the floor by the outstretched body of his chief Secret Service agent, Rufus Youngblood. Youngblood simply threw himself on top of his assignment as the limousines sped to the hospital. On arrival there, Johnson was immediately isolated by the Secret Service in a small room close to the emergency room.

In Washington, Sen. Edward M. Kennedy of Massachusetts was discharging one of the duties usually assigned to junior senators—presiding over a routine session of the Senate at lunchtime. There was a bustle in the Senate Press Gallery, a tier above and behind his rostrum, and Majority Leader Mike Mansfield appeared quickly to move that the Senate stand in recess. Then the senator was told that his brother had been shot in Dallas.

In the press gallery, the word had spread quickly after Smitty's first bulletin clattered in on the UPI wire. When the Senate recessed, reporters converged on the lobby behind the Senate chamber, the "marble room," where UPI and AP printers were grinding out a grim, first-cut at history.

Roger Mudd, a young CBS reporter, recalled rushing into that lobby to find Richard B. Russell, bent over the UPI ticker, leaning on the cabinet that encased it, with tears streaming down his face, reading aloud to a group around him as the teletype spelled out the evolving story.[33] About half an hour after Smitty's first bulletin, the official word came that the young president was dead.

Dick Russell was not in the crowd of dignitaries and ordinary folk who assembled in the darkness at Andrews Air Force Base in suburban Washington to pay respects to the two returning presidents. That sort of crowd was not his favorite milieu in any circumstance, and he was very much disturbed by the day's events. In the radio-TV gallery with Democratic leader Mansfield to say a word of condolence for the Kennedy family, he had barely been able to get through the short interview.

After the former president's casket had been lowered from the rear of Air Force One and carried by military bearers to the hearse that took it away, Johnson descended from the door at the front to receive subdued greetings. Before he boarded a marine helicopter for the short trip to the White House, Johnson made his first statement as president: "This is a sad time for all people. We have suffered a loss that cannot be weighed. For me it is a deep personal tragedy. I know the world shares the sorrow that Mrs. Kennedy and her family bear. I will do my best. That is all I can do. I ask for your help, and God's."[34]

Johnson had looked for Russell in the welcoming throng at the airport, and shortly after reaching the White House, he called and asked Russell to come to the White House the following morning. It was the first of many meetings and phone calls between the two in the ensuing days, as the new president mounted a massive campaign to maintain and dramatize continuity and responsibility in the U.S. government.[35]

As he recovered from the shock of the assassination, Russell began to take a positive view of a Johnson presidency. "Well," he said to staff members, "Lyndon Johnson has all the talents, the abilities, and the equipment to make a very good president." After a moment of reflection, he added, "And, of course, old Lyndon is going to enjoy being president. He'll enjoy every minute of it."[36] When they were together, however, there was no more "Lyndon." For Russell, by tradition, it was now unfailingly "Mr. President."

As a senior senator and old friend, Russell was a member of the Senate-House group named to escort the new president into the House chamber for the joint session of Congress shortly after noon on November 27, 1963. Johnson, in what would become a standard procedure, had asked several people to work on his short speech, which, through radio and television, would really be a speech to the nation. But he added his own touches, including the punch line that recalled Kennedy's invitation to the nation at his inauguration: "Let us begin." Johnson's reprise was: "Let us continue."[37]

"First," he said, "no memorial or eulogy could more eloquently honor President Kennedy's memory than the earliest possible passage of the civil rights bill for which he worked so long.... I urge you again, as I did in 1957 and again in 1960, to enact a civil rights law, so that we can move forward to eliminate from this nation every trace of discrimination that is based upon race and color."

Second on the agenda, he said, would be "early passage" of Kennedy's tax bill, "for which he fought all this long year." In delivering speeches, Johnson frequently numbed his audiences with a plodding delivery, startling his listeners occasionally with strident shouts; but not this time. It was a virtuoso performance, and it was received as such, interrupted twenty-seven times for applause in the crowded House chamber.

For those watching on television, there was a bit of symbolism on display in the House gallery. Seated with Lady Bird Johnson among the president's guests were Arthur Schlesinger Jr. of the Kennedy White House staff, a quintessential "Harvard" and spokesman for Democratic liberals; Robert Wagner, Democratic mayor of New York, the nation's largest ethnically diverse city; and Carl Sanders, governor of Georgia, said by pundits to epitomize the "New South."

Mindful of the controversies that still surrounded the assassination of Abraham Lincoln, Johnson was determined to put to rest rumors of conspiracy and international intrigue that immediately surrounded the

Kennedy tragedy. In the hours after the events in Dallas, he decided to set up a panel of prestigious public figures to investigate and issue an unimpeachable report on what had occurred.

Two names came to mind at once as he considered prospective members for the group. As chairman he wanted Earl Warren, Chief Justice of the Supreme Court, head of the nation's top panel for resolving controversy. And he wanted Dick Russell, whose judgment he trusted beyond all others in such matters. Carefully considering influential constituencies, he also decided on John Sherman Cooper, a much-admired moderate Republican senator from Kentucky; John J. McCloy, establishment investment banker and high-ranking federal official in several administrations; Rep. Hale Boggs of Louisiana, a friend and an able Democratic House leader; Rep. Gerald Ford, an up-and-coming GOP House member; and Allen W. Dulles, former head of the government's international intelligence agency, the CIA.

To make sure that no one declined to serve, Johnson decided to make personal appeals to each of his choices, and he heard strong objections from the first two. Warren argued that no federal judge should serve on such a panel, created in and for the government's executive branch. Johnson told Warren that it was his duty to serve his country in this civilian capacity, just as he had served in uniform in World War I. Warren finally agreed.

Russell was even more difficult. When Johnson called him in Winder, Russell was getting ready for the long and wearing civil rights battle that he knew was in prospect when the Senate reconvened. He had favored federal judge Harold Medina to head the inquiry, and he had no desire to serve with the chief justice, for whom he had had little regard since the high court's school desegregation decision ten years earlier. He told Johnson that he simply could not take on the added responsibilities of an exhaustive investigation. The new president's persuasive powers in a long telephone call did not shake Russell's resolve: he could not, would not, serve.

About an hour before formation of the Warren Commission was to be announced, Johnson called Russell again from the White House. The appointment of the commission was about to be announced, he said, and Russell's name was on the list of members. Russell would have to deal with that however he saw fit, the president said.[38]

Gen. Lauris Norstad, commander of Allied forces in Europe, greets senators Henry M. Jackson, Richard B. Russell, and Lyndon B. Johnson near Paris in 1956.

In the corridors of power, senators Richard B. Russell and John C. Stennis were among the most powerful.

*The tutor and his apprentice in Corpus Christi, Texas, in November, 1949,
just a year after Johnson joined Russell in the United States Senate*

To Dick Russell —
with thanks for dedicated service, *Lyndon B. Johnson*

The Warren Commission presents its report to the president.

Russell and Johnson conferring several months after the President announced that he would not run for re-election in 1968.

The Warren Commission, which investigated the assassination of President Kennedy: Gerald Ford, Hale Boggs, Richard Russell, Earl Warren, John Sherman Cooper, John J. McCloy, Allen W. Dulles, and Lee Rankin, counsel to the commission

Johnson and Russell among congressional leaders meeting the press after a bipartisan lunch with President Eisenhower in 1955

Two legislative giants confer in the White House.

Chapter Six

CEO AND FRIEND

1964–1965

With Johnson personally marshaling the strengthened civil rights forces for the battle ahead, Russell had no illusions about the outcome. The president had given his old friend fair warning. Sitting together a few weeks after the Johnsons had moved into the White House family quarters, the president brought up the subject of the Kennedy civil rights bill. "Dick," he said, "I love you. I owe you. But I'm going to run over you if you challenge me or get in my way. I aim to pass the civil rights bill, only this time, Dick, there will be no caviling, no compromise, no falling back. This bill is going to pass."

Silent for a moment, Russell said: "You may do just that, Mr. President. But I am here to tell you that it will not only cost you the South, it will cost you the election." It was Johnson's turn to pause for a moment, and then he replied: "Dick, my old friend, if that's the price for this bill, then I will gladly pay it."[1]

Russell knew there would be much more than civil rights legislation enacted with Johnson calling legislative signals from the White House. Kennedy, he told associates, had been whipped in congressional battles over portions of his program, but Johnson had the power to get them approved. "He'll pass them," Russell said, "whereas Kennedy could never have passed them."[2]

The Kennedy tax-cutting bill, which Johnson's speech had placed second in terms of legislative priority, got first attention. Johnson approached it obliquely—by wrestling with the proposed federal budget. Kennedy had given his aides a target of $101.5 billion for fiscal 1965. After talking with finance experts inherited from the Kennedy administration, Johnson concluded that the best thing he could do for the tax bill would be to hold the new budget under $100 billion, a sum he viewed as a psychological barrier that should not be breached.

Taking a personal interest in the process, Johnson whittled away with cuts and gimmicks and got the proposed outlays for the 1965 fiscal year down to $97.9 billion. The tax bill already had the support of GOP leader Everett Dirksen; but when Dirksen, a member of the Finance Committee, won committee approval of an amendment to cut excise taxes of luxury goods by an additional $445 million, Johnson called other committee members personally and got the committee to reverse itself.[3] After only a week of floor debate, the tax bill easily passed the Senate, and the president signed the final version late in February.

Attorney General Robert Kennedy was the administration's nominal point man for the civil rights bill, but Johnson was calling the shots. After consulting Democratic leader Mike Mansfield, he called Hubert Humphrey, the Senate Democratic whip, and commissioned him to be the battlefield commander, the floor manager for the civil rights bill.

"You have got this opportunity now, Hubert," he said, as Humphrey recalled it, "but you liberals will never deliver. You don't know the rules of the Senate, and your liberals will be out making speeches when they ought to be present in the Senate. I know you've got a great opportunity here, but I'm afraid it's going to fall between the boards."[4]

"He sized me up," Humphrey recalled. "He knew very well that I would say, 'Damn you, I'll show you!' He didn't frighten me off. He knew what he was doing, exactly, and I knew what he was doing. One thing I liked about Johnson—even when he conned me I knew what was happening to me."

Johnson also gave Humphrey what would prove to be his most important marching orders: "Now, you know the bill can't pass unless you get Ev Dirksen. . . . You and I are going to get Ev. It is going to take time. We're going to get him." To do it, Johnson told Humphrey to spend time with Dirksen, play up to him. "He's got to look good all the time."[5]

Preparing for the civil rights debate, Humphrey took a leaf from Russell's book on filibusters. With help from the Republican whip, Thomas H. Kuchel of California, he organized supporters of the bill into three alternating daily teams, as Russell had always organized his Southerners. He held daily strategy sessions and arranged to publicize the names of Senate absentees in a daily newsletter.[6]

For his side, Russell made the usual preparations and added a new gimmick. He had some of his Southerners take hotel rooms under assumed names so that they could hide away at night, unavailable to Senate functionaries seeking a quorum and reachable only by Russell. Privately, Russell told friends that the Southern group could not block the bill without outside help. Implied was his unhappy realization that, in the Senate as it now existed, the required outside help would not be available this time.

He sent the president a message by way of White House aide Bill Moyers: "You tell Lyndon that I've been expecting the rod for a long time, and I'm sorry that it's from his hand the rod must be wielded; but I'd rather it be his hand than anybody else's I know. Tell him to cry a little when he uses it."[7]

The Kennedy bill had been strengthened during its consideration in the House. Its two major deficiencies had been corrected. Title III—the provision to allow the U.S. attorney general to initiate civil rights actions, which had been stripped from the previous bills—was added in the House Judiciary Committee. A fair employment practices provision was added during House debate. The strengthened bill passed the House on February 10 by a large margin, 290 to 130. When it reached the Senate, the House-passed bill was placed directly on the calendar of measures awaiting Senate action. That step, spearheaded by Humphrey, bypassed Sen. James O. Eastland's Judiciary Committee, where the bill would surely have been weakened and perhaps derailed permanently.

A few days later Russell received a letter from a Georgia clergyman exhorting him, in effect, to see the truth and, seeing it, act as a man of God. Replying, Russell first addressed what he thought was a note of holier-than-thou. He said he had a brother, a brother-in-law, and two nephews who were "men of the cloth," one of them a strong supporter of the bill. Russell wanted it understood that he was "as honest in my position as you are in yours.

"I think I know how the fight will come out," he said, "and the fruit that it will bear after a century or two.

"I wish that I were as sure of what the 'truth' is as you are. As an humble layman and confessed sinner, I can only follow my judgment and conscience, and my judgment tells me that we will not reverse history in the United States. I have read history for half a century, and I do not know of a single instance where a mixed race has been able to maintain a great civilization—much less to establish one. In all humility, I do not believe that God's will has brought about the condition that I have seen in every country where this has been tried."[8]

Humphrey, following Johnson's orders, had been engaged in the courtship of Everett Dirksen. On a news panel show, he was asked about critical statements made by Dirksen about the civil rights bill. Years later, Humphrey recalled saying that Dirksen was a "reasonable man" whose opinions were "strongly held." He predicted that, as time passed, Dirksen would see the light.

Warming to his cause, Humphrey said, "Sen. Dirksen is not only a great senator, he is a great American. . . . I predict that before this bill is through, Sen. Dirksen will be its champion, not its opposition."[9]

Humphrey remembered that his liberal colleagues were not pleased with his TV performance, but Johnson told him he was "doing just right" and repeated his earlier advice. Humphrey, he said, must "see Dirksen . . . drink with Dirksen . . . talk to Dirksen . . . listen to Dirksen."[10]

On March 9, Democratic leader Mike Mansfield moved to take up the civil rights bill for consideration on the Senate floor. Debate began at once—not on the bill but, for the time being, on whether the Senate should take it up. From the beginning, Johnson's position was clear, as he had outlined it to Russell: this time there would be no compromise. The administration bill would be approved.

Johnson's inflexibility was only one of Russell's overwhelming number of problems. As chairman of the Senate Armed Services Committee he was trying to keep abreast of ominous events in Vietnam and Laos. The Warren Commission had started its hearings. Mansfield had again decided against round-the-clock Senate sessions to fight the filibuster, but with the civil rights debate going from morning until late at night, Russell could not attend the commission's hearings. He arranged to get transcripts of each day's session to read in his office at night. There were days and nights when he never left the U.S. Capitol complex, eating in the Senate restaurant and sleeping in his office.[11]

On March 26, the motion to take up the civil rights bill finally came to a vote. Southerners mustered only seventeen votes against it. Purists mark that vote as the beginning of the longest filibuster in the history of the U.S. Senate. It lasted fifty-seven working days—seventy-four days if the debate on the motion to take up is included; but eventually the Johnson battle plan prevailed. By early May, Humphrey, Dirksen, and Bobby Kennedy were negotiating on what should be included in a new draft. On May 26, the final draft was introduced by Dirksen and Mansfield. It contained a number of language modifications, but the only substantive change required that a "pattern or practice" of discrimination must exist in employment or public accommodations before the federal government could seek corrective action in court.

Russell did not join the bipartisan chorus of praise when Dirksen unveiled the final version of the bill, but he told the Senate he was well aware of Dirksen's prowess. "He is, without doubt, the greatest thespian who has ever trod this floor," said Russell, adding that in the civil rights debate, Dirksen had surpassed even his own Shakespearean pinnacle.[12]

Publicly, Johnson had taken the position that he would support whatever changes the negotiators agreed to. In private, he had chewed at Dirksen almost every day on the telephone. Weeks later, in a telephone call on an unrelated issue, Dirksen would complain to Johnson that the president had insisted that Dirksen accept all the major features of the House-passed bill.[13]

Russell was well aware of Johnson's involvement, but in the long days of debate he focused criticism on Bobby Kennedy's role. Supporters of the bill were led by a "troika," Russell said, identifying Humphrey, Dirksen, and Attorney General Kennedy—with Kennedy as "the lead horse."[14] After Kennedy sent a series of responses to legal questions posed by the respected Republican senator John Sherman Cooper of Kentucky, Russell wrote Kennedy, citing instances in which prior attorneys general had declined to give legal opinions to Congress on constitutional grounds, because they were members of the executive branch. Kennedy replied that he was helping the president fulfill his constitutional role of keeping Congress informed.[15]

On June 10, by a vote of 71 to 29 (at least 67 ayes were required), the Senate voted to close off debate on a civil rights bill for the first time in its history. Filibusters had successfully blocked eleven previous civil rights bills and two attempts to amend the antifilibuster rule. After the historic cloture vote, the Senate acted rapidly on remaining amendments, and Russell complained bitterly that "a lynch mob" had taken over.[16] As a last resort, he proposed that provisions of the bill be submitted to a national referendum. That proposal was overwhelmingly defeated on June 12, and on June 19 the bill passed the Senate.

On July 2 the House passed the Senate version of the bill, thereby avoiding a House-Senate conference to resolve the few differences between the two bills. Johnson signed the new law in a televised ceremony at the White House a few hours after the bill was finally approved.

A couple of weeks after the bill was signed, Russell spoke in Rome, Georgia. The occasion was a conference on the state's economic development, but Russell told a member of his staff that he wanted to insert some comments on the newly approved civil rights bill and outlined what he wanted to say. When he received the staffer's draft he materially strengthened the text.

In those comments, Russell deplored the passage of the new civil rights law and pledged to fight against further incursions into the South's way of life. More importantly, however, he said provisions of the new law were on the books and must be obeyed. It was not a conciliatory speech. Russell did not retreat. But it was a speech that reminded Georgians that they were obligated to obey the law.[17] It was, in essence, the speech Dwight D. Eisenhower never made after the Supreme Court had distressed him with its school desegregation decision ten years previously.

On July 23, three weeks after he had signed the civil rights bill, President Johnson sent Russell a note:

Dear Dick:
The statement you made in Georgia last week on the need to comply with the law was as significant as any I have heard made by a public official in this country. As the acknowledged leader of the opposition to the Civil Rights Bill, your reputation and your standing could not be higher in those areas where the adjustment to the Bill will be most difficult. Your call for compliance with the law of the land is, of course, in keeping with your personal code and I am confident it will have a great impact.
It was the right and courageous thing to do, and I am as proud and pleased as I can be.[18]

On July 25, Russell replied rather formally:

Dear Mr. President:
Permit me to express to you my deep appreciation for your very gracious note on my law and order speech in Rome, Georgia.
It is, of course, extremely gratifying to receive praise from such a source.
With assurances of personal esteem . . .[19]

The Kennedy White House had begun to focus on poverty as an area requiring legislative attention before the president died. At the time of his death, however, Kennedy, under severe budgetary constraints, had decided to concentrate for the time being on his two main legislative goals, the tax and civil rights bills.

As he advanced the Kennedy program, Johnson saw the poverty issue as one that he could adopt as his own. It was an issue that fit nicely into his own very simple vision for the nation: jobs for everyone, fair prices for the farmer, as much education as each young American could absorb, health care and retirement security guaranteed—all in a society free of racial discrimination. In his State of the Union Message he had declared "unconditional war on poverty in America," and in February he had named Jack Kennedy's brother-in-law, Sargent Shriver, to command the poverty war.

As planning went forward, Johnson found a watchword for his national goals, heralding a Great Society, with the War on Poverty as its centerpiece. By early August a bill establishing the Office of Economic Opportunity (OEO) had passed the House and was ready for Senate approval.

After the civil rights battle and in spite of his criticism of the president's efforts in dealing with another issue—dissension in the Panama Canal Zone—Russell found himself once again a member of the Johnsons' circle of intimates, frequently at the White House (often unofficially), needling his old friend as he had done in days past, and joking over the dinner table with Lynda and Luci. It was unexpected. Russell felt that Johnson had changed his mind on issues on which he was still resolute, and he was sure the president was aware of that.

However, Johnson was a man who didn't like to be by himself, Russell said, "and he would call me up, not weekly, but pretty frequently, to come down there and have supper with him. I'd go down and we'd sit around and have a highball and eat supper and talk about things and people. He was always interested in people and what they were doing . . . without getting into any argument about the matters we differed over. He was as kind to me as a man could have been to his own father."[20]

One of Johnson's kindnesses addressed a family matter that was deeply troubling to Russell as he tried to cope with his many official responsibilities. His nephew Bobby, who had ridden the "LBJ Special" in 1960 and was now a Georgia judge, had been told that he had cancer and that the prognosis was very bad. Johnson learned of the situation and, according to Mrs. Johnson, impulsively picked up the telephone and invited the Robert Russells and their five children to spend the first weekend in August at the White House, where he and Mrs. Johnson also entertained the senator and other members of the Russell family. Mrs. Johnson recalled it as "a thoroughly delightful time . . . it was one of those instances where it was apparent that Dick Russell was kind of reliving his life through his kinfolks."[21]

That week, the events in Vietnam that had been troubling Russell (and Johnson as well) finally came to a head. When Johnson became president, about 16,000 advisers from the U.S. armed services were already on duty in Vietnam, supposedly in noncombat roles. About fifty of them already had been killed in the four previous years. Assistance to the South Vietnamese was costing the United States about $400 million a year, but, like most U.S. activities overseas, the investment of personnel and money had caused little public controversy up to that time.[22]

On the afternoon of August 2, the destroyer USS *Maddox* was attacked by three North Vietnamese patrol boats in the Tonkin Gulf. A U.S. aircraft carrier provided air support, and in a twenty-minute action, the *Maddox* sank two of the patrol boats and damaged the third. No Americans were hurt in the brief action, and U.S. reaction was restrained. But the incident served to revive an idea that Johnson had shelved earlier that summer. Up to that time, U.S. assistance for South Vietnam had been extended by presidential authority, without congressional endorsement. Johnson's aides had drawn up a resolution authorizing the president to commit U.S. forces in support of any Southeast Asian nation threatened by Communist aggression, but Johnson had finally decided not to ask Congress to approve such a resolution. After the attack on the *Maddox,* however, the plan was revived in the State Department.

On the evening of August 3, in rain squalls and darkness, the destroyers *Maddox* and *C. Turner Joy* asked for air cover after radio intercepts indicated that North Vietnamese patrol boats were preparing for another attack. With visual sightings impossible, the two destroyers began evasive action on the basis of radar blips and commenced firing at their radar targets. Soundmen on the ships "heard" as many as twenty torpedoes as the two ships maneuvered wildly, firing into the darkness; but neither destroyer was hit and no sightings were made by U.S. planes in the rainswept skies overhead.

Already under attack by Barry Goldwater, who was seeking the GOP presidential nomination, for being soft on Communism—in Vietnam and all over the world—Johnson told congressional leaders on the morning of August 4 that he would retaliate against North Vietnam for its repeated attacks and would ask Congress for a resolution authorizing him to take further action if necessary.

Commanders of the *Maddox* and *C. Turner Joy* were already reassessing the nighttime melee, interviewing members of their crews, especially the operators of radar and underwater sound equipment. It developed that there had been no visual sightings of enemy patrol boats or of enemy gunfire. While attempts were being made to resolve these uncertainties, the White House announced on the evening of August 4 that retaliatory raids had been made on targets in North Vietnam for repeated attacks on U.S. armed forces.

Russell had dined with the Johnsons on the night of the initial attack on the *Maddox,* and he had participated in White House meetings before the president acted. He had not changed his mind about the advisability of full-scale U.S. intervention in Vietnam; he did not believe U.S. interests were involved there. But he made no objection when Johnson outlined his plans to congressional leaders.

Two days later, when Congress hastily approved the wide-ranging Tonkin Gulf Resolution authorizing use of U.S. forces in the area, Russell declared that national honor was at stake in the two attacks on U.S. forces, and "we cannot and will not shrink from defending it."[23] He did supply a paragraph for the approved Tonkin Gulf Resolution that provided for withdrawal of its authority by concurrent action of the Senate and House, without presidential approval or veto.

The Tonkin Gulf Resolution, offered and approved in response to this small, localized conflict, would provide the congressional underpinning for U.S. actions in Vietnam, Laos, and Cambodia over the ensuing decade. Two senators, both Democrats, voted against the resolution, Alaska's feisty Ernest Gruening and Johnson's old friend and antagonist Wayne Morse.

For all its historic importance, the Tonkin Gulf Resolution was just another incident for Johnson in the late summer of 1964. Despite the predictions of the pundits that he would win reelection easily over Barry Goldwater, his most likely opponent, Johnson was planning an all-out, nationwide campaign.

In the spring he had been forced to deal with an effort by some of the Kennedy faithful to secure the vice presidential nomination for Robert Kennedy. He squashed it in a typically devious way, by announcing that no member of the cabinet would be considered as a possible candidate for vice president. In June, he had asked Russell for advice on a vice presidential nominee, listing a number of possibilities, and Russell had favored Robert McNamara or Sen. Eugene McCarthy of Minnesota. Johnson, according to Russell's notes, said that "he could not afford to spare McNamara."[24]

In the end, until the last minute before his own nomination on August 26, the president played Johnsonian games, encouraging speculation about a series of vice presidential possibilities before settling on McCarthy's Minnesota colleague, Hubert H. Humphrey.

On the previous evening, with the Democratic National Convention already underway, Johnson had experienced another attack of self-doubt—an attack that seemed to reflect his need for new assurances that he was really wanted. He wrote out part of a statement saying that he was not the charismatic national leader who could unite people of all parties and races at that critical time. Around midnight he called George Reedy, the White House press secretary and, in a walk around the south lawn, asked Reedy to draft a formal statement withdrawing as a candidate.[25]

Reedy had been conditioned to the wide swings of Johnson's emotions, but he was panicked by this one. Johnson argued that no one wanted him as the nominee—that Democrats really wanted Bobby Kennedy; that blacks would not vote for him; that liberals saw him as a Southern redneck. He said he wanted to go back to the ranch and live out his life with his family where he was appreciated. Reedy refused to draft a withdrawal statement and pleaded with Johnson to change his mind, arguing that withdrawal would split the Democratic party and might result in a victory for Goldwater, who had just been nominated by the Republicans. Johnson would not be swayed.[26]

He had, however, shown his own short draft to Lady Bird, and as he prepared for bed, he found a short note from her. She wrote that Johnson was as brave as any of the thirty-five other men who had occupied the presidency. "To step out now would be wrong for your country," she said, "and I can see nothing but a lonely wasteland for your future. Your friends would be frozen in embarrassed silence and your enemies jeering."[27]

The next day, the withdrawal statement apparently forgotten, he flew to the convention in Atlantic City to accept its presidential nomination.

Russell was also becoming involved in political maneuvering, although he was, as usual, keeping clear of presidential politics. Though he would not face a reelection contest for another two years, he was concerned about his Senate seat. It appeared that Carl Sanders, the Georgia governor who had listened in the gallery with Lady Bird as Johnson delivered his "Let us continue" speech, was preparing to run against him in 1966, when Sanders would be barred by Georgia law from a second consecutive four-year term as governor.

As a state legislator, Sanders had been active in the 1960 Kennedy election campaign in Georgia. As governor he was managing Johnson's 1964 campaign in Georgia and, as a member of the executive committee of the governors' conference, had conferred with the president from time to time.

In the spring, Lady Bird had been invited to a Sanders reception and inquired of the Russell office if her attendance would be "embarrassing" for Russell in light of what appeared to be an impending Sanders-Russell campaign. Russell sent word that Sanders was governor of Georgia and that, as first lady, she should attend.[28]

Russell began making preparations for his first serious election challenge since he had defeated Eugene Talmadge in 1936. He brought William Bates, a former press secretary, back to his staff and assigned Bates and William Jordan, a top staff assistant, to outline a campaign to head off a campaign by the governor.[29]

In September, after the Warren Commission had reported that Lee Harvey Oswald was responsible for the death of John F. Kennedy, Johnson discharged the commission with words of praise and sent Russell a "word of personal thanks," saying that he was "particularly grateful to you and to my other old friends in the Congress who agreed to shoulder this new burden in addition to their heavy and inescapable responsibilities on the Hill."[30]

Russell had been annoyed when Johnson high-handedly announced his membership on the commission, and his distrust of Chief Justice Earl Warren had surfaced immediately. A few days after the president's announcement, Russell's suspicions were aroused when he asked Warren whether the Central Intelligence Agency knew anything about the Kennedy assassination. Russell, head of the Senate subcommittee overseeing the CIA, scrawled a note after the call, saying Warren seemed to know more about the CIA than he did.

"Something strange is happening," he wrote, noting that Warren and Attorney General Nicholas Katzenbach seemed to know everything about the role of the FBI. Russell thought they were planning to show that Lee Harvey Oswald was "the only one" to be considered in investigating the assassination.

"This to me is untenable position—I must insist on outside counsel," he wrote, commenting, "Remember Warren's blanket indictment of South."[31]

A month later, after talking "at length and around Robin Hood's barn" with J. Lee Rankin, who had been named the commission's chief counsel, Russell wrote: "For some reason Warren is stacking this staff with extreme liberals."[32]

For Russell the preparation of the commission's final report had also posed problems. Believing that commission investigators had paid insufficient attention to Oswald's wife, Marina, he found time to interview her in Dallas. Then, when a draft of the commission report was ready for consideration, he objected to language stating that Oswald had acted alone and on his own initiative.[33]

Some of the commission's deliberations had taken place during the filibuster on the civil rights bill, and Russell would later describe the period as the "most arduous" he had ever experienced. Nevertheless, he would have been glad to have the commission take a couple of extra months to do its job more thoroughly.

His early suspicions had apparently been somewhat allayed by the time the report was approved, but in 1970 he said: "I have never been completely satisfied with the report. . . . Now I don't mean by that that I think there was any great omission, but I do think it could have been made much more convincing with the evidence we had, had it been tied more closely together."[34]

As to the report's general conclusion that Oswald was the man who fired the shots and that he acted alone, "I think any other commission that you might appoint," he said, "would arrive at that conclusion." He said the material withheld from the public was largely technical, relating to the autopsy, and would not materially change the report if made public.

"I have never believed that Oswald planned [the assassination] altogether by himself," Russell said, noting especially Oswald's travels to Minsk, where the Russians educated Cuban students, and his trip to Mexico. "So as to whether it was an assignment or whether it was a conspiracy or whether he did it with the knowledge of certain people in the thought that he was helping some Communist states, I'm not prepared to say, because we didn't have enough evidence to pin it down. But I'm not completely satisfied in my own mind that he did plan and commit this act altogether on his own, without consultation with anyone else. And that's what a majority of the commission wanted to find."[35]

Russell refused to sign the initial draft report and finally negotiated a clause into the approved version stating that the commission had exhausted the evidence available to it and that any evidence that might disclose a conspiracy was beyond the jurisdiction of U.S. police bodies—the FBI and the Secret Service.[36]

With Carl Sanders running the Johnson reelection campaign in Georgia, Russell again went traveling in Europe. However, he did reply to a young state senator named Jimmy Carter, who had urged him to join the Georgia Democrats who were working for the Johnson-Humphrey ticket. Russell wrote Carter that he had said repeatedly that he would vote the straight Democratic ticket and thought that statement had been carried in every newspaper in the state.

"President Johnson and I have been personal friends since he first came to the Senate, but I do not believe that even he would ask me to stultify myself by getting out now and supporting a campaign platform endorsing and assuring enforcement of a system which changes the form of government that we have heretofore known in this country."

The recent civil rights battle not forgotten, Russell also commented sourly on the views of vice presidential candidate Humphrey "with respect to the rules of the Senate and his belief in gagging those who disagree with the majority." Humphrey, Russell said, "can charm the birds right out of the trees . . . [but] his philosophy is different from mine. . . ."[37]

Mrs. Johnson asked Russell to join her campaign train as it made its way across Georgia. He offered advice and help but declined an active role, explaining that he was unhappy with parts of the party platform and with Humphrey as the vice presidential nominee. When the first lady's aide, Liz Carpenter, called a few days later to ask that he reconsider, Russell noted "nothing but pressure, pressure to ride Lady Bird Special."[38]

Sanders's strong support of Johnson—and Russell's silence—did nothing to quiet speculation that Sanders would run for the Senate against Russell in 1966. There were even rumors that the president was urging Sanders to run against his old friend. Late in the campaign, as he had always done, Russell again announced that he would vote the straight Democratic ticket.

In mid-October a magazine poll of members of Congress and the Washington press corps named Russell the most effective senator. A few days before election day, Johnson sent Russell "heartiest congratulations and warm good wishes" on his birthday.[39] To no one's surprise, the election produced the landslide that Johnson had sought, but Georgia went for Goldwater.

Russell's European travels and his failure to campaign in his home state for his old friend while Sanders managed the unsuccessful Johnson effort provoked critical comment. Chided at one public appearance for those travels, Russell suggested that, in view of the result, it would have been better if Sanders had been the one traveling in Europe.

After the election, the president asked Russell to invite a group of top Georgia Democrats—including Sanders, Herman Talmadge, and the ailing Judge Robert Russell—for a deer hunt at the LBJ ranch. Sanders at first declined what he viewed as a secondhand invitation, extended through Russell, but changed his mind after a call from Johnson. He did attend and participated in the deer hunt, a ritual at the LBJ ranch.

After the event, acknowledging a note from Sanders, Russell wrote: "I thoroughly enjoyed our association on our trip to Texas and our visit with the President. You certainly carried off the laurels of the day by killing two deer."[40]

Weeks later, Russell sent a rather formal note to thank President and Mrs. Johnson for a Christmas remembrance, saying: "I earnestly hope and pray that Providence will vouchsafe you good health and good spirits . . . and can assure you that I will contribute in any way I can to the solution of our national problems." He added a handwritten footnote: "The deer sausages were wonderful and created more talk around Winder than Santa Claus."[41]

The 1964 Johnson landslide again strengthened the Democrats' control of Congress. One additional Senate seat and 37 seats in the House were added to Democratic ranks. In the Senate the new ratio was 68 Democrats to only 32 Republicans. The House had 259 Democrats and 140 Republicans. With margins of that sort, President Johnson set his sights on another legislative blitz.

One long-standing legislative hurdle was cleared when a presidential task force devised a formula that put an end to a long impasse over federal aid for elementary and secondary schools. With federal courts forbidding aid to church-related schools, the Roman Catholic hierarchy and other religious organizations had previously opposed federal aid bills. Johnson's task force came up with antipoverty programs offering church-related schools help in financing textbooks, technical equipment, and certain educational facilities. With these proposals quelling opposition, Johnson's education bill easily won House approval late in March and was passed by the Senate, without change, early in April. It was another major achievement for Johnson—a success where others had frequently failed.

Russell was not on hand for much of the legislative activity. Worn down by the heavy burdens of the previous congressional session, he had not really rebounded during the recess. Shortly after returning to Washington, he spent a Saturday with the Johnsons at Camp David, the presidential retreat in the Catoctin Mountains near Washington. He and Johnson needled each other amiably about prospects for new civil rights legislation, and they returned to the White House for a late supper. It was a thoroughly enjoyable day.[42]

Russell's respiratory problems had continued, however, and he was soon fighting what he first thought was bronchitis and then suspected was pneumonia. On February 2 he was admitted to Walter Reed Army Medical Center, suffering, the doctors said, from pulmonary edema—a serious congestion of fluid in the lungs. In the hospital, his condition worsened. Relatives were notified and Russell's sister Ina hurried to Washington to keep a vigil in the hospital.[43] In the White House, President Johnson, who had also been notified, immediately arranged to get periodic hospital reports on Russell's condition.[44]

When the situation became critical, doctors at Walter Reed performed a successful tracheotomy—cutting into Russell's windpipe to ease pressure and facilitate breathing. By February 5 the doctors were able to advise the White House that, although Russell was still a sick man, his condition was improved, his temperature was normal, and he was able to breathe without using an oxygen tube from time to time.[45]

On February 11, as the hospital reports showed continued improvement, Johnson dictated a note to Russell saying that "not a day goes by but my thoughts and those of the girls are not with you." He said he wanted to come out to Walter Reed for a visit but was reluctant to disrupt the hospital routine with a large contingent of trailing White House press. Lady Bird, he said, wanted Russell to know that they would be glad to accommodate any of Russell's visiting relatives at the White House.

"I lean on you so much, Dick, and not having you where I can talk to you is an unfillable void," the president said, and ended the letter by saying the Johnsons sent their love and their prayers and were awaiting Russell's full recovery. He added a handwritten postscript: "We think of you (all four of us) many times each day and are so thankful for the good nurses and doctors who are helping you. Thank them for me."[46]

On February 20, a Saturday, Johnson sat down at lunchtime in the White House to write a short note: "This morning I learned you were up and around. I hope you get away to Florida and some sunshine soon! Let me know if there is anything I can do. Love."[47] A few days later, Barboura Raesley, one of Russell's secretaries, wrote the president at Russell's direction: Russell was "overwhelmed by the flow of flowers," wanted to express his deep appreciation, and would write, himself, when he could.[48]

During the worst of Russell's illness, members of his family and staff had kept a constant watch at the hospital. On the night of the tracheotomy, Proctor Jones, a young Russell staff member, was left to stand a solitary watch, while others, advised that the operation had been successfully concluded, went to dinner. Soon after he was left alone in the waiting room, Jones was advised that the senator had regained consciousness and wanted to speak to him. Inside Russell's hospital room difficulties arose when Russell wanted to talk but had to be shown by the medical staff how to cover the new opening in his throat before he could speak. Finally he managed to ask Jones to call Harriet Orr and tell her about his condition.

Over the years, Russell's warm personal relationship with Harriet Orr had flourished. Long viewed by his colleagues—and now routinely described in the press—as a lonely old bachelor, he had continued to visit Harriet Orr, steak in hand, almost every weekend, and their close relationship had become very important to him.

Proctor Jones was one of the few people outside the Russell family who knew how important it was. Jones had been brought to Washington to complete his education while employed as a Senate elevator operator under Russell's Senate patronage. Even before he became a full-time member of Russell's staff, Jones had been the messenger who usually went to the market on Saturday to buy the steaks.

On one occasion, at the senator's request, he had double-dated with Russell and Harriet Orr when her niece was in Washington for a visit. And Jones, as a young bachelor, was the staff member who frequently drove to Winder with Russell when the Senate was not in session. More than once he had spent the night at the Orr family home on the way to Winder.[49]

As Russell requested, Jones called Harriet Orr and told her what had happened. She had seen a short item in the newspaper reporting Russell's hospitalization, but she did not know that this trip to the hospital was serious or that the tracheotomy had been performed. Soon after Jones returned to the waiting room, the diners returned, and within the hour a large bouquet of red roses was delivered with a card: Harriet Orr.[50]

Heartened as he was by a galaxy of legislative achievements, in which aid to education was the brightest but by no means the only star, Johnson could take no comfort whatever from the rapidly worsening situation in Vietnam. It was becoming clear that South Vietnamese military forces were losing their little war and the country's government was disintegrating. The president was under pressure from some of his top aides to bomb strategic targets in the North. Mindful of his campaign promise not to expand the U.S. commitment and well aware of the damage that a major military effort could inflict on his plans for a Great Society, Johnson had resisted the pressure, despite serious provocations.

On November 1, Vietcong guerrillas had conducted a mortar attack at Bien Hoa Air Base, twelve miles north of Saigon, the South Vietnamese capital. The attack had killed five Americans and two Vietnamese and wounded nearly a hundred. On Christmas Eve Vietcong agents had planted a bomb in a Saigon hotel used to house U.S. officers, killing two and injuring fifty-eight others.

In January, before he entered the hospital, Russell had stated publicly that the time had come to "re-evaluate our position in Vietnam."[51] In private, he was doing all he could to change that position. He was deeply concerned about the consequences of a growing U.S. commitment there.

He expressed his views forcefully at a meeting of the Senate Democratic Policy Committee at which the Vietnam involvement was discussed. At Russell's instigation, the committee decided to send its chairman, Mike Mansfield, to the White House on a private mission to advise the president of the committee's conviction that the United States should find a way to withdraw from Vietnam.

Nearly thirty years later, Mansfield would say: "I did as I was instructed" and told Johnson that committee members "felt strongly that we were wrong in being in Vietnam and that we should find an expeditious and honorable way to get out." The president listened, thanked Mansfield for bringing the committee's view to his attention, and, according to Mansfield, "that was about it."[52]

In early February, a few days after Russell's hospitalization, U.S. Air Force barracks at Pleiku in South Vietnam's central highlands were attacked with grenades and mortar fire by Vietcong units. Eight Americans died in the night attack, and more than 100 were wounded. Ten U.S. planes were also destroyed.

Johnson had authorized bombing of the Ho Chi Minh Trail, by which supplies from the North were reaching the Vietcong, but he had resisted pressures for more aggressive responses to the earlier attacks. Pleiku was a serious new provocation, and pressures intensified, in Washington and Saigon, for retaliatory action. When Russell's health permitted, the president went to visit him at Walter Reed Army Medical Center and found that Mansfield was also a visitor. A few days earlier, Mansfield had again expressed his concerns about Vietnam at a White House meeting with the president and his national security advisers. At the hospital it was Russell who expressed opposition to more aggressive action. As Mansfield recalled it, "He advised President Johnson not to become [further] involved in Vietnam" and pointed out "what the ultimate results would be."[53]

In retrospect, it would appear that the decisions had already been made. A few days later, Operation Rolling Thunder, involving aggressive bombing of targets in North Vietnam, got underway. Before Russell left the hospital in early March, U.S. marine ground units went ashore at Danang, ostensibly to protect the 23,000 Americans deployed in air and advisory roles in Vietnam. Less than a month later, more marines and 18,000 troops in logistics units were committed by the president, who also authorized aggressive patrolling by U.S. forces to supplement the ongoing defensive maneuvers.

For the first time, in Rolling Thunder, the president personally participated in pinpointing targets to be hit in the North by U.S. bombers, using a grid of aerial photos spread in the White House Situation Room. The bombing raids were designed to slow the infiltration of manpower and supplies from bases in North Vietnam to Communist units in the South. They also had another important objective: lifting the desperately sagging morale in Saigon and elsewhere in South Vietnam.

The raids, which occurred north of the 17th parallel, the dividing line between North and South Vietnam, marked a watershed in two respects. In Vietnam, they were a major escalation of the U.S. military effort. At home, they served to crystallize a nucleus of dissent in Congress against the hostilities 10,000 miles away and against the president's Southeast Asia policy in general. Six months earlier the Tonkin Gulf Resolution had won congressional approval by a combined vote in the House and Senate of 502 to 2. After Johnson went north with the bombing raids, he quickly had a handful of critics, and soon a double handful, publicly voicing doubts about his policies.

Early in the spring, with Russell convalescing in Georgia, history took a hand in shaping President Johnson's legislative agenda. A civil rights bill was unexpectedly added to the president's must list, and its priority resulted from an incident that took place in Selma, Alabama, on March 7, 1965, a day that became known in the civil rights movement as Black Sunday.

Although the previous civil rights bills had aimed at assuring all Americans the right to vote, their provisions had been frustrated by local voting officials in Southern states. Early in January, Martin Luther King Jr. had launched a voter registration campaign in Selma—a town of about 30,000, where only about 325 of 15,000 black residents were registered to vote. In the ensuing weeks, thousands of men, women, and children (including Dr. King) were jailed by Sheriff James Clark, and on February 18 a youthful black demonstrator was fatally shot.

King scheduled an 80-mile protest march for March 7, down the main highway from Selma to Montgomery, the state capital. Governor George Wallace banned the protest march and sent 100 state troopers to augment Sheriff Clark's forces. The marchers, about 600 blacks and a few white sympathizers, met the sheriff's combined forces, many wearing gas masks and some on horseback, at the Pettus Bridge that Sunday. Ignoring two warnings to disperse, the marchers surged forward and were attacked, first with tear gas and then by Clark's men swinging billy clubs and bullwhips.

The protesters were beaten back and forced to retreat, but the encounter was captured in all its bloody detail by television cameras, and their recording of the event provoked an outpouring of outrage across the nation. King would have settled for the public relations triumph, but some of his lieutenants and many rank-and-file marchers were determined to conduct the protest as planned. In the end, a federal judge sanctioned the march, but Governor Wallace said he could not protect the marchers.

Johnson sent U.S. marshals, FBI agents, regular troops, and federalized Alabama national guardsmen to ensure the safety of the marchers, now 1,500 strong, many of them white clergymen who had converged on the little Alabama town to join the protest. Johnson also directed the Justice Department to draft a new and tougher voting rights bill.

On March 15 at 9 p.m.—prime television time—the president addressed a joint session of Congress to ask for quick approval of a new civil rights bill designed, at long last, to assure all Americans the right to vote. The entire session lasted less than an hour, but Johnson's speech was one of the best of his presidency.

Deploring the events at Selma, Johnson declared that, after a hundred years, "emancipation is a proclamation not a fact." After a hundred years, he said, "the Negro is not equal." The president recalled his own first job after college, as a teacher in a small school for Mexican-Americans in Cotulla, Texas, where he saw for himself the effects of racial discrimination. "Somehow you never forget what poverty and hatred can do when you see its scars on the hopeful face of a young child," he said. Taking his cue from the favorite hymn of the civil rights marchers, Johnson declared that "we shall overcome," and added, "really it is all of us who must overcome the crippling legacy of bigotry and injustice."[54]

Returning to the White House after the speech, Johnson took a call from Russell, who was still convalescing in Winder. Russell said that although he obviously could not support the voting rights bill, he thought Johnson's speech was "the best speech he ever heard any president give." Johnson replied that he understood Russell's position and added that "no opinion in the world means as much to me as yours."[55]

Senate debate on the new voting rights bill began in April, with Sen. Allen J. Ellender, Democrat of Louisiana, calling signals for the Southerners in Russell's absence. Ellender used the tactics developed by Russell, but it was clear that something had gone out of the Southern opposition. Roger Mudd, who had become a prominent CBS correspondent with nightly reports from the Capitol on the 1964 debate and filibuster, would liken the antifilibuster efforts after 1964 to the achievement of the four-minute mile: once the historic cloture barrier had been broken, it was quickly broken again and again.[56]

As submitted, the voting rights bill was designed to suspend the use of poll taxes or literacy tests in areas—states or counties—where less than 50 percent of the residents of voting age were registered to vote or had voted in the 1964 presidential elections. It would allow the attorney general to appoint federal examiners to register blacks in those areas. In committee, the bill's supporters had added an outright ban on poll taxes in state and local elections, as they had been banned in federal elections by constitutional amendment in 1962.

In the Senate, opponents argued that a federal encroachment by statute on state and local elections was unconstitutional, and the ban was dropped. Russell returned to work in May and participated only briefly in the debate. Finally, after about a month of filibuster, the Senate voted 70 to 30 to close off the talk. The following day, the Senate approved the bill, 77 to 19. Early in July, the House passed its version of the bill, including a ban on poll taxes. To resolve differences, the Senate-House conference committee replaced the House-approved ban with language condemning poll taxes, and both houses approved the final version of the bill.

In other respects, Johnson's legislative blitz was rolling forward, and, as it rolled, it toppled another longtime holdout against federal intervention—health insurance for the elderly. A proposal for federal health insurance for older Americans under the Social Security system had begun as a Harry Truman initiative, but it had never been approved. In July,

Johnson was able to sign the Medicare bill, writing the Truman dream into the law books.

While the voting rights bill was being debated, the president made an important civil rights speech at the commencement ceremonies at Howard University, the prestigious black university in Washington. Tracing the progress already made in opening opportunities for blacks, he addressed the problem of expanding their achievements. He stressed the importance of strengthening the black family.

The speech was based in large part on a still unpublicized report, prepared under the direction of Assistant Secretary of Labor Daniel P. Moynihan, that focused on the deterioration of families in the nation's segregated black society, heavily settled and disproportionately unemployed in the nation's larger cities. Johnson announced that he would convene a White House conference later in the year to consider how blacks could better take advantage of the opportunities that were then opening up for them.

In August Johnson signed the new voting rights law, which would, at long last, materially change voting patterns in the Old South. A week after the bill was signed, in an ominous foretaste of things to come, a minor incident and subsequent arrest in the mostly black Watts section of Los Angeles escalated into a week of rioting, in which thousands of national guardsmen were finally called upon to quell the armed uprisings.

During Russell's illness, the illness of his nephew Bobby had reached a critical point. Russell aide Bill Bates, who had known Bobby in college, got him admitted to the cancer unit of the National Institutes of Health in Washington. The senator was not advised that Bobby was dying until he himself was out of danger. The end came in June.

On June 14, after telegraphing an expression of sympathy from himself and Lady Bird to Mrs. Robert Russell, Johnson addressed a wire to Russell, who was again in Winder: "The news of Bobby was a blow I feel in every bone. You know what a special meaning he had for me as both the nephew of a man whose friendship I cherish above all others and as my own friend too. Lady Bird and I share your grief as our own and Lynda and Luci join in sending our love and devotion and prayers."[57] Once again, this time as president of the United States, Lyndon Johnson overcame his distaste for funerals and attended church services and burial rites in the little cemetery behind the Russell farmhouse.

Although it had been expected, Bobby's death was a blow for Russell. "Life is indeed strange," he told an old friend, "when a young man of forty with five children is taken and a much older man like me manages to get back in business."[58]

In the hot Washington summer, Vietnam was becoming an obsession for the president. In May, facing increasing criticism of his policies, he had ordered a halt in the bombing of North Vietnam and sought to make diplomatic contact with North Vietnamese representatives in Moscow. The North Vietnamese would not even meet with his spokesman, and the bombing was resumed after a six-day pause.

On the ground, South Vietnamese forces were being eaten away by the Vietcong. In Saigon, Gen. William C. Westmoreland, the U.S. commander, was asking for 180,000 U.S. combat troops to prevent a total collapse. Defense Secretary Robert S. McNamara supported Westmoreland's request and proposed that reservists—mostly former servicemen—be called up to mount a massive offensive.

Johnson knew that calling up the reserves would fan the critical fires at home. In mid-July he walked unannounced into a White House staff meeting, listened for a while, and finally said: "Don't let me interrupt. But there's one thing you ought to know. Vietnam is like being in a plane without a parachute, when all the engines go out. If you jump, you'll probably be killed, and if you stay in, you'll probably burn. That's what it is." He left the room without waiting for comment.[59]

A few weeks later, Russell annoyed the president by suggesting on a TV panel show that it was "highly likely" Ho Chi Minh would win if the South Vietnamese people were asked to choose a leader in a plebescite. He said he was not convinced, by the so-called domino theory, that the other nations of Southeast Asia would fall to the Communists if South Vietnam was defeated. Defining the central problem, Russell said South Vietnam had no value "strategically," but the United States must persevere when it pledges its word, "because if our word isn't good in South Vietnam it isn't good anywhere else around the world."[60]

The president's decision on the Westmoreland troop request was announced on television—but at noon, when there would be a small TV audience. A first installment of 50,000 troops was being sent immediately, he said, but there would be no call-up of reservists. Led by Johnson's old friend and antagonist, Wayne Morse, the liberal criticism began at once; and as it mounted, word was leaked to the press that Mike Mansfield, who had previously withheld public criticism, had strongly stated his private doubts about Vietnam policies in a statement read to the president at a briefing for congressional leaders shortly before the public announcement.

Johnson's volatile spirits, so high during the intoxicating campaign of the previous summer, plunged to new lows. He saw the shadow of Bobby Kennedy lurking behind many of his adversities. The Communists and their evil influence seemed to be everywhere. He secured and read unevaluated FBI reports on some of his critics and professed, at times, to believe them. To some members of his staff his behavior went beyond the erratic to the alarming.

White House aide Richard Goodwin, who had worked for John F. Kennedy and would soon work for Robert Kennedy, had written Johnson's speech on Selma and had rejoiced with the president at its warm reception. But Goodwin, assessing Johnson's subsequent behavior, began reading psychology books about paranoia. Finally mentioning his concerns to Bill Moyers, who had replaced George Reedy as press secretary, Goodwin discovered that Moyers was also concerned. Goodwin has written that he and Moyers were so worried that each of them, without the other's knowledge, consulted a psychiatrist about the president's behavior.[61]

Russell was seldom exposed to Johnson's behavior at this low point. He was deeply involved in his efforts to prevent a 1966 campaign against him. He was making as many speeches across Georgia as his health would permit and was beginning to raise money for campaign operations if Governor Sanders did announce against him. In asking for contributions and acknowledging them, however, Russell told constituents they could expect a "rebate" or a "dividend" if all the money was not needed.[62] Early in September the *Atlanta Journal* carried a page-one report that Sanders had told friends he was going to run against Russell.[63]

Anticipating the race against a challenger who would, if successful, have to climb the Senate's seniority ladder, Russell was counting heavily on voters' appreciation of the many federal activities and installations his seniority had brought to Georgia over the years. He was, however, well aware of voters' recurring campaign question, "What have you done for me lately?" and he was following closely the Pentagon's deliberations on a major defense contract.

The giant C-5A military transport plane had just been authorized by Congress, and the $2.2 billion production contract for building the C-5A fleet would bring a weekly $3 million payroll bonanza to the state where the plane was built. Three firms—Boeing, Douglas, and Lockheed—had submitted bids, and Lockheed, if it won, planned to build the plane in Marietta, Georgia.

Russell's roles as chairman of the Senate Armed Services Committee and longtime intimate friend of Johnson's were duly noted in rumors about the contract award, but so were rumors that Russell's inactivity during the presidential campaign (with Georgia going to Goldwater) would be a factor in the final decision. In any event, the award was of such importance that the Pentagon decision would be made with strong White House input.

One evening in late September, Russell was dining with the Johnsons at the White House when the president brought up the subject of the C-5A contract. Johnson recalled that Secretary McNamara had come under heavy congressional criticism in connection with the design and production of the TFX, a fighter plane for the air force and the navy that had been pushed into production by McNamara over opposition from both services. Would Russell take care of McNamara on the Hill, Johnson asked, if Lockheed got the C-5A contract? Russell said he would do his best to protect the secretary from criticism if the contract provoked a controversy. "Well," said Johnson, "Lockheed's got it."[64]

The next morning, on the office memo that had advised him to call the White House about the dinner invitation, Russell noted: "supper with LBJ and Lady Bird—brought away loot."[65] Later, he called in the *Atlanta Journal*'s Washington correspondent, Margaret Shannon (known to him, in the best Southern locution, as "Miss Margaret") and said he could be quoted as "highly encouraged" that Lockheed would be the winner.[66] The Pentagon made it official a few days later.

At about that time, Russell had occasion to come to the president's defense in a foreign policy controversy. At issue was Johnson's action, early in the summer, dispatching marine units to the Dominican Republic, ostensibly to protect Americans and permit an orderly evacuation in what the U.S. ambassador had described as a Communist-supported uprising. Johnson had personally called the U.S. ambassador, W. Tapley Bennett Jr., to satisfy himself that the situation was critical.

Bennett had spoken to the president from under his desk, where the embassy's marine guards had urged him to take shelter from an aircraft that was, at the moment, buzzing the U.S. compound. The incident was widely publicized, and although Johnson believed he was acting to avoid the emergence of another Cuba in the Caribbean, critics contended that he had sent U.S. forces to intervene against a liberal reform movement in Santo Domingo. In early September, Sen. J. W. Fulbright took that criticism to the Senate floor, attacking the president's action and Bennett's assessment of the uprising.

"Tap" Bennett, a career foreign service officer, was a Georgian from a family well known to Russell. Russell thought Johnson had acted properly and, under the circumstances, was quite ready to say so. He responded to Fulbright's complaints in what Bennett, later U.S. ambassador to Portugal and to NATO, would describe as a "very powerful" Senate speech defending Johnson's action and Bennett personally.[67]

It was a pleasant boost for Johnson, whose troubles were multiplying elsewhere. His legislative blitz had stalled, and he was beginning to suffer setbacks on Capitol Hill. And early in October, he was taken to Bethesda Naval Hospital, where his gall bladder was removed. It was a major operation, and Johnson would have to endure a lengthy and painful convalescence.

After the operation, Russell wired the president: "With the prayers of many millions I know that you will come through in fine shape. I only wish that there might be some service, however small, that I might render. Please do not overdo things during your convalescence." Responding on the bottom of an embossed card thanking correspondents for good wishes, Lady Bird Johnson wrote: "We would have been lonesome if we hadn't heard from you. That was a sweet note. Affectionately, L. B."[68]

In a handwritten note addressed "Dear Chief" and sent in November, Russell said he had been following the daily news reports on Johnson's progress "with anxiety and concern" and had been delighted to see, in a photograph, some indication that Johnson was indeed bowing to his doctors' orders.

"If you can curb that restless spirit and turn down the dynamo for a few days I am sure it will hasten your recovery a great deal.

"The Congress is limping around and should get away in about a week. I do not envy you the administration and oversight of the fantastic amount of legislation enacted. Even more do I shudder to think of the time when any other man will have that responsibility.

"I only wish I could contribute in the slightest to your earlier recovery. Your friend, Dick Russell."[69]

Russell's solicitous attitude toward his commander in chief did not extend to the way the war was being conducted, under Johnson's leadership, halfway around the world. Russell disagreed completely with the rationale that was guiding administration policies.

Five years later Russell would say, "Personally, I never thought . . . that French Indochina, which includes South Vietnam, has any military, political, or economic values that make it worthwhile for us to go in there, even if it were to fall into the hands of the Chinese or the Russians. And I don't think it would fall into the hands of either because I thought the other would challenge them on it and stop it."[70]

That conviction had guided Russell even before he and Johnson had prevented the proposed rescue mission for Dienbienphu in 1954, but once the decision had been made to go in, he wanted to fight to win. "When Johnson got there Kennedy had sent in 18 to 20,000. They were there and they were taking part in the fighting," Russell said. "Johnson had to make the decision on whether or not to send in others or to pull those out. And my complaint with him was not for sending others in, but because we didn't go on and win the war by closing up the ports of North Vietnam. He let the timid souls in the State Department talk him out of that. He could have ended that war in six months any time."[71]

The Johnsons sent Russell a birthday greeting, as they usually did, on November 2, and the following day Russell replied that "it is an honor, indeed, to be remembered by my chief and his lovely wife on my birthday. The friendship and associations with the Lyndon B. Johnson family have been one of the most rewarding aspects of my lifetime, and I am always grateful to know that I am in your thoughts."

On the bottom of the typewritten note he wrote: "hope the press is correct that you are taking good care of yourself."[72]

Personal sentiment was not to be confused with public policy, however, and by mid-month Russell had joined one segment of the president's critics in publicly calling for a more aggressive military posture in Vietnam. He urged a major effort by U.S. and South Vietnamese forces to knock out the North Vietnamese port of Haiphong.[73]

Chapter Seven

BOARDROOM DISSENSION

1966–1967

T he president had assured Dick Russell privately that he was behind him "money, marbles, and chalk" in his anticipated race for re-election against Gov. Carl Sanders, but Johnson had made no public statement.[1] Russell told his office staff that the president had offered Sanders a couple of federal jobs to get him out of the race, but it was beginning to look as if Johnson was playing games, encouraging both campaigns and watching both candidates squirm.[2]

Involved as he was in his Georgia campaign to prevent a campaign, Dick Russell was still in close touch with the White House. Returning from a trip late in February, Lady Bird Johnson found the president huddled there with Russell and reflected that she was always glad to find the two together. All three of them had a late dinner together in the White House.[3]

The president's close relationship with Governor Sanders had again been publicized late in 1965 when Sanders came to the White House and reported to Johnson at length on a trip he and several other governors had made to survey the situation in Vietnam. In Washington again in late January, Sanders denied that he had met privately with Johnson, but it was later reported authoritatively that they had, in fact, met secretly at the White House.[4]

In retrospect it is clear that Johnson was committed, personally as well as politically, to Russell. But the president had always felt free to distance himself from his old friend. After piloting the 1964 civil rights bill to passage in the Senate, breaking the record Russell-led filibuster, Johnson had ridiculed Russell's stand in warning other adversaries not to oppose his initiatives.[5]

For his part, Russell understood—when he could be objective about it amid the anxieties of the Sanders situation—that his relationship with Johnson had changed. Shortly after the Kennedy assassination he had predicted some "head-on collisions" with Johnson and reflected that "he is President . . . I am not" and that each of them now had different responsibilities.[6]

Russell's campaigning in Georgia was nothing like his previous bids for office. In the early campaigns—for the legislature, for governor, and in his two seriously contested Senate campaigns—he had used nonstop speech making, especially to small groups—even awakening individual farmers at midnight for a handshake and a minispeech. He had, however, been one of the first to use radio when it came along, and now he was using more modern, conventional tactics. Nevertheless, it was strenuous for a convalescent, and he found it wearing.[7]

Another aspect of his campaigning was different, too. While his views on civil rights had not changed, the political realities of expanding Negro voting rolls had not escaped him. He remembered how Negro voters had been marched to the polls in groups when he was growing up.[8] Now he was seeking the votes of conservative Negro leaders.

Working with Bill Bates, he developed language for his speeches stressing that the federal programs and installations he had brought to Georgia—like the new C-5A contract—and the programs he could attract in years to come benefited Georgians of all races. All citizens, he said, would share as equal partners in the state's economic advances. It was a variation on the old political theme that a rising tide lifts all boats. He also sought support from old-line black businessmen, including Jesse Hill, longtime head of the Atlanta Life Insurance Company.[9]

To a supporter who had written him about courting various voting blocs in the state, Russell replied, "While I will, of course, lose many of the Negro votes, I agree with you that it would be a serious mistake should I write them off in their entirety. I will get a great many of them."[10]

President Johnson had told Congress in his State of the Union Address that the war in Vietnam was the "center of our concerns," and those concerns were becoming acute.[11] He was determined to succeed in Vietnam and not become the first president to lose a war, but he did not want the war in Vietnam to widen, as the war in Korea had, to involve China and perhaps even Russia. So he was resisting pressures to escalate even as he was escalating, and he believed success in Vietnam could be achieved in an honorable withdrawal. CIA Director John A. McCone thought, before he left the government in 1965, that one of Johnson's priorities (along with his status in the polls and his relations with Congress) was how to get out of Vietnam.[12]

On Christmas Eve, determined to show that he was prepared to negotiate with Hanoi and the Vietcong, he had ordered another bombing pause. Through the holidays, he had tried to get help from other world leaders to set up a dialogue, but he was unsuccessful. The North Vietnamese had not responded. With nearly 200,000 U.S. troops now deployed, the war was going better for South Vietnamese forces, but there was no end of the fighting in sight. It was becoming clear that many more U.S. troops and much more time would be needed to win the war. In Congress and across the nation, a diplomatic solution was looking better and better. That had been the rationale for the bombing halt.

Russell complained that the pause had gone on too long, and on January 31, 1966, Johnson ordered that the bombing be resumed.[13] Early in February, Chairman J. William Fulbright announced that the Senate Foreign Relations Committee would hold a series of televised public hearings on Vietnam and U.S. policies there. Fulbright had become thoroughly disenchanted with the war, and he now moved into the front rank of Johnson's Vietnam policy critics.

Hastily, to preempt the committee's headlines, Johnson scheduled a cabinet-level conference in Honolulu with Nguyen Cao Ky, now the South Vietnamese premier, and top-level aides. As planned, the conference was to focus on the peaceful reconstruction of South Vietnam—a concept outlined by Johnson in a speech at Johns Hopkins University the previous spring. The speech, in which Johnson envisioned a billion-dollar Southeast Asia development program anchored on the meandering Mekong River, had been warmly praised, even by some of the president's critics. Russell thought it one of Johnson's best.[14]

The Honolulu conference produced a hopeful communiqué pledging support for development of a modern Vietnamese society, and it gave the president an opportunity to meet with Ky and with General Westmoreland, the U.S. commander in Vietnam. But it did little to quiet the president's critics. Fulbright complained that the conference had deepened the U.S. commitment in Vietnam and made a negotiated settlement more difficult.[15]

In mid-February the president wrote Russell that he had met Lt. Col. Walter B. Russell, a Russell nephew who had been wounded in Vietnam, at a prayer breakfast in the White House. "He is a fine man," Johnson said, "and I am sure you are very proud of him. I was impressed."[16]

Another critic of the war was beginning to be heard. Robert F.

Kennedy, now the junior senator from New York, had criticized the renewed bombing,[17] and soon after the Honolulu conference, Kennedy held a press conference to propose creation of a coalition government in South Vietnam, with the Vietcong sharing power there.[18] The suggestion provoked a long and angry debate, but it had an even more important and more lasting effect on Johnson: Bobby was back. His malign shadow would again stalk the president's dreams and deepen his despair about the outcome in Vietnam. Johnson had a recurring nightmare in which Bobby Kennedy was in the forefront as Johnson was accused of losing Vietnam, as Harry Truman had been accused of "losing" mainland China. In the dream he could hear voices shouting "Coward! Traitor! Weakling!"[19]

Just as he had resisted a call-up of military reservists, Johnson had avoided any special budgeting or financing arrangements for the fighting in Vietnam. Early in the year, he again decided against a program of new taxes to finance it. When his $4.9 billion defense authorization bill was being debated, Sen. Wayne Morse offered an amendment that would have repealed the Tonkin Gulf Resolution, which was still the only congressional authority on which the war effort was based.

Opponents of the war with different shades of opinion had been searching for some aspect of Johnson's Vietnam policy that could unite them in opposition. (At one point it appeared that Russell had provided that opportunity when he proposed an amendment that would have restated the president's authority to use force in Southeast Asia, but Johnson persuaded Russell to withdraw that proposal.) Morse's amendment was clearly not the proposal to unite the president's critics, however, and it was defeated 92 to 5.

Late in 1965, with Russell campaigning and Sanders still unannounced, the Georgia press began to carry speculative stories and informal surveys suggesting that Sanders would be defeated if he did run against Russell.[20] That speculation continued, and by the spring of 1966, there were reports that Sanders had decided not to run.[21] Later, Carl Sanders would tell an interviewer that in 1965 he had indeed considered running against Russell "because Senator Russell became desperately ill" and it appeared for a while that he "possibly would die." Sanders said he "immediately withdrew my consideration" when it became apparent that Russell would recover and could serve again.[22]

On March 30 the *Atlanta Journal*'s banner headline announced: SANDERS WON'T RUN FOR SENATE, SAYS CONGRESS NEEDS RUSSELL. Russell issued a statement saying that "the governor's announcement is most gratifying, and I appreciate his generous endorsement of my candidacy for reelection. I welcome and shall try to deserve his commendation and support."[23] Russell's office sent telegrams to a few old friends: "Rejoice and be exceedingly glad. Carl E. Sanders has been had."[24]

Sanders would later acknowledge that "it would have been a very very difficult job for anybody to have tackled Dick Russell."[25] In sum, the senator's campaign to prevent a campaign had been a success, and he directed his campaign treasurer in Winder to make proportionate refunds to the people who had sent contributions in anticipation of a full-scale campaign.[26]

About $175,000 had been raised—a substantial sum in that era—but much of it already had been spent in the precampaign preparations. What was left was returned, as Russell had promised, to contributors of $100 or more, who got a rebate of about 25 percent.[27]

In Vietnam, arbitrary actions of South Vietnamese Premier Ky had antagonized Buddhists. Beginning in the old capital city of Hue, they rioted against his government, and Ky was forced to use troops to restore order. For three months, while they were engaged in the war against the Vietcong and the North Vietnamese, South Vietnamese forces were also fighting Buddhist South Vietnamese in Danang and Hue.

With these hostilities in progress, Russell was increasingly glum about prospects for a U.S. victory. In a copyrighted interview that was published in *U.S. News & World Report* and annoyed Johnson, Russell suggested that the United States conduct a careful evaluation of public opinion in South Vietnam, and if the survey showed sentiment was unfavorable to the U.S. involvement, U.S. forces should be withdrawn. If opinion was favorable, he said, the United States should aggressively step up the bombing of the North. In sum, Russell's publicized view was now "win or get out."

Johnson was avoiding all-out bombing of the North and trying to avoid civilian casualties. He personally reviewed target lists, concerned that at some point the U.S. bombing effort might provoke a response from China or the Soviet Union. He feared there were secret treaties between North Vietnam and China or Russia that might be triggered by bombing some specific target. His brother, Sam Houston Johnson, who was living in the White House at the time, described Johnson's agonizing over the war and its casualties:

Almost every morning at three o'clock he would crawl out of bed, often without ever having gone to sleep, wearily slip on his robe and slippers, then go down to the Situation Room in the basement of the White House to get the latest reports coming in from Saigon. Even the loss of one American soldier (it was never that few) could bring on a mood of sadness and frustrated anger that would keep him awake the rest of the night.

Sitting down to breakfast with him and Lady Bird, I could always tell what kind of news had come in from Vietnam. There would be dark hollows under his eyes, his face appeared somewhat gray and drawn,, his shoulders slumped forward, his voice was slightly raspy . . . I would try to make light conversation . . . It seldom did any good.[28]

Determined as he was to avoid retaliation from Russia or China, Johnson could steel himself against the mounting demands of critics like Russell, who urged more aggressive tactics. It was the Vietnam critics who opposed the bombing who really got under his skin. At a Chicago Democratic dinner in May, he lashed out at "nervous Nellies" who become frustrated and turn on their leaders and their own fighting men.[29]

That summer did have its happier moments for the two old friends. On August 6, nineteen-year-old Luci Baines Johnson was married to Patrick John Nugent at the National Shrine of the Immaculate Conception in Washington. It was the first White House wedding in fifty years and a major Washington social event.

A few days before he attended the wedding, Russell wrote the bride:

Having had the privilege of watching you develop over the years from a lovely little girl into an accomplished and beautiful young lady, I wish that I could give evidence of my devotion to you and your family by sending you, on this great day in your life, one of the world's rarest treasures.

Unfortunately, I do not enjoy working relations with a kindly genii. I hope however that you may enjoy this classic of Margaret Mitchell's as an addition to your library. The scene of this book is laid in the section of Georgia that is home to me and where some of your Johnson forebears lived before moving west.

Be assured that this small gift carries with it my devoted best wishes for your happiness, now and always.

The author was a dear friend of mine, and the area and people she described were well known to your Johnson forebears.[30]

The copy of *Gone with the Wind* was inscribed "To Luci—with affection, pride and admiration and the hope that she and Pat can find room for this book in their library."

In due course, the new Mrs. Nugent thanked "Uncle Dick" for the book and said, "We shall cherish it for its own worth but most especially because we cherish and love you. We shall miss our family dinners—and I don't know who I am going to flirt with . . ."[31]

For Russell and other Southerners in Congress the regulations for administering the growing body of civil rights law were a continuing problem. Federal guidelines for enforcing the desegregation of schools were especially troublesome to Russell, and early in the summer he joined other Southerners in a letter to the president protesting actions under the guidelines. Responding, Johnson assured Russell that the guidelines "are not designed to compel desegregation beyond that inherent in a fairly working free choice plan, to strike down freedom of choice, or to achieve 'racial balance.'"[32]

The civil rights movement was changing. After the violence in Watts, Martin Luther King's nonviolence lost its appeal for many blacks. King himself had become a critic of the Vietnam War. Leadership was passing to more militant blacks. "Black power" and, eventually, "burn baby burn" were the new watchwords, and the principal arena for civil rights activism shifted from the Southern states to urban areas in the North. During the summer, beginning again in Los Angeles, rioting swept through black communities in major cities. By year's end forty-three confrontations would result in seven deaths and 3,000 arrests in cities from coast to coast.[33]

The president's legislative program for 1966 included another civil rights bill. Its target was discrimination in the sale and rental of housing. Johnson had sent it to Congress in April, confident that the Humphrey-Dirksen collaboration could again maneuver it through the Senate. Dirksen was not playing this time, however. The national climate had changed once again. Now the uprising in Watts and not the repression in Selma was on the public mind, and Dirksen, ever sensitive, was now inclined to go slowly in the civil rights arena.

When the open housing bill reached the Senate floor, the Southerners mounted a filibuster against it. Two attempts to close off debate failed to get the necessary two-thirds vote, and in September the bill was put aside. It was another defeat for the president.

As in 1965, Russell had not been deeply involved in the debate. The behavior of some of his Southern allies had gotten on his nerves, and by the time the bill was shelved, he was out of the picture entirely.[34] On the evening of September 12 he had begun another short stay in Walter Reed Army Medical Center. He had been admitted complaining of chest pain and nausea. An allergic reaction had apparently resulted in bronchitis and aggravated the now-chronic emphysema. Johnson was advised at once.[35]

In mid-October Johnson began a frenetic seventeen-day trip to the Far East that included a visit with U.S. troops at Cam Ranh Bay in Vietnam and a conference in Manila with leaders of Pacific and Asian nations. At almost every stop he made a speech and distributed small busts of himself as mementos to heads of state and other hosts along the way. In South Korea, near the capital city of Seoul, he was cheered by a crowd estimated at two million people.[36]

Returning to Washington on November 2, Johnson and Lady Bird sent a birthday greeting to Russell, and the following day, Johnson wrote Russell an optimistic two-page letter about the trip, saying he wished Russell could have seen "the vital and exciting Asia that is forming up and will take shape if we see it through to an honorable peace in Vietnam."[37]

Johnson was still actively pursuing that honorable peace. On Thanksgiving Day he quietly sent his old New Deal friend Jim Rowe, a Catholic, as his personal emissary to enlist the help of the Pope. Johnson wanted to find out what had happened to a delegation the Pope was to have sent to Vietnam. And Rowe's principal task was to get the Pope to call for a Christmas truce in Vietnam early enough so that a U.S. bombing pause could be coordinated with it. In 1965 the Pope's initiative had come so late that the U.S. had not had time to react to it.

Rowe found the Pope "most sympathetic and friendly" to U.S. efforts to reach a negotiated peace, and later at the U.S. Embassy, he so reported in a cable to the president in Texas. On his return he reported personally on the visit to Johnson at the ranch.[38] The Pope did as he had promised, but, like other Johnson initiatives, it came to nothing.

Russell, who had been hospitalized again with respiratory problems, spent the holidays convalescing in Winder, where Johnson sent greetings and congratulations on learning that Russell had received a Georgia "Great American" award presented at a dinner honoring him in Atlanta.[39]

Hospitalized twice in the fall, Russell had concluded that his respiratory problems were chronic, and the prospect disturbed him. Early in February 1967 he dictated a letter to an unnamed governor of Georgia:

Sir:

Due to physical disability which makes it impossible for me to fully and actively discharge the duties of a Senator of the United States, I herewith submit to you my resignation from the Senate and respectfully request that it be accepted effective as of two weeks from the date of this letter.

It has been a great honor and high privilege to undertake to serve the people of my beloved Georgia in this high office, and I have given my all in the effort to deserve the confidence and trust repeatedly expressed by my people at the polls.

When it had been typed, he signed the letter and placed it in a buff-colored, nine-by-eleven-inch, franked U.S. Senate envelope on which he wrote: "Tentative Resignation—To be used and dated only on unanimous agreement of W. C. Harris, Dr. A. B. Russell and Richard B. Russell III, that I am totally and permanently disabled and incapable of ever serving actively as Senator. R. B. Russell."

Underneath, by way of explanation, he added: "Prepared to prevent a repetition of Carter Glass case in which I am the principal—"[40]

His instructions left it to his old Winder friend Clair Harris, his brother Alex, and his nephew Richard to end his career in the Senate if he was ever completely unable to serve, as had happened for a period of months during the final illness of Virginia's Carter Glass, who had been an important figure in the Senate when Russell was sworn in for the first time.

Lyndon Johnson, the nonpareil consensus maker, was in trouble. In Congress he was being urged, from right and left, to do more and do less in Vietnam. His own advisers were split on strategy.

In the Senate, Bill Fulbright continued to criticize the war, while others, such as Dick Russell and his friend John Stennis, continued to call for more aggressive tactics—including more bombing of more targets in the North. Secretary of State Dean Rusk, national security adviser Walt Rostow, and the military brass—in Washington and Saigon—favored a more aggressive stance in Vietnam. On the White House staff, however, Harry McPherson, John Roche, and Bill Moyers were beginning to have serious doubts, especially about the bombing; and in the Pentagon, Defense Secretary Robert McNamara was beginning to have doubts about whether the war could be won.

In the middle in the controversy, the president had been giving military commanders some, but not all, of the forces and authority they requested. An exchange of letters with North Vietnamese Premier Ho Chi Minh left him as far from peace negotiations as ever, and he ordered that bombing, suspended for the Tet holiday, be resumed.

The gradualism of Johnson's approach to the war was not the only Vietnam policy that troubled Russell. He felt that Johnson and his advisers had no real understanding of the depth of the feelings of the Vietnamese people in the South or in the North. In 1965 he had remarked in a Senate speech on the affection displayed in the North for Ho Chi Minh: "Whenever the people go to calling their leader 'Uncle,' you better look out," he said. "They have a man in whom they have implicit confidence, you are dealing with a very dangerous enemy."[41]

White House aide Harry McPherson got a similar cautionary word from Russell when he called on the senator before making a fact-finding visit to Vietnam early in the summer. Russell suggested that McPherson look into the practice of relocating entire villages in South Vietnam to provide "free fire" zones for U.S. and South Vietnamese troops.

"I don't like the sound of it," Russell said. "The Vietnamese people are animists. They feel very deeply about the land where their ancestors are buried. I suspect we're alienating them by moving them away from their homes, even if it's for their own safety. I know how Georgia people feel about that. When a big dam is dedicated down there, and a lot of farmers have been moved out to make way for the reservoir, I don't go to the dedication. I don't want them to see me up there on a platform built over their land."[42]

In Vietnam, McPherson found one military commander who rejected that idea and one who, sharing it, had stopped the relocation of villages in his sector.

In February, *Ramparts* magazine published an article disclosing that CIA subsidies had been paid to the National Student Association, an organization promoting international student interaction. In the following weeks, a series of disclosures revealed that the CIA had secretly supported the international activities of a number of organizations in the fields of education, religion, law, and labor.

In the resulting public outcry the subsidies were terminated, and the president decided to establish a study group to consider alternative financing methods for worthwhile activities that would now go unfunded. Johnson asked Russell to serve on the study group with other Senate and

House leaders. Russell declined, and, recalling his Warren Commission experience, he made it a point to announce to Georgia newspapers that he had declined.

Nevertheless, when the membership of the study group was announced by the White House in April, Russell's name was on the list. It was the Warren Commission all over again. Russell resisted the temptation to call a press conference and publicize his renewed refusal to serve. He decided he would simply not attend any meetings of the new group.[43]

Early in April, White House aide Marvin Watson had called at 8:40 one evening to convey the sort of impulsive invitation that Johnson often issued. Would Russell come to the White House and sit with the president at supper? On this occasion, however, Russell declined, saying he was terribly embarrassed, wished the call had come sooner, but he "simply could not come." Watson said he was sure the president would understand.[44]

Looking back with the unerring clarity of hindsight (and aided by the thoughtful insights of associates then on the scene), it is clear that Dick Russell's close personal relationship with Lyndon Johnson was becoming strained. The fabric of their friendship was spotted and unraveling a bit at the seams. Later there would be a very serious tear, but already the friendship was different. They were often together; they still enjoyed each other's company. Russell relished his role as presidential confidant and was still deeply attached to Lady Bird and the girls. But the friendship was now defined by matters like the C-5A contract, a more political and less personal association.

There was, of course, Vietnam. Eighteen months later, Russell would tell an interviewer that "it is hard to conceive of any mistake in the field of international relations or military affairs that we have not made in Vietnam."[45] In 1954 he and Johnson had helped prevent U.S. intervention to rescue the French at Dienbienphu. He did not publicly blame Johnson for getting into Vietnam, but he had come to question Johnson's judgment in not going all out to win.

Then there was the Great Society and its ever-expanding War on Poverty. As the voluminous social legislation reached the Senate, Russell had voted against many of the bills, beginning with the basic Economic Opportunity Act in 1964. But he had supported some of the programs that promised to help the poor, especially the poor farmers in Georgia. Long a proponent of federal aid for schools, he had also voted for the 1965 education bill despite his concerns about school desegregation.

Like the war in Vietnam, he thought the War on Poverty was badly managed as it expanded. He would say that "Johnson made every conceivable mistake, almost, from the standpoint of administration and organization. . . . Nobody can quarrel with the abolition of poverty, but instead of having just two or three organizations, with a minimum of components . . . every time he had a new thought he created an entirely new organization. So he wound up with four or five of them, sometimes trying to do the same thing."[46]

And, of course, there was civil rights. Russell's vision for Johnson had been of a moderate, Southern-bred president who would gradually ease the South back into the nation's political and economic mainstream. But from Russell's point of view, Johnson's philosophy had seemed to change; and in his civil rights activities as president, beginning with breaking the long filibuster in 1964, Johnson had been anything but moderate or gradual in his approach.

It was not the fact that they had emerged as opposing leaders in the major sociopolitical conflict of their time. Russell could accept that—had come to expect it would happen. More than just a question of failed judgment, what was weakening was the thread of trust that holds a friendship together in difficult times. And the times for Russell and Johnson were now frequently difficult.

Early in the spring, the president had reached Russell with an urgent call in the Senate Democratic cloakroom and had asked that Russell reply to a speech critical of his Vietnam policies by Bobby Kennedy. In the conversation, Johnson stressed that he had been trying to set up negotiations for a settlement in Vietnam. Russell thought there was nothing new in Kennedy's criticism—nothing "worthy of my involvement"—and declined.[47]

In his defense budget, Johnson had asked for $235 million to finance five fast-deployment logistic ships (FDLs). Nearly a thousand feet long, the 40,000-ton vessels were planned as floating warehouses to move military equipment and supplies into troubled areas where military manpower might one day have to be deployed. Two of the ships had been authorized the previous year, but Russell got the Senate to reject the five proposed and rescind the two previously authorized. He argued that "if it is easy for us to go anywhere and do anything we will always be going somewhere and doing something."[48] The House voted for four new ships, but in May a Senate-House conference committee went along with Russell and killed the program.

The defense bill, which did not include the FDLs, did contain the first congressional declaration on the Vietnam War since the Tonkin Gulf Resolution in 1964. It began as a resolution, offered by Democratic senator Joseph S. Clark of Pennsylvania, long a Johnson critic, stating the view of Congress that no defense funds should finance military operations "in or over" North Vietnam or increase U.S. troop strength in the South beyond 500,000. (By year's end the U.S. commitment would be near that number.)

Clark's formula was too strong for the Senate, which substituted a milder version on a 72 to 19 vote. In the House, language similar to Clark's was rejected 372 to 18, and, as finally approved in mid-March, the declaration expressed support for the troops deployed in Vietnam and simultaneously urged on the peacemakers who were seeking to end the fighting.

Despite the lopsided margins against the tougher language, dissatisfaction with the war was increasing. Martin Luther King was urging that the civil rights movement join the antiwar demonstrators in a united front.

In June, Johnson got headlines from a somewhat encouraging summit meeting with Soviet Premier Alexei Kosygin, and he raised his stock with the American Jewish community by making it clear to the Kremlin that the United States would resist any Soviet intervention to throw back Israel's victorious forces at the end of the Six-Day War. But early in July, his critics from the right and the left united against him, with Dick Russell leading the pack. At issue was a revolt in the Congo, but the critical outcry was an echo of the Vietnam discontent.

It began after forces loyal to the former president of the Congo, Moise Tshombe, revolted against forces loyal to then-President Joseph D. Mobutu. The outcome appeared to be in doubt, and Johnson, without consulting Congress, dispatched a small U.S. force—three C-130 transport planes plus maintenance and support troops, as well as protective units from the 82nd Airborne Division—to assist the Mobutu government in putting down the rebellion. Later, Secretary of State Rusk would say that lives of 3,000 Americans and others were endangered and that there were fears that a Tshombe victory might result in a wave of antiwhite unrest.

To the president's critics, however—and the Fulbright and Russell camps were together on this—the aid for Mobutu was just another intervention into a part of the world where the United States had no commitments and no vital interests. Furthermore, it was a move that could draw Soviet or Chinese forces onto the African continent. Russell reminded the Senate that "Vietnam started out with a not much larger force than that. It can swell and it will swell if a few of our forces are killed."[49]

In notes for his speech, Russell wrote that African tribal warfare had gone on for decades. His efforts to maintain the nation's military strength, he said, envisioned a force to defend the nation and not "to be a plaything of the State Department."[50]

Stung by Russell's remarks, Johnson advised him that 50,000 people, including 1,700 Americans, had been protected by the small force sent to the Congo. From Winder, Russell arranged that a response be hand-delivered to the White House for the president. After acknowledging Johnson's message, he said:

> I cannot subscribe to any policy predicated upon the assump-
> tion that the United States alone has an obligation to avoid
> domestic strife in Africa or elsewhere. Despite any great advance-
> ment that may have been made in Africa in recent years, from what
> I have been able to learn, tribal loyalties are still superior to any
> feeling of nationalism, and we are likely to have tribal rebellions
> and wars for some time to come. A number of other countries that
> have aircraft and armed forces have a much greater stake in Africa
> than the United States, and I shall continue to protest our country
> rushing in unilaterally to aid the side that we may temporarily
> favor in any African country confronted with domestic disorders
> and conflicts. . . . With assurances of personal esteem . . .[51]

Early in August, the State Department informed Russell that two of the C-130s had left the Congo and the third plane was expected to leave in about a week.[52]

The course of events and Johnson's pivotal role in them were also changing the president's attitude toward his former Senate colleague. The difference in perspective, which had begun when Johnson was vice president, was greatly expanded now that Johnson, as president, was trying to lead the nation through an unpopular war. At one point he remarked to Harry McPherson that Russell was really a nineteenth-century man adrift in the twentieth century.

Johnson was well aware that he and Russell were on different tracks. On one occasion when they were together at the White House, Johnson told Russell, "Dick, I know I have been a disappointment to you." Later, describing the incident to a Southern colleague, Russell said he had not known how to respond to the president's uncharacteristic candor.[53]

In August, Russell spent thirteen days at Walter Reed Army Medical Center with respiratory problems. The Johnsons sent flowers.[54] When he could travel, Russell headed South to recuperate.

Tight budgets with dwindling appropriations for social programs had put an economic straitjacket on the War on Poverty, and that summer the racial turmoil that had started two years earlier in Watts reached its full fury. Starting in Nashville in April, it quickly spread to Cleveland, Washington, Louisville, Montgomery, and Omaha. In May and June incidents occurred in New York, Minneapolis, Tampa, Atlanta, Birmingham, Cincinnati, San Francisco, Buffalo, Dayton, and Wichita. Early in July a full-fledged riot engulfed Boston's black Roxbury section. Newark and Detroit were next, and Johnson had to send troops to restore order in Detroit.

By summer's end 114 cities in 32 states were involved in the wave of unrest. Other cities hit included Wilmington, Toledo, South Bend, Grand Rapids, Pontiac, Milwaukee, New Haven, Providence, Saginaw, Flint, Portland (Oregon), and Cambridge (Maryland). Teach-ins and demonstrations against the war had begun on college campuses and were spreading into the streets. In June, Johnson had escalated the bombing to include attacks on petroleum storage facilities near Hanoi and the port of Haiphong.

In August the Senate Preparedness Subcommittee, headed by John Stennis, began a series of closed-door hearings on the war that became a forum in which military leaders could call for more aggressive action in Vietnam and, indirectly, criticize Johnson's policies as executed by Defense Secretary McNamara. In October more than 50,000 demonstrators ringed the Pentagon, just across the Potomac River from the Capitol, in an antiwar protest that involved scuffling with police.

In downtown Washington the preferred site for antiwar demonstrations was Lafayette Park, across the street from the White House. Inside at night Johnson would "lay awake picturing my boys flying around North Vietnam, asking myself an endless series of questions. What if one of those targets you picked today triggers off Russia or China? What happens then? Or suppose one of my boys misses his mark when he's flying around Haiphong? Suppose one of his bombs falls on one of the Russian ships in the harbor? What happens then?"

Years later he would remember: "I would then begin to picture myself lying on the battlefield in Danang. I could see an American plane circling above me in the sky. I felt safe. Then I heard a long, loud shot. The plane began to fall, faster, faster, faster. I saw it hit the ground, and as soon as it burst into flames, I couldn't stand it any more. I knew that one of my boys must have been killed that night. I jumped out of bed, put on my robe, took my flashlight, and went into the Situation Room."[55]

The nation had no hint of the agony of the president, however. In his public statements he continued ever-confident that the tide of Communism would be turned in Vietnam and an honorable peace would be achieved there. Johnson found it frustrating that critics refused to believe he was really seeking negotiations to bring the fighting and dying to an end. At one point, aides counted eighteen separate initiatives in which approaches were being made through third parties, in other capitals, to get talks started.[56] In one emotional outburst to a group of newsmen, Johnson said: "I would gladly kiss Ho's ass in Garfinckel's [a local department store's] front window at high noon to get him to the conference table."[57]

As casualties mounted in Vietnam (by year's end, more than 15,000 Americans had been killed there), Johnson's confident public statements were less and less credible to viewers who had been watching the conduct of the war as it played out on their television screens. In November Fulbright's Senate Foreign Relations Committee approved a resolution on national commitments that was, in essence, an attack on the powers of the president. Based in the constitutional power of Congress to declare war, it stated the sense of the Senate that no future commitment of U.S. troops abroad should be made without "affirmative action" by Congress.

Late in November the president announced, after word had been leaked in the press, that McNamara would leave the Pentagon to head the World Bank. McNamara had started as the president's closest adviser on military matters and the key defender of administration policy in Vietnam, but his disenchantment with events there had reached a point where he was proposing that the United States wind down its efforts. Johnson complained that McNamara's friend Bobby Kennedy had turned McNamara against the war.

With a presidential election just a year away, one poll showed the president trailing Bobby Kennedy, among presidential possibilities, by 20 percent. On November 30, however, it was not Bobby Kennedy but Sen. Eugene McCarthy who announced that he would run in at least four 1968 Democratic primaries to make a case against the administration's policies in Vietnam. In the spring McCarthy had said Bobby Kennedy would be the strongest candidate to challenge Johnson and the war. But when Kennedy made no move as months went by, McCarthy decided to make the challenge himself.[58]

Russell was away from Washington during most of this period of Johnson's declining credibility. After his convalescence in the late summer he had been hospitalized again early in October for a recurrence of the respiratory problems. He again went to Georgia to recuperate. He was back in Washington in late November, however, and dined at the White House with the President and Mrs. Johnson and General and Mrs. William Westmoreland.[59] The general had been called back to Washington to rally public support for the war.

Ailing again, Russell was unable to attend Lynda Bird Johnson's wedding early in December. Writing to acknowledge the Johnsons' Christmas greetings, Russell's holiday good wishes were restrained: "Although we are saddened by the knowledge that the tragic events of today's world have made Christmas less joyous for many American families, we have much to be thankful for and not the least among them is a nation with institutions worth defending and friendships such as yours."[60]

Chapter Eight

SEVERANCE

1968

Discussing President Johnson's problems with an aide, Dick
Russell was asked whether the president had been a victim of
bad advice. Russell thought not. "He advised with me many
times," Russell said. "I'm not going to characterize my advice as bad. He
got good advice, but he listened to the wrong advisers in many of these
instances."[1]

In Russell's opinion, one of Johnson's "wrong advisers" with respect
to Vietnam policy had been Defense Secretary Robert McNamara. Russell
complained that there had been occasions when he left the White House
confident that he had convinced the president to make an aggressive move
in Vietnam only to learn later that McNamara had persuaded Johnson not
to make it.[2]

Now McNamara was leaving, but Russell had to admit that he now
had no advice to offer. He told Harry McPherson: "For the first time in my
life, I don't have any idea what to recommend."[3]

And his private Vietnam talks with the president were sometimes
difficult now. On one occasion, summoned to the White House for a talk,
Russell told one of his aides that he did not want to be alone with the
president. Johnson got so emotional, Russell said, that he would break out
crying. Russell decided to take John Stennis along for the talk at the White
House.[4]

The situation in Vietnam had reached a new low point. A U.S. force
had been engaged in a struggle in the rolling hills around Khesanh, near the
North Vietnamese border. For a time the U.S. force was surrounded, and
there were inevitable comparisons with the final French defeat at encircled
Dienbienphu in 1954. Johnson followed the Khesanh fighting on a

sand-table model constructed in the White House Situation Room. He requested a written assurance from the Joint Chiefs of Staff that General Westmoreland would be able to hold Khesanh. "I don't want any damn Dinbinphoo," he said.[5]

But the major Communist assault was not to target Khesanh. Late in January, during a truce in observance of the Tet lunar New Year, more than a hundred cities in South Vietnam, including Saigon and thirteen of sixteen provincial capitals, came under surprise attack by Communist forces.[6] In Saigon, the U.S. Embassy was under siege for hours by a commando unit that blew a hole in the compound wall and routed South Vietnamese security guards. In many of the cities, U.S. and South Vietnamese forces quickly restored order. But in Hue, the old capital city, Communist units held parts of the city for twenty-five days, indiscriminately killing many residents who had no real ties with the South Vietnamese government.

Much later, U.S. and North Vietnamese authorities would agree that the Tet offensive was poorly planned and failed in its military objectives. At home, however, there had been dramatic television. Americans had seen the fighting at the U.S. Embassy and later had seen a top South Vietnamese police official execute a Vietcong suspect on a Saigon street with a casual pistol shot. It was getting more and more difficult to believe what the White House was saying about the war.

Johnson had appointed Clark Clifford to succeed McNamara as secretary of defense. Clifford, an influential attorney, had been a Washington insider since he came to town as a naval aide in the Truman White House, and Johnson had often turned to him for advice. Clifford had a reputation as a supporter of the war, but in its early days he had privately expressed doubts about the U.S. involvement.

The president had twice consulted Russell about a replacement for McNamara. Johnson was concerned that Paul Nitze, McNamara's deputy, might quit if an outsider was selected to run the Pentagon. Russell thought that would be no great loss. He thought Clifford was the best man for the job "by all odds" and suggested that Air Force Secretary Harold Brown succeed Nitze and possibly move up to secretary later.[7]

Clifford formally took over from McNamara on March 1, but he had been sitting in on strategy meetings and questioning experts, civilian and military, about prospects in Vietnam since his selection in January. Just three days after taking over, he was due to send the president a recommendation on a request from General Westmoreland for a 205,000-troop buildup by year's end—a buildup that would require a call-up of reservists.

Johnson sent Clifford to the Capitol to sound out Russell on calling up reservists, and Russell called in three of the top-ranking Democratic members of his Armed Services Committee—Stennis, Stuart Symington of Missouri (a close friend of Clifford's), and Henry M. (Scoop) Jackson of Washington. The four senators, all with hawkish reputations, told Clifford they could not support a reserve call-up or the large reinforcement requested by Westmoreland, and Russell took the occasion to comment that getting into Vietnam had been a mistake.[8] His notes on the meeting suggest that the war would "never end under present policies."[9]

In his report, Clifford advised the president that there was no reason to believe the war could be won by "an additional two hundred thousand American troops or double or triple that quantity." He suggested that Westmoreland be advised to abandon efforts to achieve an outright victory over Communist forces.[10]

Johnson was not persuaded by Clifford's report. He was shaken by it, however, and he deferred action on the troop request, setting the stage for an internal tug-of-war within the administration. As Westmoreland's request for more troops began to leak, first in Congress and then to the press, the internal tug-of-war gave way to public debate.

On March 12 a small but significant segment of the public expressed itself on Vietnam in a way that changed the course of events. It is almost forgotten that President Johnson actually won the Democratic primary in New Hampshire on that date. What is remembered—what stunned the pollsters and the public—is that Sen. Eugene McCarthy, whose antiwar campaign was staffed largely by youthful volunteers, received only 300 fewer votes than President Johnson in the first-in-the-nation presidential primary, with some 50,000 votes cast. Four days later Robert F. Kennedy, who had been experiencing his own internal tug-of-war, announced that he, too, would seek the Democratic presidential nomination.

Dick Russell read about some of these events in the hospital and later while convalescing. In January he had suffered another recurrence of his respiratory problem and was again admitted to Walter Reed. Clearly, his health had become a very serious problem. In addition, Harriet Orr had advised him that she was retiring to spend more time in North Carolina with her invalid mother. It was all very depressing.

He spent a very happy evening at the White House in early April, however. Following an afternoon meeting of more than twenty congressional leaders, Russell and Sen. George A. Smathers of Florida had supper with the president. Lynda and Luci were also on hand, and Russell later noted: "both kissed me on arrival and on departure (abt 1 am) and called me uncle dick." He added that the president gave him and Smathers busts—apparently similar to the busts of himself that he had distributed on his trip to Asia.[11]

An irritating patronage problem was developing for Russell at the Johnson White House. It involved a vacancy in the U.S. District Court for the Southern District of Georgia, brought about by the retirement of an old friend of Russell's. Under patronage precedents, the recommendation for an appointment to fill that vacancy was Russell's to make, and with the routine concurrence of his Georgia colleague, Herman Talmadge, he had recommended another old friend, only to learn that his nominee was unable to serve because of poor health.

Anxious to fill the vacancy, Russell, with Talmadge again concurring, had asked in February that Johnson appoint Alex Lawrence to fill the vacancy. Lawrence was a prominent Savannah attorney and also a long-time friend of the Russell family. It was a regular patronage recommendation, blessed by the appropriate senators, and in Russell's view it should have resulted in Johnson quickly sending Lawrence's nomination to the Senate for confirmation. But Johnson had not yet acted.

In public, Johnson was still calling for victory in Vietnam. In mid-March he told a business group, "We shall and we are going to win."[12] In Lafayette Park, the antiwar demonstrations continued, and their protests were routinely heard inside the White House.

A few months later, Luci Johnson Nugent, back with her family now that husband Pat was in Vietnam, could hear the tumult in her bedroom. "I'd wake up in the morning with it—'Hey, Hey, LBJ, how many kids did you kill today?' And my husband was one of those boys. And that baby sleeping next to me was his only child. Lyndon Johnson's only grandchild. . . ."

She recalled dropping in on her father in the evening, when he was watching the eleven o'clock news: "He never said anything and he never needed to, if you knew him, but he had eyes that were like laser beams. And he'd be looking at that TV set and they'd be giving reports on fatalities that day and it was as if you were looking at a man who had a knife stuck into the pit of his stomach and turned over and over and over and over. He just physically looked like he was in agony."[13]

However, Johnson could take some satisfaction from another important legislative victory. In April he signed another civil rights bill, this one focusing on his open housing proposal. The new law prohibited discrimination in sale or rental of about 80 percent of all housing units. Passed by the House in 1967, the bill had survived a six-week Senate filibuster that was finally broken on the fourth attempt at cloture, 65 to 32. Russell's hospitalization and subsequent convalescence kept him out of most of the debate and filibuster.

President Johnson had deleted a long segment on Vietnam from his State of the Union Address in January and had directed Harry McPherson to start working on another speech that would focus on Vietnam. The president had gone to the Capitol for the State of the Union Address with drafts of two final passages, one of which was an announcement that he would not run again. That announcement stayed in his pocket. He did not use it.[14]

In late March, McPherson had an inkling about things to come when he heard that the president was working with longtime aide Horace Busby on a new conclusion for the Vietnam speech now scheduled for March 30. When they talked about the speech a few hours before Johnson was to deliver it, McPherson said he thought he knew what the president's ending would be. He said he was very sorry.

"Well, I think it's best," the president said. "So long, podner."[15]

Along with cabinet officers and a few other congressional leaders, Dick Russell got a call a few minutes before the president was to speak, advising him that Johnson would announce that he would not seek reelection in an effort to enhance the prospects for peace in Vietnam. Later Russell would say that "Johnson was a victim of the war in Vietnam. It destroyed him politically."[16] In the immediate aftermath of the speech, he said the president's dramatic announcement was "a very noble individual sacrifice in an effort to secure peace. . . . I hope it will succeed, but I would be less than frank if I did not say I have very grave doubts that Hanoi will change its policy."[17]

Initially, Russell criticized as "exceedingly dangerous" the bombing pause that was announced in Johnson's Vietnam speech as an inducement for Hanoi to begin talks. A couple of days later, however, he was defending Johnson's proposal, apparently on grounds that the speech, as delivered, had been somewhat less accommodating to the Communists than it had been when he discussed it with Johnson beforehand.[18]

A day after Johnson's announcement it was reported that he and Mrs. Johnson had talked about a single full-term presidency as early as 1965 and that he had discussed withdrawal with his family during the 1967 Christmas holidays at the ranch.[19] It was later disclosed that Johnson had shown the alternative endings on the Vietnam speech to Vice President Humphrey the day before the speech was delivered and that Humphrey had urged him not to use the withdrawal statement.[20]

Daughter Luci, watching in the Oval Office as her father delivered the Vietnam speech, was still not certain that he would use it. "I thought for a moment he wouldn't do it, even when he got to it . . . he paused several moments before he started reading it," she said.[21]

The president's statement appeared to achieve its short-term goal less than a week after he made it. On April 5, Foreign Minister Nguyen Duy Trinh said the North Vietnamese were ready to meet with U.S. spokesmen at the bargaining table. But Johnson was in no position to celebrate. He faced another monumental problem. In Memphis to support a strike of garbagemen, Martin Luther King Jr. had been shot and killed by an assassin on the evening of April 4, precipitating racial unrest in fifty American cities.

In Washington, where black ghetto areas extend to within a few blocks of the Capitol complex, demonstrations began a few hours after King was killed, and vandalism began a few hours thereafter. The following morning the situation grew worse, not better.

In the White House, Johnson had called black leaders to a morning meeting prior to a memorial service for King at the Washington National Cathedral. By noon, police were overburdened with fires and incidents of looting, and it was becoming clear that Washingon's black mayor, Walter Washington, would have to ask for troops to restore order.

Russell sent his female employees home early from the office building across the street from the Capitol. He sat in his office following events on television and radio with his administrative assistant, Bill Jordan; Proctor Jones, who was just back from marine corps training; and Charles Campbell, the young attorney who had filled in for Jones during his absence.

Troops had been called in and could be seen on the streets. Smoke from the fires could also be seen from the Capitol complex. As Russell talked with his aides, there were some sour jokes about rioters burning down the nation's Capitol. Russell thought it was outrageous.

In the early evening, Russell had a nip of Jack Daniels as was his custom at cocktail hour. (As was also customary, he did not offer a drink to his staff members.) From his desk he took two pistols and announced that he was going home. He was going to carry on as usual. He would not, he said, be intimidated by the mob outside.

The staffers were not happy. They thought Russell, driving his 1963 black Chrysler with its Georgia license plates through the heart of the beleaguered city, offered too tempting a target for rioters. Russell would not be deterred. Campbell tried to get into the Chrysler with the senator, but Russell drove off without him. The others followed in Jordan's car, down Pennsylvania Avenue through the center of town.

The twenty-minute ride to Russell's apartment in the Foggy Bottom area of the District took more than an hour and a half, but the two cars made it without incident, and the staff contingent saw Russell safely inside. There he took a telephone call from the president. Johnson wanted him at the White House at 8 a.m. for a conference on Vietnam with Maxwell Taylor and other military leaders.

Russell's angry mood overrode his usual inhibitions, and after saying he would be there, he needled his old friend. "By the way, Mr. President," he said, "What are you going to do about this serious situation you got on your hands here in Washington? You going to let them burn the city down?" As Russell would later tell his staff, Johnson replied: "Oh, well, Dick, I don't know. We're working on it, doing everything we can. I'll see you in the morning, early."

Russell arrived on time to find the White House area ringed by troops who had set up checkpoints at key intersections. With his congressional license plates he had no trouble at the checkpoints, but at the southwest gate, White House police and secret service asked if Russell minded if they searched his car, saying that they were searching all incoming vehicles.

Russell was infuriated. He had driven through that gate countless times and knew he had been recognized on this occasion. (There was also the matter of one of the pistols in the glove compartment.) "Yes, I mind if you search it," he said. "I've been in Washington here for thirty-three years, and I'm a close friend of the president. I didn't want to come down here anyway. He called me up last night and asked me. . . . I feel like I have got to come if the president asks me to come. Yes, I do mind. . . ." The Chrysler was waved on.[22]

After the meeting, Johnson walked Russell back to his car, parked on Executive Avenue on the White House grounds. Russell wanted to talk about the riot, and Johnson kept changing the subject. Finally, Russell came at him again: "Well, now, Mr. President, just tell me what you are going to do about this. Are you going to let them burn this city down, or what are you planning on doing?" Again the response was: "We are doing everything we can."

"No, you're not! Why don't you arrest Stokely Carmichael?" Russell asked, referring to the black activist who, according to media accounts, had led the way in some of the early vandalism. Johnson said he had favored arresting Carmichael, but Attorney General Ramsey Clark thought that would have as serious a backlash as the King assassination.[23]

Returning to his office (where he would give staff members this account of events), Russell stopped at the Capitol as usual to get breakfast in the Senate restaurant. Armed marine guards had been posted around the building, and stopping to chat with a young marine, Russell noticed that the marine was carrying the new M-16 rifle. He asked to see one of the rounds for the gun and was told the guard had no ammunition. Other guards confirmed that no ammunition had been issued.

Thinking about it over his breakfast—guards armed, but without ammunition—he became more and more annoyed. Returning to his office, he told his staff about it, and they started checking other guard stations in the Capitol complex. The story was the same—no ammunition. Finally Russell called the White House and reached the president.

"Mr. President, after I was down there talking with you, I got up here to the Capitol and they got a whole battalion of marines up here with their rifles and bayonets. Not a single one of them has any ammunition. Not a single one. . . . this Capitol building belongs to all the American people. . . . This is just ridiculous. . . . I don't care if they burn the rest of the city of Washington down, but this Capitol building belongs to all the American people."[24]

Johnson tried to calm Russell and turned the telephone over to Gen. Earle "Buzz" Wheeler, chairman of the Joint Chiefs of Staff, who had attended the morning meeting and was still at the White House. Wheeler promised to look into the matter, and Russell sent his recently demobilized marine, Proctor Jones, back to the Capitol to investigate further.

Soon after Jones reached the Capitol building, a military staff car screeched up. A two-star general jumped out and summoned the colonel in charge, who summoned four junior officers. It turned out that ammunition was available in a truck parked nearby, but it had not been issued to the marines to avoid unauthorized shooting incidents. The delegation of officers set out at once for Russell's office to explain. The senator was somewhat mollified but not entirely satisfied.

For Russell it was simply outrageous that demonstrators had been roaming the streets of the nation's capital, burning and looting. He had always been a law-and-order man. His first burst of national publicity had come as governor when he unsuccessfully asked New Jersey authorities to extradite an escaped Georgia prisoner, author of a book (later a motion picture) called *I Am a Fugitive from a Georgia Chain Gang.* The man, Robert E. Burns, had been convicted of stealing $5.85 from a grocery store, and his book dramatized brutality experienced in the state's prison system. Russell had felt Burns should have been required to complete his sentence, and he believed the president should be acting more forcefully against rioters in the capital.

Nor was he satisfied, once order had been restored in Washington, with the White House handling of the Alex Lawrence nomination, which still had not been sent to the Senate for confirmation. Russell had submitted Lawrence's name in mid-February. Early in May he went to the White House to talk to Johnson about it.

Attorney General Ramsey Clark had already been in to see Johnson about the Lawrence nomination. He told the president that, while Lawrence was a well-regarded Savannah attorney, he had, nearly ten years previously, made a speech to a women's patriotic organization in which he sharply criticized the "tyranny" of the Supreme Court in civil rights cases. That speech was provoking opposition in Georgia, Clark said. He predicted that an American Bar Association Committee, which regularly reviewed judicial appointments, would not approve Lawrence. Clark noted that civil rights activists were then encamped near the Lincoln Memorial in downtown Washington, in a shantytown they called "resurrection city." He told the president it was the wrong time to send such a controversial nomination to the Senate for confirmation, and he could not recommend it.

After Johnson and Russell discussed the nomination at the White House, the president sent Clark to talk to Russell about it. Then Russell, at Johnson's request, wrote the president a four-page letter discussing Lawrence's qualifications. He said he was "surprised, distressed and disappointed" to learn of Clark's position and declared: "There is not the slightest doubt in my mind that as judge he will follow the law as laid down in the statutes and in the decisions of higher courts, whether he agrees with them or not."

With respect to Lawrence's remarks about the Supreme Court, Russell said they were no more extreme than criticisms voiced more recently by a committee of state chief justices or recent comments by Supreme Court Justice Hugo Black or criticisms voiced by the revered U.S. Appeals Court Judge Learned Hand.

"I do not believe Mr. Lawrence can justly be called a racist," said Russell, noting that Lawrence had been associated with benevolent and philanthropic groups in Savannah and had attacked the Ku Klux Klan. He suggested that the opposition to Lawrence originated in an organization on the "extreme left" that had sought help from Georgia chapters of the NAACP.

Noting that such appointments had always been a prerogative of Democratic senators when a Democrat was in the White House, Russell said it would be extremely embarrassing for him and for Talmadge if the nomination were not sent to the Senate, now that it had been widely discussed all over the state. He said he thought no reputable attorney in Georgia would term Lawrence unqualified.

"I have never made a personal appeal to you for a political appointment since you have occupied the exalted position of President of the United States. In this instance, however, where only a local appointment is concerned and a man of great competence and high character has been suggested, I feel justified in insisting most respectfully that you send Mr. Lawrence's name to the Senate."[25]

Johnson told his White House staff: "If we come to the final conclusion that we can't appoint him [Lawrence], then we'll come to that conclusion. We'll cross that bridge. But if there's any way at all that we can posture this in a way that he can be appointed, without doing anything to undermine the judiciary. I want to do it. I want to appoint this man."[26]

Despite the early optimism, the talks on Vietnam failed to produce a breakthrough as Johnson had hoped when he made his withdrawal statement. Sessions began in Paris amid high hopes early in May, but within a few weeks the talks were deadlocked, with the United States insisting that North Vietnam withdraw its forces from South Vietnam and the Communists insisting that the Vietcong have a role in the Saigon government.

Johnson's withdrawal had, however, opened the way for a bitter fight over the Democratic presidential nomination. Eugene McCarthy and Bobby Kennedy were fighting it out in the party primaries, and Alabama governor George Wallace had entered some primaries, too, as a hard-line conservative candidate. In state after state, the Democratic primary became a contest between the two antiwar candidates. McCarthy would later complain that once Kennedy entered the campaign, "neither he nor I could be nominated."[27] He thought Kennedy's candidacy "divided the antiwar forces and introduced the element of power politics."[28]

When Kennedy won primaries in largely rural South Dakota and very urban California on June 4, he thought he had proven that he was the antiwar candidate who could win the nomination from Vice President

Hubert Humphrey at the Democratic convention. "I've got to get free of McCarthy," he said.[29] A few hours later, taking a shortcut through a hotel kitchen in Los Angeles, he was shot and mortally wounded.

Chief Justice Earl Warren was seventy-seven years old, and he told Johnson in mid-June that he wanted to retire. Johnson decided to nominate Associate Justice Abe Fortas, his old friend and adviser, to be chief justice and name another old friend, former Texas congressman and then appeals court judge Homer Thornberry, to fill the Warren vacancy. He called Russell in Winder to sound him out on the two nominations.

During that initial talk, Russell made it clear that he could support Thornberry but was somewhat equivocal about Fortas as chief justice.[30] Johnson told his White House liaison staff to let him deal with Russell, and in subsequent talks he got a commitment from Russell to support the Supreme Court package.

Sen. Robert P. Griffin, Republican of Michigan, was leading the opposition to the Fortas nomination, and he called on Russell to sound him out on the appointment. They met alone in Russell's inner office. In retrospect it would appear that Russell told Griffin that, although he was committed to vote for Fortas, if the appointment became embroiled in a filibuster, he and the Southerners could not, on principle, vote for cloture to force the nomination to a vote.[31]

Russell's main interest in judgeship nominations was the still-unnominated Alex Lawrence.[32] When the president sent White House aides Harry McPherson and Larry Temple to Russell's office to talk about Fortas and Thornberry, Russell talked about Lawrence.[33]

As he thought about it, Russell began to wonder whether the delay on Lawrence was being extended to keep him in line on the Fortas nomination. (Once before, after President Truman had named Russell's brother Bob to the U.S. Court of Appeals, there had been a similar incident, and an angry Russell finally had to be persuaded that his brother's nomination was not being held hostage to assure his support for another judgeship nominee in Georgia.)

After talking with Lawrence, Russell had advised Johnson that, although Lawrence's controversial speech had reflected his strongly held views in 1958 when he made it, Lawrence fully understood that Supreme Court decisions represented the law of the land and, if nominated, would under no circumstances try to impose his own feelings or judgments.

Johnson met personally with the American Bar Association committee that was considering Lawrence's nomination to ask that an on-the-spot inquiry be made in Savannah with respect to his qualifications. In June Johnson visited Russell in Walter Reed, where the senator was again hospitalized, and a few days later Russell supplied a petition signed by all living former presidents of the Georgia Bar Association supporting Lawrence. However, Ramsey Clark was still dragging his feet, and Johnson did not want to nominate a judge over the head of his attorney general.

The attorney general was not the president's only source on the Lawrence matter. Johnson had an aide solicit the views of two distinguished Georgia journalists—former *Atlanta Constitution* editor Ralph McGill and McGill's successor, Eugene Patterson. McGill did not fully support a Lawrence nomination, and Patterson said he would be unhappy with it, though he said Lawrence had backed away from some of his controversial views.[34] That seemed to bear out Clark's judgment that serious opposition to Lawrence could be expected in Georgia.

On June 25, Russell talked with Johnson in the Oval Office about the nomination and then dined with the Johnsons and White House aides Tom Johnson and Mary Rather. It was all very cordial, but mulling over the situation afterwards, Russell decided that it was time to force the Lawrence issue. He believed Johnson's position on Lawrence had to be challenged directly. He thought it was simply ridiculous that the president was being deterred by the flimsy rationale advanced by Attorney General Ramsey Clark. He knew that less than a year previously, Johnson himself had been bitter about Clark's refusal to side with draft director Lewis Hershey in a troublesome controversy. Russell considered Clark incompetent and thought Johnson should have fired him.[35]

Russell had also told Georgia newsman Wayne Kelley that he had angrily advised the president that civil rights advocate H. Rap Brown should be indicted for his rabble-rousing activities, and Johnson had replied that Ramsey Clark was against that. He said he asked Johnson: "Who is President? Are you President or is Ramsey Clark President?" It had reached a point, Russell said, where he just didn't understand Johnson anymore.[36]

On July 1, Russell began drafting another letter to Johnson. In thinking about the Lawrence matter, he had lost all patience and with it much of his temper. Between two close friends of twenty years standing, the letter Russell completed was unusual. Between two long-standing friends and political allies—between a powerful senator and a sitting president—it was perhaps unique.

Russell began by reminding Johnson that he and Talmadge had made their urgent request on behalf of Lawrence more than four and a half months previously "based on public need" for a district judge. Three months later, at Johnson's suggestion, he recalled, he had written Johnson about Lawrence's qualifications "and concluded by making a personal appeal (the first that I have made to any President of the United States)." In asking that Lawrence's nomination be submitted to the Senate, Russell said, "I was only insisting on that which every Democratic Senator has had a right to expect since the formation of our party."

He then stated that he had never submitted a recommendation to any president for a lawyer better qualified than Lawrence and added that no lawyer recommended had been "more universally endorsed by the bench, bar and those who were likely to be litigants in the courts of the district." "An overwhelming majority of the leading citizens of all races, creeds and colors in the Southern District," Russell wrote, "have . . . expressed their complete confidence in Mr. Lawrence and his fairness as judge."

From his discussions with the president, Russell said, he had almost become convinced that Johnson would appoint Lawrence "despite the protests of the person who serves as your Attorney General." In their recent evening talk, Russell recalled, Johnson had said he would even name Lawrence to the U.S. Circuit Court of Appeals if Lawrence, Talmadge, and Russell desired it.

"To be perfectly frank, even after so many years in the Senate, I was so naive I had not even suspected that this man's nomination was being withheld from the Senate due to the changes expected on the Supreme Court of the United States until after you sent the nominations of Fortas and Thornberry while still holding the recommendation for the nomination of Mr. Lawrence either in your office or in the Department of Justice." That, said Russell, put him in a position where, if he supported Johnson's high court nominations, "it will appear that I have done so out of my fears that you would not nominate Mr. Lawrence."

Placed in a similar position by President Truman, Russell said, "when he nominated my own beloved brother to be a judge of the United States Circuit Court, I told Mr. Truman that he had best withdraw that nomination as I did not intend to be blackmailed . . . even to secure a circuit judgeship for a brother who was as close to me as two men could be. I still dislike being treated as a child or a patronage seeking ward heeler.

"When I came to the United States Senate some thirty odd years ago, I did not possess much except my self respect. When I leave—either voluntarily, carried in a box, or at the request of a majority of the people of Georgia—I still intend to carry my self respect back to Georgia.

"This is, therefore, to advise you that, in view of the long delay in handling and the juggling of this nomination, I consider myself released from any statements that I may have made to you with respect to your nominations, and you are at liberty to deal with the recommendations as to Mr. Lawrence in any way you see fit. I shall undertake to deal objectively with the nominations you have made to the Supreme Court, but, however I may vote, I want you to understand that it is not done with any expectation that I am buying or insuring the nomination of Mr. Lawrence to either the District Court or the Circuit Court and that I do not propose to make any future endorsements to you for judicial appointments even in my own state."

Russell said he would have told Johnson this when they spoke on the telephone earlier in the week, but he wanted to see Lawrence and advise him of what he proposed to do. "He and his family have already been humiliated beyond what decent and honorable persons should be required to bear at the hands of a motley collection of fanatics, mystics, and publicity seekers."[37]

Sending the letter did not have any noticeable cathartic effect on Russell's surging adrenaline. Nor did sleeping on the matter. The following day he wrote a U.S. circuit judge who had supported Lawrence: "I have never been as disappointed in a man as I am in Johnson for being frightened by the prospect of opposition. . . ."[38]

In the White House, Russell's letter to the president had the same effect as the fabled two-by-four that the Georgia farmer applied to the tail of his mule—it got his attention. Johnson realized that his temporizing, in an effort not to cross his attorney general, had deeply offended his old friend.

Ramsey Clark's father, Tom C. Clark, had favored Johnson against Coke Stevenson in the contested Texas Senate election of 1948, and Johnson had been slow to criticize his son; but he called to say, "Ramsey, I'm very unhappy. I think your foot-dragging on this has destroyed one of the great friendships I've had with one of the great men that has ever served this country." He told Clark to proceed with the processing of the Lawrence nomination. "I want to go ahead and nominate him."[39]

Proposed responses to the Russell letter were drafted by McPherson and by Temple, but they did not suit Johnson.[40] Finally, a couple of days after Russell's letter was received, Johnson telephoned Russell to say that he was returning it. "Dick," he said, "I have your letter here in my hand.

I don't think this letter reflects creditably upon you as a statesman. I don't think it reflects very well upon me as your President. I don't think it reflects very well on our long friendship. I don't think it is the kind of letter that I want to have in my file for historians to see. Now I don't want it in my file. . . . I'm going to send it back to you. I'm not going to make a copy of it. . . . I hope you'll destroy it. Whatever you do with it is your decision, because it's your letter. It's not mine."

Johnson added that he did not feel he had any commitment from Russell on Fortas or Thornberry and that he knew Russell would, as he always did, decide on those nominations as his conscience dictated. He said he would nominate Lawrence to the district judgeship, "but it's not a quid pro quo. It wasn't and isn't now."[41]

White House aide Tom Johnson, born in Macon, Georgia, was dispatched to the Capitol with the letter. He delivered the returned letter to Russell's office with a personal letter of his own, saying he knew for a fact that action on the Lawrence nomination was "in no way related" to the nominations of Fortas and Thornberry.[42]

Johnson's conciliatory statements and the return of the letter put Russell in a position to treat the controversy as a relatively minor patronage flap, one of those misunderstandings that occasionally occur in the interplay between two friends. If it had been just the Lawrence matter, Russell might have been inclined to do that, but for Russell it was not just the judgeship dispute. That was simply the final chapter in a much longer story.

The president's decision to finally send the Lawrence nomination to the Senate was made easier by the report of the Bar Association committee. The committee reported that Lawrence's controversial speech had been made by a younger man who had now matured. The committee found Lawrence exceptionally well qualified for the appointment. That enabled Ramsey Clark to withdraw his opposition and get on board, and President Johnson did not have to override his attorney general.

The controversy over the Lawrence nomination profoundly altered the personal relationship between Russell and Johnson. If it did not quite destroy the friendship, as Johnson had feared in his reprimand to Ramsey Clark, it reduced it, except for occasional nostalgic intervals, to little more than a formal playing out of ritual courtesies.

For his part, Russell would deny published reports that the friendship had cooled and would say he had no ill feeling toward the president about the Lawrence matter.[43] It is clear that Johnson, when he realized that he had hurt his old friend, tried to redeem himself but without any real success, and the informal breakfasts and suppers at the White House stopped.

For Russell, along with the element of trust, the relationship had now lost the element of deep affection that had characterized it from the beginning. When pressed, he would remark that he and Johnson had had their "sharp differences" over the years; and he would blame Clark for the controversy over Lawrence, who was formally nominated, as Johnson had promised, and was confirmed by the Senate without major opposition.[44]

It was, in other respects, not a good time for the president. The stalemate continued in Vietnam. As the Democratic National Convention approached, unrest in the cities and on the campuses increased. In his bid for the nomination, Humphrey was trying to distance himself from Johnson's policies, and Johnson was determined to keep Hubert in line.

The Republicans nominated Richard Nixon; and when Humphrey did win the Democratic nomination, demonstrations and rioting in Chicago, the convention city, kept Johnson from attending to address the delegates and receive a last hurrah. The defeated Eugene McCarthy then withdrew to the Riviera to pout, as the Humphrey presidential campaign got off to an uncertain and underfinanced start.

When Johnson received Russell's explosive letter in early July, informal White House nose counts showed 73 Senate votes in favor of Fortas as chief justice.[45] In addition to Russell, the president had sought and secured the support of GOP leader Everett Dirksen, and that is what had vaulted Senator Griffin to lead the fight against Fortas. Up to that time, opposition had been based on Fortas's reputation as a liberal justice and on his role as adviser and crony to Johnson while he was serving as a Supreme Court justice. Senate sentiment began to harden, however, when Judiciary Committee hearings disclosed that Justice Fortas had accepted fees totaling $15,000 for teaching a series of nine legal seminars at the American University, with the money coming from corporate givers—clients of his former law firm—who might one day have business before the Supreme Court.

It is indicative of the soured Russell-Johnson relationship that Russell felt constrained to state his decision on the Fortas nomination in another formal letter to the president. "Because I am well aware of Justice Abe Fortas' great legal ability," Russell wrote, "and of your profound interest in this nomination, it is with deep regret that I am impelled to tell you that I cannot vote to confirm his nomination as Chief Justice of the Supreme Court."

Russell said 95 percent of more than a thousand letters from Georgians—including lawyers and judges—were opposed to Fortas's nomination, but he had accepted those protests without making any public statement. It was the $15,000 honorarium and the way it was handled, he said, that "make it impossible for me to support Justice Fortas." The $15,000 would have seemed "excessive, even exorbitant," said Russell, if the money had come from the university. "But the fact that these funds were collected by a former law partner from the most affluent clients of the law firm (people who have an interest, direct or indirect, in every decision which touches the economy of our country) in my opinion raises a very grave question of ethics and propriety," Russell declared. "Due to all of these circumstances, I felt in duty bound to tell you frankly and in all candor of the conclusions to which I have been driven in this case. With assurances of respect and esteem, I am, Sincerely, ..."[46]

The day after Russell wrote his letter, Dirksen withdrew his support. As expected, opponents had launched a filibuster to prevent a vote on the Fortas nomination, and when Democratic leader Mike Mansfield tried to close off debate, the vote in favor was 45 to 43, considerably less than the required two-thirds. Fortas asked that his nomination as chief justice be withdrawn.

Though their personal relationship had soured, Johnson still regarded Russell as a valued adviser and bellwether of opinion in the Senate. In mid-October, trying to jump start the Paris talks on Vietnam, he called Russell to the White House to meet with the secretaries of state and defense and the chairman of the Joint Chiefs of Staff on a proposal for a bombing halt conveyed through Moscow. In declining health (he now used oxygen tanks at home and at the Capitol) and uncertain in his own mind, Russell said he had come to the White House meeting "only to listen.

"This is the most agonizing decision any president or any secretary of state or defense could face. Whatever you do, you will be charged with politics. But everyone wants an end to the war. It's been miserable—worse than Korea."

Johnson replied that he knew he would be accused of trying to influence the election if he approved the bombing halt. "But if this doesn't work I don't think I will have another opportunity."

"I guess it's worth a try," Russell said.[47]

Subsequently he urged Johnson to call Gen. Creighton Abrams, now the U.S. commander in Vietnam, back to Washington as the most effective spokesman to sell a bombing halt;[48] but Russell quickly came to believe that stopping the bombing was a "totally useless gesture." His basic view on Vietnam was still "win or get out."[49]

Shortly after he announced that he would not run again, Johnson had started making plans for a presidential library and public affairs center at the University of Texas in Austin. With help from the university, interviews were begun at once for an oral history collection to record events of the Johnson presidency in the words of the individuals who participated.

One of the university interviewers called Russell in October to arrange for an interview. Russell declined, on grounds that the chronicle of a presidency should not be written while the president himself was still in the White House. Johnson sought help, unsuccessfully, first from Russell staff members whom he knew and eventually from his most persuasive advocate, Lady Bird.[50] Russell would not be swayed and gave no interview.

Early in November, the president wrote Russell his usual birthday note, stressing their long friendship and extending Lady Bird's birthday greetings with his own.[51] A few days later, he announced the appointment of a longtime Russell staff member, William Darden, to the U.S. Court of Military Appeals.[52]

In December, as the Johnsons prepared to vacate the White House, Russell laid out his win-or-get-out views on Vietnam explicitly and at some length for his Georgia constituents. In a long interview conducted by Wayne Kelley, Washington correspondent for the *Atlanta Journal*, and published in *Atlanta* magazine, Russell said the newly elected president should "quarantine North Vietnam" by closing all its ports or else "bring our troops home." A quarantine should have been employed at the outset, Russell said, and "the war could have been brought to an end in six months. . . . I still think it could be done in six months. And we could do it without losing many more American lives, if we wanted to, by bombing the dikes that control the rice fields of North Vietnam."

Asked at the end of the wide-ranging interview whether his friendship with President Johnson had "cooled," Russell replied: "I think our personal relations are just as they have always been. We have had some rather sharp differences of opinion on political matters and issues. President Johnson has known me pretty well. He never did expect me to be spoon-fed by his philosophy."

Pressed for his reactions to Johnson's delay in appointing Alex Lawrence, Russell said: "Oh, well, I didn't have any feeling toward the president on that. I thought that the attorney general of the United States acted like a child about it. And I still think so. I very frankly do not feel that the present attorney general [Ramsey Clark] is qualified to fill that position."[53]

It was a disingenuous appraisal of his torn relations with the outgoing president, and there were hints that Russell would have an enthusiastic patron in the incoming president. Shortly after the election, President-elect Richard Nixon had called. Russell thought later that he had "responded perhaps too warmly" with assurances of cooperation on national security issues and kind words for Nixon's campaign calls for a stronger defense posture.[54]

In December, Melvin Laird, the new president's choice for secretary of defense, also called to touch base and solicit Russell's help in the days ahead. Russell had known Laird as a member of the House. He felt Laird was a good man for the job and told him so.[55]

Chapter Nine

NEW MANAGEMENT

1969–71

In his final State of the Union Address, President Lyndon Baines Johnson singled out Dick Russell and a few other House and Senate leaders for a special word of thanks, and a few days before he left the White House he wrote, in a "Dear Dick" letter: "The time of my departure grows near, but I leave with a sense of pride in the quality of friends I have made over the years.

"I am indeed proud to call you 'my friend'—a good friend, a steadfast friend, a loyal friend.

"You have helped lighten the load that I have carried as President and you have enriched my life. Thank you from the bottom of my heart."[1]

Despite its personal message, the letter was signed formally: "Lyndon B. Johnson"; and Russell may have viewed it as a mass-produced farewell. In any event, Johnson's thank-you note appears to have elicited no reply.

They were together a couple of times during the final days of the Johnson presidency. In mid-January, Russell attended the last meeting of the Democratic Congressional leadership with the president at the White House. The following day, Johnson called and they talked, according to Russell's note, about "things in general," with Russell bragging about a couple of young men from Georgia who had won the Congressional Medal of Honor. Just a few minutes later, the Johnsons attended a reception at the Capitol, and Russell "helped escort in Lady Bird, Lynda, Luci and Lynn" (the president's grandson).[2]

Russell was not present, however, on the day when senators, by prearrangement, rose ritually in the Senate chamber to pay respects to their former leader as he began his Texas retirement. Russell was again in Walter Reed Army Medical Center, where President Nixon sent him a note deploring his illness. Russell responded that his condition was no more than "a heavy cold."[3]

As is customary after such Senate ceremonials, the special *Congressional Record* containing the farewell tributes to Johnson was kept open temporarily so that absentees could add their encomia before the *Record* was printed in a memorial booklet. When nothing was forthcoming from Russell, well known to Senate functionaries as Johnson's friend and mentor, a clerk made inquiries at Russell's office.

It fell to the new press secretary, Powell Moore, to raise the matter with Russell, and he did so several times. Each time Russell insisted that he did not want to make any statement about Johnson's presidency. Finally, Moore suggested that Russell submit a farewell statement confined to their long personal relationship. Russell reluctantly agreed but told Moore to prepare it. Moore's draft was eventually submitted as written, except for one nostalgic paragraph, added by Russell, recalling their attendance together at baseball games many years previously.[4]

In his note to the hospital and with other courtesies, Nixon was clearly cultivating Russell. As senators, Nixon and Russell had not been close. Nixon did not serve on the armed services or appropriations committees, and they had no everyday relationship. However, Nixon was well aware of Russell's stature in the Senate, and it is not surprising that, as president, he sought to establish himself in Russell's good graces.[5]

As his began his presidency, Nixon had good political reasons to cultivate congressional Democrats. For the first time in more than 100 years, an incoming Republican president would have to cope with a Congress in which both the House and Senate were controlled by Democrats. And Russell, now more than ever, was the senator to cultivate. With the retirement of Sen. Carl Hayden of Arizona, Russell became chairman of the Appropriations Committee, minder of the government purse strings. He was also elected to succeed Hayden as president pro tempore, presiding officer for the Senate when the vice president is not present—an honor traditionally bestowed on the majority party's senior senator. As president pro tem, Russell was entitled to use a chauffeured limousine, a perk he enjoyed. In the new role, however, because he was now an officer of the Senate, he gave up the chairmanship of the caucus of Southern senators.

Russell was well aware of the irony of the fact that he had reached a pinnacle of Senate power at a time when his poor health was diminishing his capacity, but he threw himself into the Senate's business. In late January, at Nixon's request, Russell began attending meetings of the joint congressional leadership with the new president.[6] At a White House meeting early in March to hear Nixon talk about his recent trip to Europe, Russell's notes indicate that he cautioned Nixon against sounding "flat" in talking publicly about Vietnam, with American boys dying there.[7]

Before the month was out, Russell had a new and serious health problem. A check-up at Walter Reed disclosed a cancerous growth in his left lung, and he began a series of treatments with radioactive cobalt. After a news conference announcing the new problem, Dr. Willis Hurst—who also had Johnson as a patient—called the Texas ranch and reported on the situation to Johnson aide Mary Rather, who wrote the former president a note. Dr. Hurst, she said, reported that Russell had cancer but felt all right and was in good spirits. Hurst predicted that Russell's doctors would keep him going, Rather continued, and added that "obviously Senator Russell loves you very much."[8] Johnson called Russell to voice his concern.[9]

For about eight weeks Russell received intensive radiation therapy, and one day in May his doctors told him that the treatment had been successful and that no trace of the tumor remained. It was, he thought, a cause for celebration. Sister Ina was in town for a visit, and Russell took her and his former fiancée, Pat Collins, now the widowed Mrs. Sal Andretta, out for an expensive dinner.[10]

In the long view, the celebration was unwarranted, and Russell's recovery from lung cancer would, in a sense, mark a new low in his health history. He was still plagued by emphysema, and in destroying the cancer, the cobalt radiation had also destroyed most of what was left of his left lung, further reducing his ability to breathe. His stamina and mobility were now very seriously impaired.

Recently he had been telling associates, "I just can't keep up. Things are going too fast for me."[11] Now he was forced to ask other senators to make motions he would have made in better times, or make speeches he would have made. That was the case in the Senate debate that began in May on President Nixon's Safeguard antiballistic missile system (ABM), which barely survived in the Senate.[12]

In Texas, the first months of Johnson's retirement were a time of deep depression, but he worked out of it. He occupied himself with day-to-day operations of the ranch, the business of the television station, and development of the Johnson Library in Austin. He also, as daughter Luci would remark, discovered play and his grandchildren and found that retirement has its compensations.

"One of the things I enjoyed most was being able to go to bed after the ten o'clock news at night and sleep until daylight the next morning. I don't remember ever having an experience like that in the five years I was in the White House," he would recall.[13]

In early August, Russell wrote Johnson to extend an invitation from the Blue Key Society at the University of Georgia, asking the former president to make a speech. Declining, Johnson said: "Lady Bird and I hope you are progressing toward full recovery from the radium treatment." He thanked Russell for information supplied for his presidential memoirs, then in preparation, and added: "You know the invitation is always out for you to visit with us at the ranch."[14]

Replying a few days later, Russell said he was sorry Johnson couldn't accept the Blue Key invitation and glad that the information he had supplied was helpful, adding: "It has been much too long since I have been fortunate enough to visit the Ranch, and I would like very much to do so. However, you know as well as anyone the interminable demands which are imposed on us here."

Russell went on to say he was glad to report that he was feeling fine. The doctors at Walter Reed were well pleased with a recent check-up, "and while I still have the old scourge of emphysema to limit me, I am doing as well as I have any right to expect."[15]

Despite that note of optimism, Russell's health continued to deteriorate. He went each day to get oxygen at the office of the Capitol attending physician and dosed himself with various medications under the direction of the doctors at Walter Reed, carefully noting the time of each day's dosages on memo slips that cluttered his desk.

In December, with the holidays approaching, he and Johnson talked on the telephone, and afterwards Johnson wrote: "Hearing your voice was a great pleasure. Our telephone visit did my heart good.

"Lady Bird and I continue to pray and hope that your health improves. No one could wish that more than we do. Warmest regards." Signing the note, Johnson added a handwritten postscript: "So sorry about the virus. Do take care."[16]

A few days before Christmas, a glass bowl—a gift from the Johnsons—arrived in Winder, where Russell was spending the holiday recess. Unfortunately (though perhaps symbolically) it arrived in pieces, having been damaged in the mail. In his thank you (addressed "Dear Lady Bird and Mr. President"), Russell advised the Johnsons that the bowl had been smashed, "but that does not in any way diminish my appreciation for being in your thoughts." Russell said he hoped the Johnsons had enjoyed their finest

Christmas ever, "and I know how much you must enjoy the two grandchildren." The Russells, he said, had had a "real, good old country Christmas," and he concluded "with warm regards and with the hope that 1970 will be the best year ever for you both." He signed it "Richard B. Russell."[17]

Johnson immediately arranged to have a replacement hand-delivered to Russell's Washington office rather than entrust another bowl to the postal service.[18] When he returned to Washington, Russell found "the very handsome bowl" and wrote the Johnsons: "I had certainly not intended for you to replace the one that was shattered on its way to Georgia, but I am delighted to have the new one. It will be a treasured memento of the friendship that we have enjoyed for these many years, and I deeply appreciate your kindness in thinking of me." This time he ended "with cordial good wishes and warm regards, sincerely," but again he signed it "Richard B. Russell."[19]

In Winder, Russell had granted a series of interviews to Atlanta television station WSB, which was preparing a three-part documentary, "Georgia Giant," on the life and career of Georgia's senior senator. The interviews were conducted by Hal Suit, a professionally (and, it would develop, politically) ambitious journalist. The programs were to be unveiled at a February 1970 reception in Washington honoring Russell, to which many of Russell's present and former associates—including Johnson—were invited.

However, aide Tom Johnson, on the former president's behalf, advised Cox Broadcasting, owners of WSB, that "much as he would like to participate," Johnson would be out of the country on the day of the reception.[20] Among the joys of retirement that Johnson had discovered was Acapulco, the Mexican beach resort, where he could relax in the sun with friends in a villa owned by the former president of Mexico, Miguel Aleman.[21]

In June Johnson declined an invitation to attend the dedication of the Richard B. Russell Agricultural Research Center at the University of Georgia in Athens. To the sponsors, he sent best wishes "as you honor a great American." In June, he wrote Russell declining another invitation to attend a Blue Key banquet. He was, he said, busy with his memoirs, and "right now, I don't feel I can plan any speaking engagement."[22]

In Winder early in July, Russell met briefly with Jimmy Carter. The state legislator, whose family was well known to the Russells, had informed Russell that he planned to run for governor and had been trying for some time to arrange a meeting. They sat on the porch and had a cordial talk, but

Russell said later that the visit from the young man he scarcely knew really hadn't made much sense.[23]

The senator's declining health was apparent at the annual Russell family reunion that summer when he did not walk back to the cemetery for the ceremony that was always held there, but went upstairs to rest instead. Now more than ever Russell needed oxygen whenever he exerted himself. He had a device to supply it that could be carried as a backpack, and when the weather was good, he would walk in the woods with Proctor Jones, who was now his constant companion. He was telling friends that he didn't expect to be around for long.[24]

It was a tight little household—Russell, Proctor Jones, and Modine Thomas, the black housekeeper who had been hired as a part-time worker by Russell's mother many years previously and had stayed on, eventually to become caretaker for the house when Russell was in Washington. Sometimes, when Jones took a few hours off to visit his fiancée, it was just Russell and Modine. He had never lost his love for sports, and that summer he watched a lot of baseball on television. Sometimes Modine was invited to watch, too.[25]

Jimmy Carter's opponent in the race for the Democratic gubernatorial nomination was Carl Sanders, eligible to serve again after sitting out a term. Stories were quickly circulated that Carter had met with Russell and that Russell had pledged his support to Carter's candidacy. It reached a point where Russell felt obligated to issue a statement saying that he had never endorsed any candidate for governor in a Democratic primary, and Carter called to apologize.[26]

This time the winner of the Democratic primary would not be an automatic winner in the general election. Hal Suit, the WSB correspondent who had, in effect, costarred with Russell in the WSB television programs, was now the Republican candidate for governor and was campaigning actively across the state.

In August, Johnson wrote Russell that he could not fit a speech at the University of Georgia Law Day into his schedule for the following May. "We think of you often and hope you are doing well," he said. "Warm personal regards, as always."[27]

In listing the various invitations, courteously extended and courteously declined, it is hard to avoid speculation about what might have happened if one of the invitations had been accepted and the two old friends had found an opportunity to sit down and talk—the coolness warmed, perhaps, by a bit of Cutty Sark in one glass and Jack Daniels in the other.

In the best of times they had occasionally survived periods of annoyance with each other; and although the original relationship almost certainly could not have been recovered, they might have resumed a more regular political friendship.[28]

Russell returned to Washington in August, but it was clear to his colleagues that the Georgia Giant was now a frail old man. Earlier, when his mobility was first impaired by shortness of breath, he had tried a cane, but he disliked and abandoned it. Now he had a motorized cart to get around. To improve his breathing he had tried a regimen prescribed at the Duke University hospital, and he used an oxygen device developed by the space agency, NASA; but nothing helped much. Every cough was painful, and every cold was a crisis. When he felt poorly he did not like to stay in his apartment alone, and on several occasions he asked Proctor Jones to spend the night there with him.[29]

In September, on a weekend when the Nixons intended to go to Camp David, the presidential hideaway in the nearby Catoctin Mountains, President Nixon turned the White House over to Russell for a party with his family and friends. A showing of the movie *Patton* was featured. Mrs. Mamie Eisenhower came from Gettysburg to attend, along with David and Julie Eisenhower and Tricia Nixon, and there were more than fifty guests.[30]

A few weeks later Russell's health took another serious turn, and after intervals in and out of the hospital, he went first to Key West and then to Winder. Jimmy Carter had won the Democratic nomination for governor and was now in the state's first real general election campaign against Hal Suit. Both were running as Russell intimates—Suit as the admiring, friendly companion of the recent television series and Carter as an old family friend and, as the campaign progressed, as a young man who had sought his old friend's fatherly advice at every important turn in his career.[31]

At least twice during this period there were calls from the LBJ ranch inquiring about Russell's health. As election day approached, reporters began calling the Russell home to get Russell's comments. Russell was willing to meet with the reporters, some of whom were old friends, but he had suffered a serious fall on the stairs and landed on his head. Proctor Jones took one look at the senator's face—drawn, scarred, and still a nasty black and blue—and suggested that Russell take phone calls from a few of the reporters he knew instead.

Russell was determined to take his usual pre-election stance: "Like I've always said," he told one of the callers, "I vote the straight Democratic ticket. I never struck a Democratic ticket in all my life, and it's too late for me to start now." Was that an endorsement of Carter? the reporter asked. "Well," Russell replied, "he's the Democratic candidate, isn't he?"[32]

Throughout his career Russell had avoided involvement in state politics, and he had never endorsed a gubernatorial candidate in the years when the Democratic primary was the real election in Georgia. After the phone call, however, it was duly reported statewide that, for the first time, Sen. Richard B. Russell had endorsed a candidate for governor.[33]

Back in Washington after Thanksgiving, Russell was ill much of the time. Sister Ina came from Georgia to stay in the apartment with him. Late in November he was admitted to Walter Reed, but he checked himself out on December 3 to vote against deleting from a pending appropriations bill $390 million in development funds for the supersonic transport plane. The bill was strongly supported by Sen. Henry M. Jackson, Russell's friend and longtime ally on the Senate Armed Services Committee.

Readmitted to the hospital, Russell was not at first entirely bedridden. He worked in the hospital's VIP quarters, where Senate aides brought papers to him. He had planned to go to Winder for the holidays, but as his condition worsened, his doctors became concerned about the rigors of the trip.[34] President Nixon had offered the use of Air Force One, with its many creature comforts, and in Winder, Modine was looking forward to the holidays. She viewed the occasions when "Mr. R. B." was in residence as her "happiest time" and could not believe he would not arrange for Christmas at home. She bought a tree and decorated it herself, but Russell reluctantly decided not to make the trip.

Instead, a family Christmas was arranged in the hospital. Brother Fielding and his wife, Virginia, brought their children to join sister Ina and the senator for the holidays. During their visit, President Nixon brought Secretary of State Henry Kissinger to the hospital to brief the senator on the world situation. It was a tonic for Russell's sagging spirits.

He had told his sister that he was going to die. She objected, saying that Russell had been as ill before and had gotten well. "No," he said, "this time I'm not going to get well and I don't want to, because I don't want to go through this again." Declaring that he was "not one for deathbed scenes," he nonetheless told Ina, before Christmas, to advise the family that if they wanted to see him alive, "they had better come up now." With help from Proctor Jones, she did pass that word, and close relatives arranged to visit him in the ensuing weeks.[35]

Get-well messages and calls poured in. Many were from his congressional colleagues and other dignitaries. One message of encouragement and support was sent by the black waitresses who worked in the Senate dining room, for whom Russell had been both wailing wall and court of last resort over the years.

January 12, 1971, marked thirty-eight years of Senate service for Russell, but he did not feel well enough to discuss an anniversary press statement that Powell Moore had drafted for him. Moore returned to the hospital the following day to work on the statement with Russell, and when they were finished, Russell told Moore to write a memo to the Senate comptroller raising Moore's salary. Moore thanked Russell and began gathering his papers.

Russell commented sharply that if Moore didn't want the raise he need not write the memo. "You mean right this minute?" Moore asked. "Certainly I want you to write it right this minute," Russell said testily. "I might not be here fifteen minutes from now." Moore found a typewriter at the nurses' station and wrote the memo. Russell signed it.[36]

In the organization of the new Senate, a battle had developed over the job of Senate Democratic whip. Sen. Edward M. Kennedy of Massachusetts, who had held the post in the previous Congress, faced a challenge from Sen. Robert Byrd of West Virginia in a contest that would be settled in the Democratic caucus scheduled for January 21. Several days beforehand Russell signed a proxy directing that his vote in the caucus be cast for Senator Byrd.

On Tuesday, January 19, Johnson learned at the ranch that Russell had suffered a stroke during the night and had lost consciousness in mid-afternoon. Tom Johnson had been advised by the Russell staff that they did not think Russell would last another night. The *Atlanta Constitution* was asking for a statement from the former president, and Tom Johnson began drafting one—a task that eventually would be taken over by Lyndon and Lady Bird.[37]

But in Washington, Russell rallied and seemed to improve. He was intermittently in and out of consciousness, and for about thirty-six hours it appeared that Ina might be right and that he would again recover. She was with him in his room early in the afternoon on January 21 when he died.[38] He was seventy-four. After thirty-eight years as a senator, his final proxy had been voted a few hours earlier in Byrd's successful effort to unseat Kennedy as Democratic whip.

As Russell had directed, Proctor Jones placed a call only a few minutes after Russell's death, but it was several hours before he was able to reach Harriet Orr.[39]

From the ranch Johnson and Lady Bird sent a telegram to Russell's nephew, Richard B. Russell III: "We send our deepest sympathy on the death of your uncle, our old and dear friend. He was an uncommon man with an uncommon devotion to duty. He will be sorely missed. To quote a poet on another great leader, 'He fell like a kingly cedar tree and left a lonesome place against the sky.' Please extend our condolences to Dick's brothers and sisters."[40]

Russell had long since selected the spot in the family cemetery where he intended to be buried, next to his mother. He had told his aides that he wanted his friend John Stennis, who had succeeded him as chairman of the Senate Armed Services Committee, to speak at his funeral.[41] To accommodate the expected crowd, a dais was erected in an open field adjoining the small fenced graveyard, so the burial service could be conducted there.[42]

Russell had left instructions that there be no ceremony in Washington marking his death. On the way to the airport, however, the hearse and funeral cortege slowly moved through the plaza past the east front of the Capitol, where his colleagues stood on the steps to pay their respects. In Atlanta, on the way to Winder, Russell's body lay in state for a day in the Capitol, President and Mrs. Nixon laid a wreath there, and the president spoke briefly as Georgians by the thousands paid their own final tributes. Three military transport planes, carrying the vice president, senators, other dignitaries, friends, and staff left Andrews Air Force Base in the Washington suburbs for Dobbins Air Force Base near Winder on the morning of the Russell funeral. As they approached the airport, visibility was seriously restricted by clouds and heavy rains. One of the three orbiting transports, the staff plane, made three attempts to land. Each time the pilot was forced to pull up.[43]

John Stennis, who was to deliver the eulogy, and the Senate chaplain, who was to conduct the funeral service, were on board one of the diverted VIP aircraft. At the Russell home, Russell's brother Jeb prepared to conduct the service. The three transports were rerouted to the air force base at Charleston, South Carolina. There, through a hastily assembled telephone and television hookup, Stennis was able to speak to the mourners gathered in Winder, who watched borrowed TV monitors in the rain.

One senator, who had been traveling independently and was not airborne with his colleagues, was able to attend. Before the service, as the rain poured down outside, Russell's longtime personal secretary, Barboura Raesley, answered a knock at the front door of the Russell home. There on the porch stood a thoroughly drenched Hubert H. Humphrey, whom

Russell had described as a "damn fool" on his arrival in the Senate more than twenty years previously. Away from Washington on business, Humphrey had reached Winder by bus and the head of the lane to the Russell home by taxi and had trudged to the doorway in the downpour to pay his last respects.[44]

In several phone conversations with Proctor Jones and members of the Russell family, Harriet Orr was deeply troubled about whether she should attend and finally decided against it.

In Texas at the ranch, Johnson arranged to attend the ceremony. An air force plane was positioned at nearby Bergstrom Air Force Base to provide transportation for the Johnsons. At departure time, however, the violent rainstorms that prevented the landing of the planes from Washington prevented the former president's plane from obtaining clearance for a north Georgia flight.[45]

Johnson was himself experiencing health difficulties. As it had been in 1955, the problem was his heart. For almost a year he had been suffering late-afternoon attacks of angina—intense chest pain with shortness of breath. At the time of Russell's death, he had just recovered from a touch of viral pneumonia, and, unable to attend the funeral, he headed for Acapulco instead for rest and sun.[46]

AFTERWORD

Lyndon Johnson used to tell friends that the Johnson men tended to die out at sixty.[1] In the months after Dick Russell's death, Johnson's heart problem persisted. As Russell had done—but for his painful angina rather than for a respiratory problem—he now kept an oxygen supply close by for difficult times.

Unlike other former presidents before and since, he made few public appearances. His family and his life in retirement kept him occupied, especially supervising the hour-by-hour operations of the ranch. If he agonized over developments in Vietnam and the unraveling of his War on Poverty, he kept his concerns pretty much to himself.

He was coming to grips with his own mortality. Through much of his career he had hated funerals and avoided attending them. Now he attended when he thought it was appropriate. He made it a point, late in 1972, to travel to Independence, Missouri, for the funeral of Harry S. Truman.

On January 22, 1973, resting alone in his bedroom after an active day, Johnson had a heart attack. He called the ranch switchboard for help, but he died before help could reach him. He was sixty-four.

He had had a last hurrah of sorts in December, driving his snowmobile from the ranch in snow and ice to participate in a civil rights symposium at the Johnson Library in Austin. Though not feeling well, he made a speech to the assemblage, which included Chief Justice Warren, Hubert Humphrey, and other dignitaries, hailing civil rights progress but warning that much remained to be done. Then he had to use his old conciliatory skills to keep the peace among leaders of the various civil rights factions on hand.[2]

As Dick Russell said, Vietnam destroyed Lyndon Johnson politically, and his rehabilitation—as the Vietnam War recedes into the history books—is inhibited by a perception of Johnson as an unprincipled political manipulator interested only in power and, later, in personal wealth. Psychologists, sociologists, and political analysts will be worrying about Johnson and writing about him for years to come.

In assessing his complex and often devious maneuverings, these scholars will do well to keep their eye on a few simplicities. As a boy and young man Lyndon Johnson was dominated by his mother in a way understood long before Freud. He was programmed—the computer term is useful here—to succeed by Rebekah. He was occasionally rebellious (running away to California after high school, for example); but in the end, as she prescribed, he relentlessly sought success; and power and money were its negotiable currencies.

Until he married, he experienced none of the gentling forces that might have tempered Rebekah's determination. (In this aspect of his development his father's influence was largely negative.) His formal education was minimal, and he did not read independently. He had no real friends, and religion was one of the conditioners employed in his mother's program.

As he matured, he was not without a simple principle, however. He was dedicated, as a leader, to carrying others upward with him. Once reasonable family incomes were assured, once education was provided for all youths—to the extent it could be absorbed—and old age was made secure for everyone, all the "pee-pul" of whom he so often spoke could realize their dreams and be successful, too. This simple philosophy emerged in educating Latino children in Cotulla and in providing electricity for Pedernales farms. It continued with aid to education, Social Security and Medicare, and it came to be applied equally, without racial bias.

His simple philosophy was to have had its triumph in the realization of Johnson's vision of a Great Society; but that concept, with its many disorganized, poorly planned, expensive programs, was caught up in prosecuting and financing the Vietnam War. In this respect also, Johnson was destroyed by Vietnam.[3]

Dick Russell was the quintessential senator, admired by his colleagues—liberals as well as conservatives—even while he was championing an increasingly unpopular cause. It was Eugene McCarthy who described Russell as "a classical senator [who] was also a classical victim of his times, since it fell to him to defend segregation and to lead the anti–civil rights movement in the Senate."[4]

He never hesitated in shouldering that burden. Over the years Russell's admirers and critics have wondered why a man of his civility and understanding never shed his regional biases or moderated his stance on racial mixing as other more virulent segregationists had done. Of all the opponents of civil rights initiatives, Russell had seemed to many to be the most reasonable.

Johnson and newsman Roger Mudd probably had part of the answer when they said (in almost identical language, on different occasions) that Russell was a nineteenth-century man adrift in the twentieth century.[5] Russell himself said that as he got older, he became more conservative. Generally unreceptive to change, as he grew older he grew more resistant to it. He did come to realize that his outright resistance to civil rights initiatives would fail, and he consciously began to conduct a delaying action against measures he had previously tried to block. In his campaign to prevent a campaign in 1966, like any prudent and foresighted politician, he was even trying to corral votes of conservative blacks. But his views on racial mixing did not change.

It was not difficult for Lyndon Johnson to espouse racial equality. Growing up in a part of Texas where there were almost no blacks—an area where German settlers had opposed the Confederacy—he had little of the Southern heritage to fix his attitudes. He had seen minorities oppressed as a young teacher in Cotulla, and before he became a senator—before he gave his first Senate speech in the Southern cause—he had begun to express misgivings about blacks' lack of rights.

Russell, on the other hand, was a product of the Deep South. Ina Russell taught her children that the Negroes (never "niggers") were to be respected and, in a sense, protected. She monitored the tenant houses, ministered to the sick, and sent Dick running to Winder for the doctor when someone was seriously ill. (There was even a family story that Arch Barnes, the teenage son of one of the black tenant families who had been threatened by vigilantes, spent a night on the floor of the kitchen in the main house while young Dick slept in the adjoining dining room with his rifle at hand.)[6]

But there was no doubt that the Negroes lived in a separate, inferior society. Years after the Supreme Court's 1954 school desegregation decision, Dick Russell would recall that black children in Winder went to schools known to be inferior, but that desegregated facilities were never even discussed in his childhood.[7]

It is argued persuasively that many Southerners, in and out of politics and from just such a background, did change their views. Outspoken, Deep South opponents of civil rights for blacks, including George Wallace, Strom Thurmond, and James Eastland, underwent a change.

For Russell, however, deciding that racial mixing was right would have involved more than outliving regional biases and commitments of his past. More thoughtful and contemplative than many of his contemporaries, Russell had developed a rationale based in large part on his reading of history. He believed that racial mixing was wrong even as he acknowledged that it was going to occur. The pages of history told him (wrongly, as most historians will assert) that racial mixing had led to the collapse of societies through the ages. As he told the clergyman who wrote him before the 1964 civil rights debate, he knew of no civilization that had been able to survive it (see p. 105).[8]

What did he mean? Here the evidence is sketchy. He surely believed that Rome began to decay as centurions brought wives and slaves to Rome from other parts of the expanding empire into the Roman bloodline. He may have meant the Spanish civilization after the Moors and the disappearance, for centuries, of the Egyptian culture as its racial lines were thinned. Whatever the evidence (and no matter how flawed), for Russell, the study of history produced a strong and reasoned conviction that buttressed the regional biases and commitments of a lifetime and left them impervious to change.

In later years he found support for these racial views in his own experience. Ramey Air Force Base in Puerto Rico was one of the sunny havens where he occasionally convalesced after respiratory difficulties, and it seemed quite clear to him that the Spanish strain there had been irretrievably corrupted. He thought Brazil's was another civilization where racial mixing (beginning with slavery) had produced decay.[9]

With his nineteenth-century concepts and boyhood biases reinforced by these conclusions, Dick Russell was simply not in a position to change his mind. As an intelligent man, he could see that racial mixing was coming, and as an able politician, he tried to adapt to that. But he would not have seriously entertained the idea that racial mixing was right.

It serves no purpose to speculate, to wonder what might have happened if, at an early age, Russell's reading could have been broadened to provide exposure to different racial views. It is important to understand that if he had changed his views on race, he could never have been elected to public office in the Georgia of his time. Always a cautious politician, he saw himself as already at the risky edge of the mainstream, and a candidate who was too enlightened and moderate on racial questions was always in danger of being "outsegged" or "outniggered" by opportunistic foes.

Russell and Johnson became close personal friends late in the 1940s.

They were doing much the same job and often working at it together. They enjoyed each other's company, and each saw features in the other that he admired. Politically, each believed the other had a potential that could be exploited in the future.

It is usually assumed that the friendship ended in 1968 after the dispute over the judgeship nomination for Alex Lawrence. I have included incidents and correspondence to indicate that the change in the relationship was more complex. The intimacy ended—there were no more impromptu breakfasts, dinners, and the like—but Russell remained an adviser on important issues, and a show of friendship was maintained.

Personally and politically, many things had changed in their relationship before Russell sent Lawrence's name to the White House. He and Johnson were now in different jobs, and their perspectives were different. Many of the potentials that each had seen in the other had been realized, but for Russell at least, the outcome was not as he had envisioned it. Russell aides and colleagues agree that there came a time, before the dispute over Lawrence, when Russell simply did not trust Johnson.

Communications continued, albeit formally and sporadically after the dispute, and Russell publicly denied that there had been a serious break. In an interview in mid-October 1968, months after the incident, he said his relations with Johnson were "just as they have always been," and he reported almost a year later that he had recently had a "very intimate" letter from the former president.[10] If there is such a thing as a pro forma friendship, this one dragged along on that basis.

Hundreds of Johnson associates from his public and private life were interviewed for an extensive oral history collection at the imposing eight-story Lyndon B. Johnson Library and Public Affairs Center in Austin, Texas. After Johnson left the White House, Dick Russell remained adamant and was never interviewed for that collection.

A much smaller collection of oral history interviews of Russell friends and associates has been assembled in the more modest Richard B. Russell Memorial Library in Athens, Georgia. Though Lady Bird Johnson contributed a warm and perceptive interview, Lyndon Johnson is not represented.

RETROSPECTIVE, 1998

In the five years since this book was delivered to the original publisher a flood of information, relevant to the events described, has come into the public domain. Some of this was speeded by an Act of Congress. Much of this new information is presented in the words of Lyndon B. Johnson, Richard B. Russell and their associates.

In 1992, after nearly thirty years of speculation and controversy about the death of John F. Kennedy, Congress passed the John F. Kennedy Records Collection Act. Bowing to journalists and historians who had complained over the years that the truth about the young president's death might be hidden in government files, that act required that all U.S. government archives make public all unclassified data relating to Kennedy's assassination in Dallas on 22 November 1963.

In 1973, four years after leaving the White House, Lyndon Johnson directed that the tapes of recordings that he had made there—of telephone calls and office discussions—be kept secret for fifty years and then reviewed for possible release. Under the 1992 law, however, the Lyndon B. Johnson Library in Austin, Texas, a government archive, was required to make public its tapes dealing with the assassination, including those involving formation of the Warren Commission. In 1993 the Johnson Library and the National Archives, in Washington, began releasing the assassination tapes. Under these circumstances, Lady Bird Johnson and Harry Middleton, Director of the Johnson Library, decided to make public all the tapes made by President Johnson during his five years in the White House.

Early in 1998, the Richard B. Russell Library, where much of this book originated, opened "Exhibit B," documents that had been kept under seal since Russell's death in 1971. Many of those documents are memos, scribbled or dictated by Russell after calls from or meetings with Johnson. (A few of them describe calls that are also now available in the tapes.) Much of the information has relevance to the friendship between Richard B. Russell and Lyndon B. Johnson.

There is a sense of finality for a writer who sends a book like this one off to the printer. But he is quickly confronted with new information vitally important to the events he has described. Rarely does he have an opportunity to review and supplement what is already in print. Here in this new edition is a look back from a 1998 perspective at events described here in 1993.

Talking to and about one another in the tapes and memos, Russell and Johnson reveal a great deal about the devolution of their long friendship. Their talk was colloquial, often profane, and occasionally earthy. They slipped frequently into a slangy patois where, even for the polished and usually urbane Russell, things are "gonna" happen or perhaps they "aint." Johnson often called to seek Russell's advice on a specific problem, but they usually digressed to discuss a number of concerns. Invited to the White House for dinner on 9 June 1967, ostensibly to discuss "a very important matter"—whether Johnson should meet with Soviet Premier Alexei Kosygin when Kosygin visted U.N. headquarters—Russell noted afterwards that he concluded that Johnson just "wanted someone to eat supper with . . . [someone] with whom he felt at home." Nor were they always concerned with affairs of state. Russell had asked Johnson to appoint Georgia Tech football coach Bobby Dodd to succeed Bud Wilkinson as the White House adviser on physical fitness. On 4 February 1964, however, he was persuaded to go along with St. Louis Cardinal star, Stan Musial, also an admired acquaintance.

As he had when they were colleagues in the Senate, Russell occasionally needled the new president. He had, of course, noticed the presence of Georgia's young governor, Carl Sanders, along with other dignitaries, in Lady Bird Johnson's box when Johnson made his "Let Us Continue" speech, after Kennedy's death (see p. 100). When Johnson on 15 January 1964 asked Russell for names of "top men" from Georgia who might serve in his new administration, Russell suggested that he find something for Sanders "and quit running him against me for the Senate." He was teasing, he later admitted, but he had read in the Georgia press that "Sanders is Johnson's favorite."

Johnson showed great affection for his old friend and mentor. He was often solicitous about Russell's health. Would Russell like to come down to the White House on 7 December 1963 for a swim in the warm pool? When Russell ruled out a swim because of his breathing difficulties, Johnson quickly asked if there was any reason why Russell couldn't come down for a little sherry and some lunch. Russell could think of none, and Johnson said, ". . . the car will be at the side door there waiting for you," just a few steps from Russell's office.

One of the tapes discloses that Johnson was aware of Russell's weekend dates (see p. 92), but did not know whom he was dating. Always inquisitive, Johnson wanted to know more. He called on Saturday, 11 January 1964, to invite Russell to fly up to Camp David, the presidential retreat in nearby Maryland, with the Robert McNamaras to "have a quiet dinner in front of the fireplace and a drink or two and philosophize a little bit" and return late Sunday. Russell declined, saying he had a date, and Johnson quickly said he thought Russell's dates were on Friday. Russell said he had postponed it, but now: "I've already bought two big steaks and got them in the icebox." Johnson then invited Russell to fly up for Sunday lunch and Russell, who had never been to Camp David, accepted. "Is there any lady you'd like to bring?" Johnson asked. "No, " Russell replied. "Kinfolk?" "Not here," said Russell. "Anybody around? No companion you'd like to have?" Russell said, "No," and Johnson joked that Russell was "just going to be a bachelor." "Well, I think I'm about past the point of no return on that," Russell replied.

Another call on 15 January 1964 made clear that their relationship was, at this point, a secure friendship characterized by devotion and trust. Johnson had called to confide that France planned formally to recognize the Mao Tse Tung Communist government in China. As they talked, eight years before President Nixon ended the long freeze with his historic visit to China, Russell commented that "the time's gonna come when we're gonna have to recognize Red China." Johnson agreed, and Russell suggested that it probably should have been done "three or four years ago." "I think so," Johnson said, with Russell adding, "Politically, right now, it's poison of course." It was an extraordinary exchange, and it could indeed have had poisonous consequences for both men had it become public. It stands now as a frank and casual exchange between good friends, full of good sense, made with confidence that it would not reach other ears, and it did not.

One of Johnson's initiatives in the first days of his presidency was formation of the Warren Commission, and the account here (see pp. 100-101) is supported by the Johnson tapes, with one important addition: transcripts show clearly that in the immediate aftermath of Kennedy's assassination President Johnson was strongly opposed to the idea of a presidential commission. He had, in fact, made his own arrangement to investigate Kennedy's death in Dallas.

Transcripts of Johnson tapes indicate that the idea of a presidential commission first came to the attention of the White House in a call to Johnson aide Bill Moyers from Eugene Rostow, Dean of the Yale Law School, three days after the Kennedy assassination. Rostow had already discussed the idea with Deputy Attorney General Nicholas Katzenbach, who was then acting as head of the Justice Department, since Attorney General Robert Kennedy was in seclusion after the death of his brother. Moyers thought it a "good suggestion" and said he would pass it on."

By the next morning Johnson had heard all about the idea, and he told FBI Director J. Edgar Hoover he was dead set against it. He had heard that "some lawyer in Justice is lobbying the [Washington] *Post*" for an editorial advocating such a commission "which we think would be very bad." The White House, he said, couldn't be investigating "every shooting scrape." He told Hoover that he had arranged for Texas Attorney General Waggoner Carr to impanel a special state Court of Inquiry to look into Kennedy's death. He directed Hoover to put "every facility at your command" into compiling a full FBI report on the assassination to the (U.S.) Attorney General. Then he told Hoover to offer "full cooperation" to the Texas inquiry.

The tapes do not reveal how Johnson was persuaded to change his mind. He would surely have been annoyed when the *Washington Post* editorial did appear, but three days after trashing the plan, the tapes find him discussing the creation of a commission with Senator James O. Eastland, D-Miss., Chairman of the Senate Judiciary Committee, one of several congressional committees that had been discussing their own investigations of the Kennedy killing. Eastland said a commission "would suit me all right."

It is clear that Johnson had become concerned that several competing congressional committees could hold televised hearings on the Kennedy assassination. He had lunched with Russell who agreed that it would be bad to have Senate and House inquiries, as the President said, "running all over the lot." That was clearly an important factor in Johnson's decision to adopt the commission idea. The killing of Lee Harvey Oswald by Jack Ruby meant that no court would ever deliberate and reach a verdict on the assassination, and that was surely a factor.

Johnson referred in the tapes to discussing the assassination with an attorney whom he did not identify. The attorney was probably Abe Fortas, Johnson's friend from New Deal days, and Fortas was very probably influential in Johnson's change of mind. Fortas had been Johnson's attorney of last resort since he helped assure Johnson's election to the Senate in 1948 (see p. 9). In any event, it was to Fortas that Johnson turned the following day, Friday, 29 November, to line up the membership of his commission. In early afternoon, in the first of two talks, Johnson and Fortas arrived at the final Commission membership. It would be Chief Justice Earl Warren, Senators Russell and John Sherman Cooper, R-Ky., House members Hale Boggs, D-La., and Gerald Ford, R-Mich., plus former CIA Director Allen Dulles and Wall Street attorney John McCloy. Fortas had arranged that Katzenbach and Solicitor General Archibald Cox meet with Warren and ask him to serve. He and Johnson agreed that Johnson himself should call the other prospective members. Johnson was in no mood to beg or beseech: "I think we ought to order them to do it and let them bellyache," he said.

Johnson had been clearing the idea of an investigating commission with Senate and House leaders in both parties, asking that they "protect my flanks" when the plan was publicized. In those calls, he digressed occasionally to conduct some timely lobbying on behalf of the legislative program he had inherited from President Kennedy. "Let's get the tax bill out," he urged Senate Republican Leader Everett M. Dirksen, R-Ill., who was a member of the Finance Committee where Kennedy's tax bill had stalled. Later he would make the same plea to other members of that Committee.

After advising J. Edgar Hoover that appointment of a commission seemed to be "the only way we can stop" a flock of competing congressional inquiries, Johnson turned to calling prospective commission members. He began with Russell, and he was immediately in trouble (as reported here p. 101). "Oh no, no, no, get somebody else now," Russell said, interrupting when Johnson included him as he began to name his commission, "I declare I don't want to serve. . . . I haven't got time." They discussed other subjects and then returned to the commission plan. Johnson had not advised Russell that he wanted Chief Justice Warren to head the commission, and Russell agreed to try to think of another justice who might serve as Chairman. The matter of Russell's role was not resolved.

It becomes clear in the tapes that Chief Justice Warren had declined the request from Johnson's messengers and, in a call to Senate Minority Whip Thomas H. Kuchel, R-Cal., the president told how he got Warren to serve: "So I just called him and sat him down here and said, 'Now listen, you'd get into a World War I uniform and you'd go and fight if you thought it would save one American life. . . . I'm asking you to do something and you're saying no' . . . Tears just came into his eyes . . . you never saw anything like it . . . he said, 'I can't say no.' . . . He's a patriot."

In late afternoon, Fortas reported that he had talked to Texas Attorney General Carr who was "very much for" the president's commission and said his Texas inquiry would defer to it. Fortas dictated a draft press release to a White House aide, announcing the creation of what would emerge as the "Warren Commission." Now Russell was the only holdout, and Johnson waited until nearly nine p.m.—after, not just before (see p. 100)—the announcement had been made, to call and read him the final press statement listing Russell among the commission members. Russell's emphatic objections were now personal: "Well now Mr. President, I don't have to tell you of my devotion to you but I just can't serve on that Commission. I'm highly honored . . . but I couldn't serve on it . . . with Chief Justice Warren. . . . I don't like the man. . . . I don't have any confidence in him at all." A possible foreign involvement in Kennedy's death had been much discussed in the press, and as he did in persuading the Chief Justice, Johnson raised the specter of 40 million casualties in a war that might result from international misunderstandings about the assassination. "You can do anything for your country," he told his old friend, "and don't go giving me that kind of stuff about you can't serve with anybody." Johnson told Russell that he begged Warren to serve "as much as I'm begging you." "You've never begged, you've always told me," Russell replied.

Johnson then put a close friend, Texas cattleman and County Judge A. W Moursund, on the telephone for a diversionary chat with Russell. When they talked again, Johnson said Russell could give Warren "some confidence

. . . God damn it . . . associate with him. . . . I'm not afraid to put your intelligence against Warren's." Russell was weakening: "If it's for the good of the country," he said, "you know damned well I'll do it. . . . I'll do it for you, for that matter," and eventually: "I'm at your command. . . . I'll do anything you want me to do." Acquiescing, he said he hoped the President would be "a little more deliberate and considerate" with his requests in the future. That provoked a new outburst from Johnson, who said he planned to have Russell involved in "a good God damned many things that I have to decide," and he didn't give a damn "if you have to serve with a Republican . . . if you have to serve with a communist . . . with a negro . . . or if you have to serve with a thug . . . or if you have to serve with A. W. Moursund." Russell answered that he could serve with each of the above, but he had had enough of the Johnson treatment. He concluded: ". . . we won't discuss it any further Mr. President, I'll serve."

As noted (see pp. 113-114), Russell's hostility to Warren would later extend to the Commission staff as well. The tapes show that he complained to the president about late nights spent reading voluminous commission material. "You destroyed me, putting me on this commission," Russell complained on 7 December 1963. He was not always properly informed of Commission meetings, though he was rarely able to attend them. The newly released Russell files include a letter to Johnson, in final form, written toward the end of the inquiry, in which he resigns from the Warren Commission altogether. He apparently changed his mind and did not send it to the White House.

But as the Commission completed its final report, a conversation shows that while the Report was finally unanimous the final drafting sessions were by no means harmonious. On 18 September 1964 Johnson called Russell at his home in Winder, Georgia. Russell said those sessions "whipped me down so" that he fled there without even a toothbrush. The president was trying to learn what the Commission would say in its report. Russell said he disagreed with one theory, advanced by the commission staff, that the same bullet in the Dallas shooting hit both Kennedy and Texas Governor John Connally. Johnson said he also disagreed with that so-called "single bullet" theory.

The recently released Russell files show that Russell had actually prepared drafts, to be included in the Report, dissenting with the single bullet concept and also (see p. 114) with the draft report's proposed finding that Lee Harvey Oswald acted alone, without involvement from abroad. His draft dissents argued that Oswald's first and third shots hit Kennedy and the second bullet (which was never accounted for) hit Governor Connally. He wrote that evidence of Oswald's involvement in any possible foreign conspiracy was "beyond the reach" of U.S. investigative agencies. In the end, both dissents were withheld, in the interests of presenting a unanimous

Commission Report after Russell and other dissenters negotiated softened language on these points into the final Report.

Unquestionably, speculation about events in Dallas that November day in 1963 will continue into the new century. But one effect of this new information will be to narrow the field for conspiracy theorists. With Johnson on the record at the outset as strongly opposed to the Commission idea, it will be hard to argue that he cooked up the plan as an assassination cover up. With key members of the Commission at odds, at the beginning and the end of the inquiry, it is also hard to envision a conspiracy in which they might have been participants.

Along the way, Johnson got Russell to agree to a compromise that would ease a long and troublesome dispute in the Senate. Russell had always opposed any enlargement of his six member subcommittee that rode herd on intelligence activities including the CIA. (This was the group to which he had named Johnson in 1957 (see p. 59) as a junior senator.) Pausing as he pressed Russell to join his new commission, Johnson referred to the desire of members of the Foreign Relations Committee to share in intelligence oversight and asked Russell "how much of a problem" it would cause if Foreign Relations Chairman, J. William Fulbright, D-Ark., and ranking minority member, Bourke Hickenlooper, R-Ia., were to sit with the special committee "by invitation." Russell had no objection, "as long as it is confined to those two." Johnson quickly called Fulbright and Hickenlooper and told them to await Russell's invitation.

Johnson frequently asked Russell for advice on problems erupting abroad. The first crisis erupted in Panama where the American flag flying at a school produced riots and unrest. They discussed the situation at length in several calls, and Russell attended a White House meeting on the problem in late January. Russell believed Cuban Premier Fidel Castro had incited Communist activists in Panama, and urged Johnson to take a tough line to protect vital U.S. interests in the Panama Canal. When a diplomatic solution appeared to be at hand, on 25 January 1964 he warned Johnson that the State Department would use the settlement agreement to "gradually renegotiate that (Panama Canal) treaty away."

Before that problem was defused, there was trouble in Cuba itself, when Castro turned off the water supply to the U.S. Naval Base at Guantanamo Bay in a dispute over U.S. Coast Guard seizure of Cuban fishing boats. Soviet Premier Nikita Khrushchev, supporting Castro, accused the U.S. of an act of piracy. Johnson's advisors were divided, but the tapes show Russell, on 7 February, backing Johnson who had adopted Defense Secretary McNamara's plan to make the Naval Base fully independent by making its own water and reducing the number of Cuban laborers employed. "What do Americans think about the situation there?" Johnson asked. "They're just tired of Castro urinating on us and getting away with it," Russell replied.

Russell was not happy later that evening when Johnson called to read him, paragraph by paragraph, the final settlement of the Panama dispute. He was still afraid that it would result in a change in the canal treaty, but he finally said the arrangement was "not nearly as bad as I thought you'd be driven to." "Don't go to needling me, Dick," Johnson said brusquely, noting that he was still at work and had had no dinner. "I wouldn't be your friend if I didn't tell you what I thought," Russell replied. Johnson insisted he didn't retreat in the Panama negotiations. Russell said "you've left the door open to get out."

Johnson changed the subject to Vietnam, which had been a matter of their mutual concern since the start of Johnson's presidency. In early December, when Johnson mentioned Vietnam and Korea among nations that needed U.S. financial aid. Russell immediately recalled their having opposed U.S. air support for French forces in Vietnam in 1954 when President Eisenhower was considering intervention there. (see pp. 38-39). "We should get out," said Russell, "but I don't know any way to get out." He recalled warning Eisenhower in 1954 that "we'd never get out, be in there fifty years from now."

At that point Johnson wanted Russell to be one of a small group of advisers to meet with McNamara, "a private deal" to talk about what should be done in Vietnam. "I'm afraid I won't be able to help you much," Russell said, adding that he had thought about the problem "in the still marches of the night and I just don't know. . . ." "You go to sleep thinking about it tonight," Johnson said.

As the situation in Vietnam deteriorated, the view from Washington worsened. By late May, when Johnson called Russell for advice on "this Vietnam thing," Russell said: "I just don't know what to do," but he put his finger on the continuing dilemma: "We've either got to move in or move out," he said and Johnson replied: "That's about what it is." Russell said there must be some "middle ground somewhere," but he could not locate it. If a South Vietnamese leader would demand that the U.S. withdraw, he said, that would "give us a good excuse."

Intervening aggressively, they agreed, had terrible risks. As Russell put it: "If we go in there and get 'em up against the wall, the Chinese Communists are gonna come in." That was Johnson's judgment as well. That conviction would haunt him later, when he spent time in the White House situation room personally approving bombing targets, fearful that one wrong decision would bring Chinese troops into the conflict. The president was also concerned about public opinion: "They'd impeach a President though, that would run out, wouldn't they?" he asked, noting that most of the voices he hears, including "all the Republicans," favor going in with force. Looking ahead to the forthcoming presidential election, Johnson predicted the Republicans would make an issue of his inaction at a time when Americans were being killed in Vietnam. That was, said Russell, "the only issue they've got." Johnson also worried that the U.S. was constrained by treaty, as a member of the Southeast Asia Treaty Organization (SEATO). Russell replied: "Yeah, but we're the only ones paying any attention to it."

They talked for nearly half an hour, foreseeing many of the problems that would arise in the months ahead. Russell was concerned that McNamara had "been kicked around on it so where I'm not sure he's as objective as he ought to be in surveying the conditions out there." Johnson said, "I don't think the people of this country know much about Vietnam and I think they care a hell of a lot less." Johnson questioned the military plan for massive bombing to intercept supplies moving down the supply trail from the north and Russell exploded: "Oh hell, that ain't worth a hoot. That's just impossible." "I wish I could help you, God knows I do," Russell said, as the long conversation ended. "It's a terrific quandary that we're in over there. We're just in the quicksands up to our very necks, and I just don't know what the hell is the best way to do about it." "I love you and I'll be calling you," Johnson replied.

In that long conversation, Johnson told Russell of his dissatisfaction with the performance of Henry Cabot Lodge, the U.S. Ambassador in Saigon. When they talked again on 11 June, Lodge was about to resign. Johnson and Russell discussed possible successors but reached no conclusion. Johnson said he was at wits end. "I don't believe the American people ever want me to run [away]. If I lose it. I think that they'll say that I've lost. I've pulled in. At the same time, I don't want to commit us to a war. And I'm in a hell of a shape." Russell said it would take half a million men to clean up in Vietnam, "and they'd be bogged down in there for ten years." Johnson said he had asked experts to study the effect of a U.S. withdrawal, "whether Malaysia will necessarily go and India'll go," and with what damage to U.S. prestige worldwide. Russell was no less perplexed: ". . .we're in there and I don't know how in the hell you can tell the American people you're coming out. They'll think you've just been whipped . . . ruined . . . you're scared. It'd be disastrous," he said. But a moment later: "I don't think the American people want to stay in there. They've got enough sense to realize that it's just a matter of face, that we can't just walk off and leave those people down there."

By early August (see p. 110), when word of an attack by North Vietnamese torpedo boats on the destroyer U.S.S. Maddox put Vietnam on the nation's front pages, Johnson's uncertain attitude toward Southeast Asia was already beginning to edge away from Russell's. Mindful of adverse public reaction, Russell would have liked to get out. Mindful of the risks, Johnson could not see himself as the first president to lose a war and leaned toward getting in.

During much of that summer, Russell and the president went head to head in the historic congressional confrontation that would produce the Civil Rights Act of 1964 (see p. 107), but the tapes suggest that they said very little to one another in their private conversations about the debate itself and talked around the edges about its consequences. In January, months before the Senate debate began, Johnson urged Russell to persuade two of his influential southern allies, Senators Harry F. Byrd, D-Va., and George Smathers, D-Fla., to report the tax bill out of the Finance Committee of which Byrd was chairman and Smathers a member. Johnson warned that Russell could come under heavy fire from business leaders if the tax bill was pending while a long Senate filibuster blocked all other Senate business. "I'm slipping, and I'm getting senile but I'm not that bad," said Russell, "I saw that coming way back yonder last fall and I got after Harry about it." Playing all sides of the street, Johnson had warned Senator Eugene D. McCarthy, D-Minn., another Finance Committee member, that Russell hoped the tax bill would be stalled behind the civil rights bill. In rallying supporters of the civil rights bill, Johnson was quite ready to cast Russell as the evil genius of the opposition who must be outwitted. In the Oval Office for less than two weeks, an agitated Johnson predicted to Katherine Graham, publisher of the *Washington Post* on 2 December 1963 that Russell would exploit delays by House and Senate leaders, "and by the time you get him, he will screw them to death, because he's so much smarter than they are."

In April the governor of Mississippi asked to meet with Johnson about civil rights problems in his state, and Johnson called to get Russell's advice on how to respond. The situation there was explosive, at the outset of what would be called "Freedom Summer," and Johnson told Russell that "every nigger family's got a gun." Russell thought that a president should meet with any governor when requested to do so, but they agreed that a meeting should be postponed until after the Senate civil rights debate. When Johnson asked when debate would end, Russell replied that it might be mid-June. "Oh, Dick, now! You're not going to keep 'em there till June?" said Johnson.

On June 11, the day after the Senate voted to close debate, which assured that the civil rights bill would be passed, the president called Russell to talk about a meeting of congressional leaders to discuss administering the bill's provisions. After a call on July 26, several weeks after the bill had become law, Russell wrote a memo noting that Johnson had "talked down his part" in pushing the bill to passage. Russell wasn't deceived by the president's disclaimer, he said.

The tapes reveal some flat out errors in events as reported here—or not reported. The tapes disclose that Johnson also asked Russell to help solve other problems by intervening with his southern allies in the Senate. Senator B. Everett Jordan, D-N.C., chaired a committee looking into the activities of Johnson's former aide Bobby Baker. As noted here, much of Baker's free wheeling took place after Johnson left the Senate, (see p. 24) but Baker had given Johnson an expensive hi-fi set during their Senate years and Baker had arranged that a friend sell Johnson insurance. In that deal, some of the commission went to purchase advertising on the Johnson television station in Austin, Texas. Republicans on Jordan's Committee were hammering away on those events and insisting that Johnson's long-time chief-of-staff, Walter Jenkins, be called to testify about the deal. Russell had no part in the inquiry, but Johnson asked that he get Jordan to shut it down. In a call on 29 January Johnson complained to Russell about Jordan's abilities, and Russell commented wryly, "He labors very earnestly to understand that two and two is four." The matter flared up again in May, and Russell, in a call in which Jordan also participated, told Johnson he was "doing the best I can" to convince Senate Republican Leader Dirksen to quash the inquiry. He finally suggested that Jordan let the Republicans on his committee discuss one of their proposals for committee action and then vote it down with the committee's Democratic majority. That plan was accepted by Johnson.

Politics, and especially Johnson's campaign to win the White House on his own in 1964, figured in many of the phone calls. Eventually, in late July, the president called to ask Russell about blocking the drive by Kennedy loyalists to install Attorney General Bobby Kennedy as the Vice Presidential nominee (see p. 111) at the Democratic National Convention in late August. Russell noted that he advised the president to deal with it now, "so he would have time to control adverse reactions when they developed." At that time, 26 July, Russell noted, "I believe he'll end up with Gene McCarthy" as his running mate.

Four days later, in a taped call, Johnson read Russell his statement saying that he believed it "inadvisable" to select any member of his cabinet, or anyone who meets with the cabinet, to be the vice presidential nominee. Russell said the statement would "eliminate a whole lot of" potential candidates. Johnson replied "I just had to eliminate one," and Russell dryly said, "I understood it the first time you read it. . . . I think that's very wise, to get it out of the way now."

After a call on 21 August just before the convention opened, Russell noted that he "again" told Johnson that he was "prejudiced" against Senator Hubert H. Humphrey, D-Minn., as the nominee "on account of the rulings he would make as presiding officer and for other reasons." (He was concerned that Humphrey's adverse interpretation of Senate's rules during civil rights debates might force him to round up votes and try to overrule the Vice President.) Russell said he also told Johnson that Humphrey, was "so ebullient" that he would cause the president "more troubles over the next four years than Nikita K." (Khrushchev). Russell believed that Johnson "does not want Humphrey" but the president's many references to labor, negro, and small business leaders led Russell to believe that "he is the man."

At a dinner with Russell the previous evening, a handwritten Russell memo notes, Johnson produced polls and charts, boasting that his own candidacy was showing the "most phenomenal political strength ever registered" and "indicating runaway everywhere except the South." Russell also noted that J. Edgar Hoover had apparently been "turned loose" and wiretapping was widespread, including a "whorehouse in Maryland" —thought to be somehow involved in the Bobby Baker inquiry—Barry Goldwater's "boys" vacationing in Hawaii, and "ML King." He wrote that Johnson said it "took him hours each night to read them all," and added: "But he loves it."

Another individual included on the wiretap list was Washington attorney Joseph Rauh. Long associated with liberal Democratic causes, he was at that time being eavesdropped upon in his calls to leaders of Mississippi's Freedom Democratic Party. The party had chosen a slate of black Mississippi Democrats to contest the elected lily-white state delegation for Mississippi's seats at the convention. When the convention opened three days later, that black-white battle threatened to disrupt the proceedings completely.

Johnson's happy talk of polls and political invincibility, turned to unhappy complaints about the convention and its leaders. He asked Russell, among others, for advice as he schemed in Washington to quell the dispute emerging at the convention meeting in Atlantic City. On 24 August, as the convention opened, Martin Luther King had wired asking Johnson to oppose the seating of the white Mississippi delegation. Russell had heard King on the radio, "openly threatening" to withdraw black support from the Democratic Party. Johnson had told Russell five days earlier that it would be "ever so much better" if he could stay out of the convention maneuvering. Now he thought Bobby Kennedy was trying to get him into it. "I think this is Bobby's trap," he said.

Johnson asked Russell to persuade Senator Eastland to help engineer a compromise and on the morning of 25 August, still in a mood of frustration and self doubt (see p. 112), he called Russell to say that he had decided he was not the man to lead the nation and would announce that he would not run for reelection. Russell's hand written memo included an aside stating that he would not want to dictate his reactions to this call, even to his trusted confidential secretary.

Johnson called at 8:15 a.m. and began with complaints about the "Kennedy crowd" and other party leaders in Atlantic City. "I sensed," noted Russell, "that he was in one of his more depressed and extreme moods." Johnson gave Russell the same sad story he had given to Lady Bird and would give a few others: that he had tried and failed to achieve party unity, that his "enemies and the negro leaders had taken over the convention," and that he would go to Atlantic City and say "he had too many scars—could not unite the country in today's troubled world, and tell them to get some fresh figure to nominate and elect, and he would try to hold country together until January."

The president added, as Russell recalled it, "that he had only accepted V.P. nomination (in 1960) to avoid dropping dead on the Senate floor as majority leader and was looking for peace and quiet of V.P. job." "Begging forgiveness for frankness," said Russell, "I told him he was talking like a child—and a spoiled one at that." Russell "knew that he was not serious—and my advice was to take a tranquilizer and get a couple of hours sleep.

"It was easy," Russell wrote, "to see the L.B.J. who must be up to his neck in actual operations—and who was disgusted and frustrated that convention was not going exactly as he wished." Russell told Johnson he must get a "tougher hide and not be sensitive to such criticism." Johnson replied that he *was* "sensitive and had done his best to achieve unity."

In the ensuing conversation, Russell recalled Abraham Lincoln's efforts to unite the war torn nation "and how he was attacked and vilified." Johnson returned to his statement that "he had not had any overriding ambition (to me! of all people) to be Pres. but sought inactive place as V.P." When the conversation turned to Lincoln's unfortunate successor, Andrew Johnson, Russell told Johnson his troubles were "as a small wart on finger" compared to Andrew Johnson's "cancerous pancreas—kidney—and lungs. . . ."

"He persisted, however, that he could not get unity nor even control the convention," Russell wrote, and mentioned the dispute over the feuding Mississippi delegations. When Johnson asked whether he should make his announcement at a press conference or at the convention, Russell pretended to think Johnson was talking about announcing his choice of a Vice Presidential candidate, "but he recurred to his determination to retire," and Russell recalled a time when Johnson, as Senate minority leader "wept for half an hour over something I had said on [the Senate] floor." Russell wrote:

This complex and usually ruthless man was bitter in his disappointment as a child and had to cry on some one's shoulder. He knew or should have that I knew he was as likely to try to swim the Atlantic as he was to retire—If he had been at Atlantic City to work with people and issues he would never have had this depressed and bitter mood.

A final paragraph noted that Johnson called Russell again in early afternoon to say that a compromise plan had been developed to give the black freedom party delegation, two additional convention votes that would not be subtracted from the vote of the elected white delegates. "I was tired and finally told him it seemed most unusual but might be the best way out," Russell said.

Except for a few that relate to the Warren Commission Report, the now available LBJ tapes end at the end of August 1964, with events in Vietnam again moving to center stage. Russell's Exhibit B files cover the rest of the Russell/Johnson friendship but sparingly. More tapes will be needed for the full, coherent story. But it is clear that the relationship between the two friends already had started to change. In a sense, change began with Johnson's presidency. Resisting service on the Warren Commission, Russell said petulantly that Johnson never begged him but always ordered. That had not been true in their Senate years, but Russell foresaw that it would be true in the future. Indeed, when Johnson asked him , a few weeks later, to attend a short morning briefing at the White House, Russell said: "I'm at your order, sir. You're the President of the United States."

On 11 October 1964, after attending a swearing in ceremony at the White House, Russell noted that Johnson "marched me out" and demanded that Russell, as a member of the Senate leadership, arrange a six weeks Congressional recess. "This President," he wrote, "will demand a subservient Congress when reelected—will operate with an iron hand."

The tapes are sprinkled with expressions of affection, especially by Johnson. Russell, in the call on 26 July, thanked the president for the weekend White House visit of his ailing nephew, Bobby, and his family, (see p. 109) describing it as "one of the kindest, most charitable things you all have done." The intimate meetings at the White House continued, and Russell was pleased when the Johnson girls treated him "with the affection of close relatives."

But it is evident in Russell's jottings that he was confronting a new Johnson—Johnson as the assertive chief executive—and that his dream of his Texas friend as a southern president who would gradually ease the south into the national mainstream was fading. The occasional Russell memos suggest that it faded away with the passing years.

Johnson found it difficult to isolate his personal feelings for Russell from the hostility he built toward Russell's southern allies in the Senate. On 29 July 1964, Representative Hale Boggs, D-La., called about plans for the Democratic National Convention. He had heard that some Georgia

Democrats thought Russell would make a seconding speech for Johnson if the president would request it. Johnson told Boggs that he knows Russell better than that and dismissed the idea. He had already had arranged for Governor Sanders to invite Russell to be a member of the Georgia convention delegation, and Russell had declined. Johnson remarked that Russell had avoided conventions since his unhappy experience in 1952 (see pp. 28-30). "He'll probably vote for me," Johnson said, "but he feels obligated to Goldwater for helping him on cloture" (in the recent civil rights debate) and for other things. "He would feel like a traitor if he ran out on him." That was a very strange comment for Johnson to make. From his experience as Senate Democratic Leader, he knew very well that no Arizona Senator had ever voted to close off a Senate debate, because a filibuster helped the Arizona territory become a state, and that Russell was not obligated to Goldwater at all. Boggs may well have known it too, but he replied that it would be helpful if one southern senator would make a seconding speech. Responding, Johnson bitterly named a number of prominent southern senators and said: "They can't be for a man who's for the civil rights bill. The southern senators won't go to the convention for me."

The senatorial hopes of Georgia Governor Carl Sanders, joked about in December, began to be a source of tension between the old friends. In a typed, 4 May 1964, memo, Russell described a Johnson call the previous day, in which the president said he had been asked by Sanders to get former President Truman to speak at a political dinner in Atlanta. Russell said Johnson "wanted to clear it with me before getting involved." Russell told the president to go ahead with the request to Truman. Referring to what he called "rumors" that Sanders would seek his Senate seat, Russell said that if Johnson would just "leave it alone . . . I would beat the hell out of him in a campaign." Johnson said he would leave it alone, but he wanted Russell to know (as Russell would later tell his staff), that he was for Russell "lock, stock and barrel; money, marbles and chalk."

The president then disclosed his recent comments to two very influential Georgia newsmen, Eugene Patterson and Ralph McGill. He said he told them that, from his days as assistant Democratic leader in the Senate, Russell "had been more responsible for his (Johnson's) political success than any other man." Johnson said Patterson then reported that he had that day asked Russell about his current relationship with Johnson and was told that "it was fine." Russell noted that he found that "hard to believe," and did not remember his comments to Patterson "quite that way." He recalled that he praised the president's abilities in his talk with Patterson, but was "not sure as to how our personal relations were as of that date."

By 4 February 1966 a Sanders candidacy was looking more and more likely. Johnson and Russell talked about that after a White House conference on food shipments to India where Russell's "unvarnished" views, he wrote, caused "a great many shocked looks among those present." The president, Russell wrote, reported that Sanders had been to see him and explained that he could not succeed himself as governor (see p. 112) and that, if he wanted to continue a political career, he would have to "become a candidate for some other office." The governor added that he did not believe he would be appointed to succeed Russell if Russell should die. In the ensuing conversation, as Russell reported it, Sanders said he knew of Johnson's friendship with Russell and asked for no commitment in a senatorial contest. But he pointed out that he was working for Johnson in Georgia during Johnson's campaign for the White House, while Russell was away in Spain. Sanders said he supported Johnson and his program "and would give it more than lip service" in the Senate.

Johnson's response, as noted by Russell, was that he had a brotherly feeling for Sanders but viewed Russell as a father. He told Russell, however, that he had to admire Sanders's "steely and courageous approach to him on this matter" and thought Sanders might be a "cool and confident person with plenty of guts." That was "certainly my estimate," Russell said, adding that he still hoped Sanders would not run, but if he did, there was "no doubt in my mind that I would defeat him . . . so overwhelmingly that there would be no chance for him to run for the Senate, when and if I had passed away."

A handwritten addition to the typewritten memo stated that the president also talked of offering federal jobs to Sanders who said he was not interested in judicial appointments but did not say directly how he felt about appointment as the Director of the Office of Emergency Planning. When Johnson offered to hold that job open for him, however, Sanders did not ask that it be held. Some six weeks later Sanders bowed out (see p. 132). In their February talk about the Sanders situation, Russell and Johnson had again talked about the worsening situation in Vietnam, which was bringing the president under increasing fire, especially from some of Russell's associates in the Senate. Russell noted that Johnson, "expressed some annoyance that I had not been more active in defending him on the floor of the Senate but had left him, as he said, to the mercies of the Fulbrights and the Mansfields."

Russell was also more than a bit annoyed with the progress of the war. A month earlier, on 25 January at a White House meeting, he had noted: "We should not be there . . . patience has ceased to be a virtue . . . should withdraw or go all out in the bombing." Those were now the Russell alternatives—all out or get out.

On 28 June 1966 Russell reported on a pleasant evening at the White House. Finding Johnson in a "high good humor," he learned that the president had made an important decision to bomb petroleum installations in Hanoi and Haiphong, beginning in about an hour, Washington time. As the evening ended, President and Mrs. Johnson departed with daughter Luci, who had called at the president's request and located a church where they could attend a service. Noting that the church was Catholic, Russell assumed that they were going to pray for the success of the raids and the safety of the participants.

Almost a year later, Russell described another White House encounter where the church visit figured prominently. Two Russell memos, one scribbled on sheets from a small, pink, Senate memo pad, and the other apparently dictated from those jottings, referred to a dinner on 12 May 1967. Russell had arrived at the Oval Office to find the president with a small group that included Johnson's former aide Harry McPherson. They had been discussing tariff negotiations and had adjourned for dinner when the discussion turned first to Vietnam. Johnson asked Russell's opinion on knocking out the last major power station in Hanoi, which was dangerously close to Ho Chi Minh's headquarters. Defense Secretary McNamara favored bombing it. Secretary of State Rusk was opposed. Russell said: "I again stated my views that individual targets in North Vietnam are all incidental and that the war could not be concluded without invading North Vietnam, which everyone was determined to avoid, unless Haiphong harbor and the other ports in North Vietnam were closed to shipments of materiel of war which were already growing much more sophisticated." Then, Russell wrote, they went through "the usual discussion of whether or not this would bring the Russians into the war" and if so, with what effect.

The president then criticized U.S. officials who attended diplomatic functions at the Soviet Embassy, and McPherson (Russell thought he had been a guest there) said they were just trying to promote a sensible dialogue with the Russians. Then Johnson began what Russell described as a "bitter denunciation, amounting to a tirade" against the press—apparently the press who covered Lady Bird and, reading between the lines, it was press reports of the president's going to mass at Luci's church that had offended him. It appears that these reports originated at a social affair—a White House reception for the Judiciary.

Russell's jottings report that Johnson was "lecturing Lady Bird" and denouncing her press secretary, Liz Carpenter. Russell said he tried to change the subject a few times with no success, even praising social coverage at the White House. Johnson declared that he didn't want press people in the White House "eating his food and drinking his whisky and champagne." After he had "ranted" for twenty-five or thirty minutes, Russell wrote, Lady Bird "rejoined with surprising spirit" saying that the White House belonged to the people of the country who paid for the whisky and champagne, and that "all should be represented." She soon "left the room," leaving it to Russell to suggest that it was late and time that both he and the president retire for the evening.

One newly released Russell file lays out the full story of the Alex Lawrence nomination and reveals a significant epilogue to the account here (see pp. 155-160). It begins with a calendar card for 11 May 1968, when Russell met with Attorney General Ramsey Clark. The card bore a terse Russell notation: "Unhappy experience, Lawrence vetoed." Drafts and the final version of Russell's explosive letter of 1 July 1968 are in the file with a copy of Johnson's reply dated 3 July 1968 (which was not reported here.) In it the president aggressively defended his actions in the Lawrence matter. A Russell memo attached to the reply read: "This does not sound like the President, and I do not think he wrote it—he probably did not see it. . . ."

A two-page, typed memo discloses a final, angry face-to-face argument about the Lawrence nomination between Russell and Johnson more than a week after the angry exchange of letters. Russell wrote on 13 July 1968 that he was called to the White House for an 11 a.m. meeting and, after "a little chaff and comment," was shown formal nomination papers and forwarding letters for Georgia judgeships including Alex Lawrence. There followed a discussion of Johnson's plan to nominate Abe Fortas and Texas Congressman Homer Thornberry to the Supreme Court.

Russell reported that "almost an hour had passed," and he had opened the door to leave, "when the lid blew off." Johnson "criticized me vigorously for my letter written July 1st," he wrote, "stated it was not factual and that somebody had undoubtedly poisoned my mind . . . that I had known all the time he had intended to appoint Lawrence but was only waiting to build up a case in his behalf." The president, Russell said, "referred particularly to his accomplishments with McGill and Patterson," apparently referring to his glowing appraisal of his relationship with Russell, made to the two Georgia newsmen more than four years previously.

"I told him that I had not been perfectly sure (about the appointment) for the first several weeks, " Russell said, because Johnson would outline actions Russell should take and then say "he wanted me to understand that it was not a firm commitment to appoint." Johnson then insisted, according to Russell's memo, that Russell had surely known that he would appoint Lawrence since they met together early in May."

In the course of the argument, Johnson outlined all the steps he had taken with respect to the Lawrence nomination, including "submitting the file to Fortas and (Clark) Clifford" (a step that may have come as a surprise to Russell.) Both of them, Russell wrote, said they would have appointed Lawrence. Russell found it very strange that the original letter from the American Bar Association panel on Lawrence found him exceptionally well qualified, (the highest ABA endorsement) and the ABA letter now presented on Lawrence's behalf only found him "well qualified." Johnson, wrote the Georgia Senator, "kept saying and insinuating that some evil or malign influence had caused me to write the letter." He stated also that he told the president he would not try to "lead any movement" against the Fortas and Thornberry nominations to the Supreme Court. He said he "made no statement" to the president as to how he would vote on Fortas but twice said he would support Thornberry for Chief Justice.

As members of Russell's staff concluded, the time came when Russell simply did not trust Johnson. Future tapes may provide more detail, but the broad outlines of the friendship's collapse are clear. Small things surely had a part in it, including Johnson's increased assertiveness as he settled into the presidency and his occasional erratic behavior that was carefully chronicled by Russell and tucked away in a confidential file. It was certainly not heartening for Russell that Johnson was secretly taping their telephone conversations. Russell discovered it in the first year of Johnson's presidency. On a memo describing a call on 20 August, He scribbled: "Guess recorded. He records."

There were other, more important factors. Russell had expected that they would be adversaries on civil rights legislation. When, however, he became convinced that U.S. policy for Vietnam must be all out or get out, he found his old friend and ally in defense matters unable to commit fully to either of those alternatives. Beyond Vietnam, he felt that the nation's defense was eroding under Johnson. On a White House pad, while attending a 23 August 1968 conference on Vietnam, Russell's notes are not sequential but they are revealing: "We are much weaker militarily, vís-a-vís the Soviets," and separately: "We are depending on NATO (which was penciled out and replaced by UN); they on military strength."

Johnson's dispatch of a small U.S. unit to the Congo (see pp. 141-142) was especially distasteful for Russell. After a call from Secretary of State Rusk on 9 July 1967, he wrote that the State Department seems to be playing God, and evidently intends to involve the United States in "every internal affair in Africa to meet whims of Americans of African descent."

For Russell, one of the most troubling aspects of the Johnson presidency was what he viewed as a further weakening of the already weak Supreme Court. At dinner in the White House on 12 May 1967, the president had told Russell that he planned to appoint black civil rights attorney Thurgood Marshall to succeed Justice Tom Clark who was retiring. A Russell note indicates that he told Johnson that he had expected it, but "that I did not think it was a good appointment." He wrote that he thought Johnson himself feared Marshall "because of his extreme liberal views on law enforcement."

A month later, on 19 June, dining alone with Johnson at the White House, Russell, never an admirer of the retiring Justice Clark, wrote that he stated, without regard to Marshall's race, that Johnson "was destroying the Constitution by appointing a Court composed entirely of extreme and violent liberals (if not radicals.)" Further, "I said, in my opinion, it was a shame that he did not have one traditionalist on the Supreme Court, that while (John Marshall) Harlan, (Potter) Stewart, and (Byron R.) White occasionally deviated from the Warren line of 'No rules but what you want,' there should be one, at least, traditionalist who had the courage to adhere to some consistent line of reasoning and to quote some part of the Constitution other than the 14th Amendment which is used solely, now, for striking down the rest of the Constitution." Russell wrote that Johnson then offered to appoint Russell to the high court "if I could get (Hugo) Black to retire," and Russell replied that, even if he had any judicial aspirations, Johnson knew he was too old to serve.

These comments certainly bring Russell's ambivalence about the Fortas nomination into focus. There are also, in Exhibit B, jottings and telephone messages suggesting that an FBI acquaintance was fueling (if he did not initially plant) Russell's suspicion that Ramsey Clark's Justice Department was holding the Lawrence nomination hostage in return for Russell's support for Fortas. (see p. 159)

As is so often the case when assessing Johnson's actions, the factors contributing to his behavior here are not easily discerned. He was attentive to the superficialities of the Russell friendship right up to the break over Lawrence, but fundamentally he was determined to assume the role of president of "all the peepul," and by the time of the break that determination had overrun his Southern commitment, which (see p. 181) was never that of a deep Southerner.

With respect to Vietnam, Johnson felt that he was the one who had been abandoned. Dick Russell, the ally with whom he worked to avoid intervention in Indochina during the Eisenhower years, had now left him to the mercy of the Fulbrights and the Mansfields. And Johnson, who sometimes felt himself beset by demons, told Russell in their argument at the end of the Lawrence affair that some malign influence had been at work, turning his friend against him.

A few items in the Russell files relate to his activities in 1969, as Nixon moved into the White House, and Johnson was settling into life on the LBJ Ranch. Still another Kennedy, Senator Edward Kennedy, D-Mass., reported to Russell that some young Senate liberals, notably Birch Bayh, D-Ind, were unhappy about their committee assignments. Russell replied pointedly that Kennedy was present at a Steering Committee meeting where the assignments were proposed. A full folder contains many mimeographed minutes of meetings of the Senate Democratic Policy Committee, and most of them list the often ailing Russell among the absentees.

He did attend one Policy Committee meeting, however, on 3 February 1969, scribbling on the back of an envelope his reflections regarding the session with a Republican president now in the White House: "role changed absolutely—support President except where have better plans to substitute—not opposition for the sake of opposition." It might have been the blueprint that he and Johnson had crafted for dealing with President Eisenhower in the early, happy days of their friendship when expectations were high and trust was mutual and unending.

Publication of this edition is made possible by a grant from the Richard B. Russell Foundation. In the preparation of this retrospective, I am again indebted to the staff of the Russell Library for guiding me through the recently released Exhibit B and to the Johnson Library staff for providing a data base for the LBJ tapes and for promptly providing the tapes that I ordered. The new Maryland facility of the National Archives made available transcripts of LBJ tapes from its assassination files. At Mercer University Press I want to thank my editor, Andrew Manis, publisher Cecil P. Staton Jr., and assistant publisher Marc Jolley for their efforts in developing this edition.

In this retrospective, the data with respect to formation of the Warren Commission is drawn from transcripts of taped Johnson telephone calls released under the congressional edict and from tapes K6311.05, K6312.05 and K 64.02, from the Assassination Series at the Johnson Library, which also supplied pertinent tapes from the White House Series. I have relied especially on those numbered WH 6401.06, WH6401.09, WH6401.12, WH6401.14, WH6401.21, WH6401.24, WH6402.08, WH6402.09, WH6403.07, WH6404.06, WH6405.06, WH6405.10, WH6406.05, WH 6407.17, WH6407.20, WH6408.09, WH6408.34. Russell's notes and memos are to be found at the Russell Library for Political Research and Studies, Athens, Georgia. Scholars should search the recently released "Exhibit B," in Boxes labeled: Red Line File, Personal, and Political, largely in the Red Line File.

Some of the LBJ tapes, recorded with now antiquated equipment, are difficult to understand. Russell's handwritten notes, with abbreviations, omitted articles and verbs, are not always easy to decipher. I have tried to make this account readable while preserving the flavor of the spoken and written word and sticking to the principals' intents as I understand them.

Historian Michael Beschloss has excerpted many of the now available LBJ tapes in a valuable book, *Taking Charge: The Johnson White House Tapes, 1963-1964* (New York, Simon & Schuster, 1997) which first suggested that a review of tapes involving Russell and Johnson would enhance this new edition. Beschloss has promised additional books as tapes are released chronologically by the Johnson Library.

John A. Goldsmith
Franconia, Virginia
13 July 1998

NOTES

Richard B. Russell made and kept copious notes. After a telephone call he often jotted comments on his tear-off calendar pad or on the staff memo advising him to return a call. Those jottings were removed from his desk each day and saved. In meetings with the president and his advisers, he often made notes on a scratch pad. Occasionally, after an important meeting, he would return to his office and dictate an account of what had been said. Now filed at the Richard B. Russell Memorial Library, University of Georgia Libraries in Athens, Georgia, many of those notes of all sorts are cited here.

Abbreviations in the Notes are as follows:

CR	*Congressional Record*
LBJL	Lyndon Baines Johnson Library, Austin, Texas
OH	Oral History
RBRC	Richard B. Russell Collection
RBRL	Richard B. Russell Memorial Library, University of Georgia Libraries, Athens, Georgia

RESUMÉS 1948

1. Henry E. (Jeb) Russell, OH, 21 June 1974, RBRC, RBRL.
2. Fielding Russell, OH, 5 September 1974, RBRC, RBRL.
3. Ibid.
4. For a detailed account of Russell's life before he and Johnson became colleagues, see Gilbert C. Fite, *Richard B. Russell Jr., Senator from Georgia* (Chapel Hill: University of North Carolina Press, 1991).
5. CR, 26 January 1938, beginning at p. 1101; 3 March 1949, p. 1811; 9 March 1949, p. 2042; 8 May 1950, pp. 6618–19.

6. CR, 17 November 1942, p. 8904.
7. Carl Vinson, OH, 24 May 1970, LBJL.
8. For an extensive account of Johnson's career during this period, see Robert A. Caro, *The Years of Lyndon Johnson: The Path to Power* (New York: Alfred A. Knopf, 1982).

TRAINING 1949–1952

1. The 87-vote margin was reported by the Texas Election Bureau, a newspaper organization that collected county results, which were often released in dribs and drabs. When the state Democratic convention later rejected Coke Stevenson's strenuous protest and declared Johnson the party candidate for the U.S. Senate, it did not announce an official count and thereby set the stage for the continuing controversy.

2. Doris Kearns, *Lyndon Johnson and the American Dream* (New York: Harper & Row, 1976), 103. Apparently Johnson was less than candid in these remarks. Correspondence at the Lyndon Baines Johnson Library, Austin, Texas, suggests that he explored the possibility of joining the powerful Appropriations Committee and even the Agriculture Committee before opting for Armed Services. Since Russell was a senior member of the Appropriations Committee and chairman of its Agriculture Subcommittee, Johnson would have been able to pursue the courtship of Richard B. Russell had he been given either of these assignments.

3. Doris Kearns, *Lyndon Johnson*, 104.

4. Carl Vinson, OH, 24 May 1970, LBJL. Mr. Vinson warmly praised Johnson's contributions and stated that Johnson "was invaluable to me" as a member of Vinson's Naval Affairs Committee before Johnson moved to the Senate.

5. From the television series "Georgia Giant," printed with the permission of WSB-TV, Doc. #3, p. 21.

6. See Sidney Blumenthal's letter to the editor, *New York Times Book Review*, 31 March 1991. For further assertions that Stevenson supporters were involved, see Merle Miller, *Lyndon: An Oral Biography* (New York: G. P. Putnam's Sons, 1980), 87, and the recollection of Johnson campaign worker James Blundell: "There's no question about it in my mind. It wasn't O'Daniel that beat Johnson. It was Coke Stevenson and the fact that a lot of people wanted him to be Governor. . . ." Blundell comments that the Johnson lead dwindled every day and adds: "Now I don't know if the Stevenson people had been withholding their votes or were just waiting to see how many votes they needed . . . but whatever it was, apparently it was effective." What had happened between 1941 and 1948 was that George Parr, powerful boss in the "Valley," had a falling out with Coke Stevenson and in 1948 switched his support—and votes—to oppose Stevenson.

7. Richard B. Russell to Gov. J. Strom Thurmond of South Carolina, 17 February 1948, Dictation Series, Political Files, RBRC, RBRL.

8. From the television series "Georgia Giant," printed with the permission of WSB-TV, Doc. #3, p. 21.

9. Ibid.

10. Ibid., p. 19. For an appraisal of Johnson's less than intense interest in a baseball game as such, see George Reedy, *Lyndon B. Johnson: A Memoir* (New York: Andrews and McMeel, 1982), 72.

11. Other senators, knowledgeable reporters, and even black waiters and waitresses on the Senate dining room staff all took their problems to Russell at his breakfast table.

12. From the television series "Georgia Giant," printed with the permission of WSB-TV, Doc. #3, pp. 21–22.

13. Mrs. Ina Russell Stacy, interview, Winder, Ga., 10 December 1988.

14. Claudia Taylor "Lady Bird" Johnson, OH, 28 June 1977, RBRC, RBRL.

15. Ibid. Mrs. Johnson also recalled that Hubert Horatio Humphrey was "Uncle Hubie" to her girls.

16. From the television series "Georgia Giant," printed with the permission of WSB-TV, Doc. #3, p. 22.

17. From the television series "Georgia Giant," printed with the permission of WSB-TV, unedited tapes, RBRL.

18. In 1969, Russell described the invitation and Johnson's acceptance in an interview for the television series "Georgia Giant" (Doc. #3, p. 21, printed with the permission of WSB-TV); but Thomas H. Gaskin, in his paper written at Everett (Wash.) Community College for the Southern Historical Association meeting in Lexington, Ky., 10 November 1989, cites contemporary newspaper reports in reporting that Johnson did not attend the publicized strategy meeting of the Southerners on 13 January 1949. Russell might well have called an earlier meeting, attended by Johnson, that eluded press scrutiny.

19. Richard B. Russell to several constituents, January 1949, Dictation Series, Political Files, RBRC, RBRL. Russell advised constituents that he would offer the relocation plan as an amendment to a civil rights bill to demonstrate the "hypocrisy" of civil rights advocates.

20. CR, 9 March 1949, p. 2069.

21. The Johnson speech on 9 March 1949 begins on p. 2042 of that day's *Congressional Record.* When he finished it (p. 2049), Russell, in his role as tactician for the South, suggested the absence of a quorum, a regular tactic in long civil rights debates. CR, 17 March 1949, p. 2722.

22. Richard B. Russell to Ina Dillard Russell, 22 March 1949, Winder Files, RBRC, RBRL.

23. Richard B. Russell to Judge Frank M. Scarlett, U.S. District Court, Brunswick, Ga., 24 July 1950, Dictation Series, Civil Rights Files, RBRC, RBRL.

24. Richard B. Russell to Lawrence E. Spivak, 25 February 1950, Dictation Series, Civil Rights Files, RBRC, RBRL.

25. For several comments on the Longoria incident, including reflections of Lady Bird Johnson, see Merle Miller, *Lyndon,* 144.

26. Lyndon B. Johnson to Richard B. Russell, 17 October 1949, Congressional File, Russell, Richard B., LBJL.

27. James Rowe, OH, 9 September 1969, LBJL. For all the criticism of Johnson's role, the fight over the Olds nomination was not a clear-cut, Republican-Democrat or liberal-conservative test. Harold Ickes, who had been Roosevelt's interior secretary, and Johnson's friend Abe Fortas, who had been undersecretary, strongly opposed Olds. In the end, 21 Democrats voted to reject the nomination and only 13 supported it, and Olds was rejected 53 to 15.

28. William H. Darden, OH, 13 August 1975, LBJL.

29. Richard B. Russell to Lyndon B. Johnson, 25 November 1949, Congressional File, Russell, Richard B., LBJL.

30. Richard B. Russell to Ina Dillard Russell, 1 June 1950, Winder Files, RBRC, RBRL.

31. Lyndon B. and Lady Bird Johnson to Ina Dillard Russell, 11 May 1950, Congressional File, Russell, Richard B., LBJL.

32. Lister Hill, OH, 1 February 1971, RBRC, RBRL.

33. Sam Houston Johnson, *My Brother Lyndon* (New York: Cowles Book Company, 1969), 82.

34. Richard B. Russell to Lyndon B. Johnson, 8 September 1950, Legislative Series, Armed Services Files, RBRC, RBRL.

35. Hubert H. Humphrey, OH, 17 August 1971, LBJL.

36. Ibid. Also in his book, *The Education of a Public Man: My Life and Politics* (Garden City, N.Y.: Doubleday & Company, 1976), 124.

37. Hubert H. Humphrey, OH, 17 August 1971, LBJL

38. From the television series "Georgia Giant," printed with the permission of WSB-TV, unedited tapes, RBRC, RBRL. Russell provided a somewhat different rationale for a Southern colleague: ". . . You and I know that as a general rule the South is blamed for everything which does not meet with the approval of our critics. I feel that for a Southerner to be in the position of majority leader would cause criticism of his acts to fall on the South as a whole rather than upon the individual involved, though this would not, of course, be the case with a leader coming from any other section of the country. For this reason, as well as many others, I am sure that I cannot accept." Richard B. Russell to (Alabama senator) John J. Sparkman, 1 December 1950, Dictation Series, Political Files, RBRC, RBRL.

39. From the television series "Georgia Giant," printed with the permission of WSB-TV, unedited tapes, RBRL.

40. For an account of Baker's learning experience, see Bobby Baker with Larry L. King, *Wheeling and Dealing: Confessions of a Capitol Hill Operator* (New York: W. W. Norton & Co., 1978), 28–80.

41. From the television series "Georgia Giant," printed with the permission of WSB-TV, unedited tapes, RBRL. Russell felt that MacArthur's firing, while justified, was "botched very badly down at the White House" in that the general was not notified by Truman or a presidential emissary before his dismissal was announced in Washington. From the television series "Georgia Giant," printed with the permission of WSB-TV, Doc. #2, pp. 32–33.

42. George E. Reedy, *The U.S. Senate: Paralysis or a Search for Consensus* (New York: Crown Publishers, 1966), 14–15.

43. RBR calendar note, 5 May 1951, Intraoffice Files, RBRC, RBRL.

44. RBR calendar note, 25 June 1951, Intraoffice Files, RBRC, RBRL.

45. Reedy, *The U.S. Senate*, pp. 32–33, pp. 92–93, and correspondence with the author.

46. William Bates, OH, 16 March 1971, RBRC, RBRL.

47. Ina Russell Stacy, OH, 5 April 1971, RBRC, RBRL.

48. A Russell memorandum for the record, Winder Files, RBRC, RBRL. Dictated after this session with President Truman, the memorandum is the basis for this account. The quoted Truman statements are as Russell's memo attributed them to the president.

49. Writing about Russell's great ability and his presidential hopes three years later, President Truman would comment that ". . . being from Georgia, where the race issue was so heated, he did not have a serious chance of being nominated. I believe that if Russell had been from Indiana or Missouri or Kentucky, he may very well have been the President of the United States." Harry S. Truman, *Memoirs, Vol. 2: Years of Trial and Hope* (Garden City, N.Y.: Doubleday & Co., 1956), 494.

50. Embossed copies of the Walter George nominating speech are in the Winder Files, RBRC, RBRL. One of the copies is inscribed to "Mrs. Ina Dillard Russell—the great mother of a great son, Senator Dick Russell—great in victory—great in defeat. He will always bring pride to you. Sincerely, Walter F. George."

51. Rayburn's major test was on the seating of delegates from three Southern states—Virginia, Louisiana, and South Carolina—that had refused to pledge that they would support the eventual party ticket and were threatening to leave the convention. Rayburn's tactics as presiding officer in the showdown, which occurred during the balloting for the presidential nominee, are described by D. B. Hardeman and Donald C. Bacon in *Rayburn: A Biography* (Austin: Texas Monthly Press, 1987), 363–367.

52. From the television series "Georgia Giant," printed with the permission of WSB-TV, Doc. #2, pp. 37–38, which provides Russell's own account of Sparkman's selection as summarized here. It has been reported in several books about Johnson that he and Russell had made a preconvention deal that Johnson would support Russell for the presidential nomination, and if unsuccessful, Russell would support Johnson for the second spot on the ticket. One such account quotes Johnson's brother, Sam Houston Johnson, as saying that Lyndon told him that Russell actually urged Stevenson to select Lyndon. This account simply does not hold water. When Russell and Johnson first discussed a Russell presidential candidacy, both knew Russell could not succeed, and they were simply seeking to avoid a party-splitting fight. George Reedy, who sat in on the Johnson-Russell preconvention discussions, calls the alleged deal "nonsense," and it would not have been the only bit of nonsense that Lyndon inflicted on Sam Houston. Russell was not particularly close to Sparkman, however, and it appears likely, in retrospect, that Sparkman was one of several names he mentioned when his views on a vice presidential candidate were solicited.

53. Ibid., p. 36.

54. A 19-page memo and 2-page addendum written by Russell, in the Winder Files at the RBRL, are the basis for this account of the Taft-Hartley incident. In retrospect, the difference between supplanting Taft-Hartley with a new labor law and outright repeal does not seem terribly significant. The incident is summarized here because Russell, in talks with staff and reporters, repeatedly cited it as a major embarrassment.

55. From the television series "Georgia Giant," printed with the permission of WSB-TV, Doc. #1, p. 9.

56. Claudia Taylor "Lady Bird" Johnson, OH, 28 June 1977, RBRC, RBRL. Some observers, including longtime Johnson intimate Jim Rowe (OH, 9 September 1969, LBJL), have described Russell as "embittered" by his rejected candidacy in 1952. In our association, I did not find him to be so; asked about his reaction in a 1970 interview, Russell said, "It didn't make me bitter because I recognized it as a fact of life when I got to the Senate and I have recognized it ever since" that a Southerner could not be nominated. From the television series "Georgia Giant," printed with the permission of WSB-TV, Doc. #2, p. 39.

57. James M. Cain, M.D., to Richard B. Russell, 3 September 1952, Winder Files, RBRC, RBRL.

Journeyman 1953-1956

1. Accounts of Johnson's campaign to become leader vary as to whether Russell first called Johnson or vice versa. This version is as Johnson told it to George Reedy, who was called to Texas by Johnson during these early talks.

2. Russell's handwritten notes for his speech to the caucus on 2 January 1953 are in Senate Papers, Box 364, LBJL.

3. Hubert H. Humphrey, OH, 20 June 1977, LBJL.

4. Russell discussed his early Senate advancement in the television series "Georgia Giant," Doc. #1, pp. 28–29, printed with the permission of WSB-TV.

5. Hubert H. Humphrey, OH, 20 June 1977, LBJL.

6. Hubert H. Humphrey, OH, 17 August 1971, LBJL.

7. D. B. Hardeman and Donald C. Bacon in *Rayburn* report that Eisenhower often wondered why he got along better with the congressional Democrats than with the Republicans.

8. Claudia Taylor "Lady Bird" Johnson, OH, 12 August 1977, RBRC, RBRL.

9. Russell's calendars and daysheets during the 1950s show calls from both of the Johnsons and from Johnson's office to set the time and place for informal social engagements, some also involving Speaker Sam Rayburn. They also reflect the many turn-downs and the exceptions made for Churchill and DiMaggio.

10. Ina Russell Stacy, interview with the author, 15 December 1988.

11. Richard B. Russell to Lyndon B. Johnson, 5 August 1953, Congressional File, LBJL.

12. Lyndon B. Johnson to Richard B. Russell, 18 August 1953, Congressional File, LBJL.

13. The postfuneral correspondence is quoted in Thomas M. Gaskin's paper "Lyndon B. Johnson and Senator Richard B. Russell: Death of a Friendship," presented at the Southern Historical Association meeting in Lexington, Ky., 10 November 1989.

14. Hubert H. Humphrey, OH, 17 August 1971, LBJL.

15. Quoted by Caroline F. Ziemke in her paper "Senator Richard B. Russell and the 'Lost Cause' in Vietnam, 1954–1968," *The Georgia Historical Quarterly*, Vol. LXXII, Spring 1988.

16. Russell's notes on the meeting of 3 April 1954 are in the Red Line Files, RBRC, RBRL.

17. George Reedy, who was present as a member of the Policy Committee staff, described the tenor of the meeting in a letter to the author, 23 June 1989.

18. Meeting of 5 May 1954, Red Line File, RBRC, RBRL.

19. For an account of these events in Vietnam, see Stanley Karnow, *Vietnam: A History* (New York: Penguin Books, 1983), 189–198.

20. Robert Dallek, *Lone Star Rising: Lyndon Johnson and His Times, 1908–1960* (New York: Oxford University Press, 1991), 445.

21. This short summary of the events preceding McCarthy's censure is derived from a number of the books listed at the end of the Acknowledgments. (See p. xiii.)

22. Hubert H. Humphrey, OH, 20 June 1977, LBJL.

23. Russell B. Long, interview with the author, 5 April 1991.

24. Hubert H. Humphrey, OH, 20 June 1977, LBJL.

25. Ibid.

26. James Rowe to Lyndon B. Johnson, 20 July 1954. Sen. Joseph McCarthy Special File, Box 374, LBJL.

27. Notes of Johnson's confidential telephone conversation with McClellan are in the same Sen. Joseph McCarthy Special File, LBJL. The minutes, more accurate summaries of these Policy Committee meetings, are available in the same file, LBJL.

28. Ibid. Some accounts assert that Johnson, in discussing the committee membership with Knowland, handpicked the GOP members as well as naming the Democrats. For example, see Robert Dallek, *Lone Star Rising*, 457.

29. Robert Dallek, *Lone Star Rising*, 456.

30. Hubert H. Humphrey, OH, 17 August 1971, LBJL.

31. Hubert H. Humphrey, OH, 20 June 1977, LBJL.

32. D. B. Hardeman and Donald C. Bacon, *Rayburn*, 395.

33. Democratic Policy Committee letter to Lyndon B. Johnson, 7 July 1955, Congressional File, Russell, Richard B., LBJL.

34. George E. Reedy, correspondence with the author.

35. Carl Vinson, OH, 24 May 1970, LBJL.

36. Richard B. Russell to Lyndon B. Johnson, 5 November 1955, Congressional File, Russell, Richard B., LBJL.

37. Richard B. Russell to Lyndon B. Johnson, 16 November 1955, Congressional File, Russell, Richard B., LBJL.

38. Strom Thurmond, OH, 7 May 1979, LBJL, notes that Russell gave this rationale when he advised the Southern caucus that Johnson would not sign the manifesto.

39. George E. Reedy, in correspondence and in a discussion with the author.

40. Robert Dallek, *Lone Star Rising*, 500.

41. From the television series "Georgia Giant," printed with the permission of WSB-TV, unedited tapes, RBRC, RBRL.

42. George Reedy, who was present at the convention (as was the author) believes that Johnson never had any illusions about his candidacy and that he simply wanted to maintain control of the Texas delegation; but Russell's change of plans and caustic comments by Speaker Rayburn suggest that Johnson fell prey to the presidential virus for perhaps 36 hours.

43. Russell's views on Johnson's 1956 candidacy are reported in detail by Gilbert C. Fite in *Richard B. Russell Jr.: Senator from Georgia* (Chapel Hill: University of North Carolina Press, 1991), 312–313.

44. James Rowe, OH, 9 September 1969, LBJL.

45. Lyndon B. Johnson to Richard B. Russell, 31 October 1956, Congressional File, Russell, Richard B., LBJL.

FOREMAN 1957–1960

1. Horace Busby, Smithsonian LBJ Seminar, 26 November 1990.

2. From the television series "Georgia Giant," printed with the permission of WSB-TV, Doc. #3, p. 22.

3. See William Manchester, *The Glory and the Dream*, Vol. 1 (New York: Bantam Books, 1975), 822, and Harry McPherson, *A Political Education* (Boston: Houghton Mifflin Company, 1988), 116.

4. Richard B. Russell to Lyndon B. Johnson, 20 February 1957; Lyndon B. Johnson to Richard B. Russell, 26 February 1957; Congressional File, Russell, Richard B., LBJL.

5. For a detailed account, see Rowland Evans and Robert Novak, *Lyndon B. Johnson: The Exercise of Power* (New York: New American Library, Inc., 1966), 129–130.

6. Russell's preliminary speech, on 2 July 1957, begins at p. 10771 of the CR for that date.

7. From the television series "Georgia Giant," printed with the permission of WSB-TV, Doc. #3, p. 4.

8. Clinton P. Anderson, OH, 20 May 1969, LBJL.

9. CR, 15 July 1957, p. 11623.

10. George E. Reedy, OH, 12 December 1968, LBJL, and discussion with the author.

11. CR, 26 July 1957, p. 12820.
12. Ibid., 1 August 1957, p. 13472.
13. Strom Thurmond, OH, 7 May 1979, LBJL.
14. Unsigned telegram, Senate Papers, 23 September 1957, LBJL.
15. Strom Thurmond, OH, 7 May 1979, LBJL.
16. Herman Talmadge, OH, 15 July 1969, LBJL.
17. Allen J. Ellender, OH, 30 July 1969, LBJL.
18. Lister Hill, OH, 1 February 1971, LBJL.
19. Lyndon B. Johnson to Richard B. Russell, 23 August 1957, Congressional File, Russell, Richard B., LBJL.
20. For data on Russell's interests and plans, see Little Rock File, RBRC, RBRL.
21. Memo, George E. Reedy to Lyndon B. Johnson, 11 September 1957, Senate Papers, LBJL.
22. Harry McPherson, *Political Education*, 133.
23. Proctor Jones, OH, 3 March 1971, RBRC, RBRL, and discussions with the author.
24. Lyndon B. Johnson to Richard B. Russell, 24 August 1958, Congressional File, Russell, Richard B., LBJL.
25. William Proxmire, OH, 20 April 1971, RBRC, RBRL. Looking back, Proxmire was inclined to agree that his judgment had not been very good.
26. Harry McPherson, *Political Education*, 130.
27. Richard B. Russell to William E. Smith, 30 November 1960, Dictation Files, Political, RBRC, RBRL.
28. Richard B. Russell to Price Daniel, 18 November 1959, Dictation Files, Political, RBRC, RBRL.
29. Herman E. Talmadge, OH, 15 July 1969, LBJL.
30. Some accounts have attributed these attacks on Kennedy's father to partisans speaking on behalf of Johnson. The author heard Johnson himself make them in impromptu speeches to convention delegations in Los Angeles.
31. Most accounts present the Speaker as strongly opposed to Johnson accepting the vice presidency, including D. B. Hardeman and Donald C. Bacon in *Rayburn*, 439–444. But Tip O'Neill's account in *Man of the House: The Life and Political Memoirs of Speaker Tip O'Neill* (New York: Random House, 1987), 93–95, and Robert Dallek in *Lone Star Rising*, 575–581, show Rayburn more amenable to Johnson on the ticket.
32. Tip O'Neill, *Man of the House*, 93–95.
33. D. B. Hardeman and Donald C. Bacon, *Rayburn*, 441.
34. Eugene C. Patterson, OH, 11 March 1969, LBJL.
35. Richard B. Russell to John F. Kennedy, telegram, 15 July 1960, Dictation Files, Political, RBRC, RBRL.
36. Russell notes on the daysheet, 19 July 1960, Intraoffice Files, RBRC, RBRL. The daysheet also notes that Johnson described a "brawl" between Bobby

Kennedy, Rayburn, and Johnson aide John Connally, apparently a reference to the incident in which Robert Kennedy, unaware that his brother and Johnson had agreed that Johnson would be on the ticket, visited Johnson's hotel suite to talk him out of accepting.

37. Richard B. Russell to Judge John J. Jones, 19 July 1960, Dictation Files, Political, RBRC, RBRL.

38. Richard B. Russell to Rev. Thomas M. Lee, 29 September 1960, Dictation Files, Political, RBRC, RBRL.

39. Richard B. Russell, letter to Rufus C. Harris, president of Mercer University, 7 October 1960, Dictation File, Political, RBRC, RBRL.

40. Richard B. Russell to Hon. Harvey J. Kennedy, 17 November 1960, Dictation Series, Political, RBRC, RBRL; Bill Bates, discussions with the author. Texts of a Russell press conference and speeches for Johnson in Texas are in Congressional File, Russell, Richard B., LBJL.

41. Richard B. Russell to Lyndon B. Johnson, 21 December 1960, Senate Papers, LBJL.

Shop Steward 1961–1963

1. Hubert H. Humphrey, OH, 17 August 1971, LBJL.

2. Bobby Baker, *Wheeling and Dealing*, 135.

3. Hubert H. Humphrey, OH, 17 August 1971, LBJL.

4. Wyckliffe A. Knox, Jr., OH, 24 February 1971, RBRC, RBRL. A young man seeking to join Russell's student patronage program in Washington, Wyck Knox went to Winder with his father for an interview during his 1960 Christmas vacation, a few days after press reports of Bobby Kennedy as attorney general began to appear. In their conversation, Russell described the President-elect as "a good boy" but took a dim view of Bobby. He said Jack Kennedy had told him personally that Bobby would not be appointed attorney general: "The senator had asked him, was he going to do that. The president-elect told him he was not," Knox said.

5. Russell memo, 15 December 1960, Red Line File, Winder Inventory, RBRC, RBRL. It is now clear that about this time, the president-elect sent his own attorney, Clark Clifford, to persuade Joseph Kennedy, the Kennedy patriarch, that Bobby should not be attorney general. Joe Kennedy heard Clifford out, but he would not be persuaded, and Jack Kennedy bowed to his father's wishes. Clark Clifford with Richard Holbrooke, *Counsel to the President* (New York: Random House, 1991), 335–337.

6. Bobby Baker, *Wheeling and Dealing*, 138.

7. Ibid.

8. Ibid., 139.

9. Richard B. Russell to Joe Hornsby, 31 July 1963, Dictation Files, Political, RBRC, RBRL.

10. Bobby Baker, *Wheeling and Dealing*, 139–140.

11. Rowland Evans and Robert Novak, *Lyndon B. Johnson*, 308–309.

12. There are a number of versions of the visit by Bobby Kennedy to Johnson's suite that morning, and most of them leave Johnson and his aides angry at Bobby's intervention.

13. George E. Reedy, OH, 12 December 1968, LBJL.

14. Elie Abel, *The Missile Crisis* (Philadelphia: J. B. Lippincott Co., 1963), 53.

15. The Russell note, headed "told the pres," also contended that the quarantine would be more likely to lead to nuclear war than the "fait accompli of having done what we told them we would do." 23 October 1962, General, Red Line File, Special Presidential, 1954–1962–1966, RBRC, RBRL.

16. Elie Abel, *The Missile Crisis*, 119.

17. George Reedy, himself Irish, recalls an incident when Johnson was unable to reach agreement on a labor bill with a liberal senator whose assistant, also Irish, Reedy had known in his days as a young socialist. Exasperated, Johnson finally told the senator: "You send your Irish socialist down to talk to my Irish socialist and we'll let them straighten it out."

18. Bobby Baker, *Wheeling and Dealing*, 145.

19. For details, see Rowland Evans and Robert Novak, *The Exercise of Power*, 325–330.

20. From the television series "Georgia Giant," printed with the permission of WSB-TV, unedited tapes, RBRC, RBRL.

21. Proctor Jones, OH, 3 March 1971, RBRC, RBRL.

22. From the television series "Georgia Giant," printed with the permission of WSB-TV, Doc. #3, p. 20.

23. Russell telephone conversation with President Kennedy, 9 November 1961, Transcript, Red Line File, Winder Inventory, Presidential, RBRC, RBRL.

24. Johnson's sarcasm was also directed at White House aide Harry McPherson, who was interested in the activities of a church on Capitol Hill. In *A Political Education*, 167, McPherson quotes the president as saying: "Nobody's around when I need him. Russell's home reading Plato, and Harry's off somewhere reading the Bible."

25. Proctor Jones, OH, 3 March 1971, RBRC, RBRL. Friends who occasionally rode with Russell into the Northern Virginia countryside recalled that he would remark on little-known Civil War skirmishes at crossroads along the way. Herman Talmadge, interview with the author, 5 December 1991.

26. Proctor Jones, OH, 3 March 1971, RBRC, RBRL. Proctor Jones was one who double-dated in this fashion.

27. Daysheets and pages from Russell's desk calendar for November and December 1960 and early January 1961 reflect frequent phone conversations with Johnson, mostly about legislation in the coming Congress and appointments to the new Kennedy cabinet. However, Russell's handwritten notes on calendar pages for November 17 and 18 contain reminders to be conveyed to the new vice president. On November 17: "Johnson—tell South depending on him—he elected"; and on November 18: "LBJ . . . South elected on acct LBJ and looking squarely to him to protect." Intraoffice Files, RBRC, RBRL.

28. Eugene McCarthy, *Up 'Til Now* (New York: Harcourt Brace Jovanovich, 1987), 58.

218   COLLEAGUES

29. Proctor Jones memo, November 1961, Intraoffice Files, date uncertain, RBRC, RBRL.

30. Proctor Jones memo, 29 August 1963, Intraoffice Files, RBRC, RBRL.

31. George E. Reedy, correspondence with the author.

32. The extensive quotations from this interview are from a videotape of the program "Portrait," as aired by CBS, 17 July 1963. Used with permission.

33. Roger Mudd, OH, 4 March 1971, RBRC, RBRL.

34. The statement is quoted by Merle Miller in *Lyndon: An Oral Biography* (New York: Ballantine Books, 1981), 395.

35. Russell's meetings and phone calls with the new president are detailed by Gilbert C. Fite in *Richard B. Russell*, 405.

36. Earl T. Leonard Jr., OH, 15 February 1971, RBRC, RBRL.

37. CR, 27 November 1963, pp. 2238–2239.

38. Russell himself and several of his aides were the sources for this account of his appointment to the Warren Commission. Former Sen. Eugene McCarthy, to whom Russell had confided it, included it in *Up 'Til Now*, 152–153. Russell's favoring Medina is from the television series "Georgia Giant," printed with the permission of WSB-TV, unedited tapes, RBRC, RBRL.

CEO AND FRIEND 1964–1965

1. Jack Valenti, *Washington Post*, 5 August 1990, p. 5. Valenti sat in on this talk, and the quotes are as he reports them.

2. Russell is quoted by D. W. Brooks in OH, 25 March 1971, RBRC, RBRL, and in an interview with the author, 6 December 1991. Brooks, an agronomy professor at the University of Georgia, organized Depression-ridden farmers in the 1930s to form the Cotton Producers Association (now Gold Kist). He was Russell's principal adviser over the years on farm issues and analyzed farm legislation for him.

3. Sam Houston Johnson, *My Brother Lyndon* (New York: Cowles Book Company, 1969), 141.

4. Hubert H. Humphrey, OH, 21 June 1977, LBJL.

5. Ibid.

6. Ibid.

7. Bill Moyers, OH, quoted by Merle Miller in *Lyndon*, 369.

8. Richard B. Russell to Rev. Hal S. Daniell Jr., 5 March 1964, Dictation Series, Political Files, RBRC, RBRL.

9. Hubert H. Humphrey, OH, 21 June 1977, LBJL.

10. Ibid.

11. Barboura G. Raesley, OH, 16 June 1975, RBRC, RBRL.

12. CR, 26 May 1964, p. 11943.

13. Doris Kearns, *Lyndon Johnson*, 183.

14. See, for example, CR, 26 May 1964, p. 11921.

15. CR, 26 May 1964, p. 11940.

16. CR, 10 June 1964, p. 13329.

17. In a talk with the author, Bill Bates said he drafted law-and-order language at Russell's request for this speech, and in delivering it, Russell departed from the text, as he often did, to strengthen the proposed language.

18. Lyndon B. Johnson to Richard B. Russell, 23 July 1964, White House Central File, Name File, Russell, Richard B., LBJL. Red Line Files, RBRC, RBRL.

19. Richard B. Russell to Lyndon B. Johnson, 25 July 1964, White House Central File, Name File, Russell, Richard B., LBJL. Red Line Files, RBRC, RBRL.

20. From the television series "Georgia Giant," printed with the permission of WSB-TV, Doc. #3, p. 26.

21. Claudia Taylor "Lady Bird" Johnson, OH, 28 June 1977, RBRC, RBRL.

22. In tracing the events of the war in Vietnam, I have relied heavily on Stanley Karnow, *Vietnam: A History* (New York: Penguin Books, 1983).

23. Stanley Karnow, *Vietnam*, 375.

24. Russell memo, 15 June 1964, Intraoffice File, RBRC, RBRL.

25. George E. Reedy, *Lyndon B. Johnson: A Memoir* (New York: Andrews and McMeel, 1982), 55.

26. Ibid., 56.

27. Doris Kearns, *Lyndon Johnson*, 204–205.

28. Staff memo, 2 May 1964, Intraoffice File, RBRC, RBRL.

29. Newspaper clippings in the Russell scrapbooks show speculative stories throughout this period suggesting a Sanders-Russell race in 1966. Bill Bates, in his oral history at the Russell Library, says the race was "an accepted fact" in the Russell office by the time he returned to work there in 1964.

30. Lyndon B. Johnson to Richard B. Russell, 24 September 1964, White House Central File, Name File, Russell, Richard B., LBJL. Red Line Files, RBRC, RBRL.

31. Russell memo, 5 December 1965, Red Line File, Winder Inventory, RBRC, RBRL.

32. Russell memo, 7 January 1964, Intraoffice File, RBRC, RBRL.

33. From the television series "Georgia Giant," printed with the permission of WSB-TV, Doc. #3, p. 30.

34. Ibid., 28.

35. Ibid., 32.

36. Ibid., 30.

37. Richard B. Russell to Jimmy Carter, 1 September 1964, Dictation Series, Political Correspondence Files, RBRC, RBRL.

38. Russell memo, 12 September 1964 (Lady Bird); Russell memo, 10 October 1964 (Liz Carpenter), Intraoffice File, RBRC, RBRL.

39. Lyndon B. Johnson to Richard B. Russell, 2 November 1964, White House Central File, Name File, Russell, Richard B., LBJL.

40. Richard B. Russell to Carl Sanders, 8 December 1964, Dictation Series, Political Correspondence Files, RBRC, RBRL.

41. Richard B. Russell to Lyndon B. Johnson, 30 December 1964, White House Social Files (Alpha), Russell, Sen. Richard B., LBJL. Venison sausage and Texas pralines were standard Christmas remembrances from the Johnsons, and members of the Johnson staff crisscrossed the capital and its suburbs in the days before Christmas, delivering parcels to senators, staff members, reporters, and other associates. Recipients who had sampled both generally preferred the pralines.

42. Margaret Shannon, *Atlanta Journal*, 17 January 1965.

43. Ina Russell Stacy, OH, 5 April 1971, RBRC, RBRL.

44. Memo, 2 February 1985, to President Johnson, White House Central File, Name File, Russell, Richard B., LBJL. The memo indicates that the president was advised of Russell's admission to Walter Reed and, with Lady Bird, sent flowers.

45. Memo, 5 February 1985, to President Johnson, White House Central File, Name File, Russell, Richard B., LBJL.

46. Lyndon B. Johnson to Richard B. Russell, 11 February 1965, White House Central File, Name File, Russell, Richard B., LBJL.

47. Lyndon B. Johnson to Richard B. Russell, 20 February 1965, White House Central file, Name File, Russell, Richard B., LBJL.

48. Barboura Raesley to Lyndon B. Johnson, 25 February 1965, White House Central File, Name File, Russell, Richard B., LBJL.

49. Proctor Jones, OH, 3 March 1971, RBRC, RBRL.

50. Ibid.

51. Stanley Karnow, *Vietnam*, 410.

52. Michael J. Mansfield, interview with the author, 17 August 1992.

53. Michael J. Mansfield, OH, 22 April 1971, RBRC, RBRL.

54. CR, 15 March 1965, pp. 5059–5061.

55. Richard N. Goodwin, *Remembering America: A Voice from the Sixties* (Boston: Little, Brown & Company, 1988), 337. The quotes are as Goodwin attributed them to Johnson.

56. Roger Mudd, OH, 4 March 1971, RBRC, RBRL.

57. Lyndon B. Johnson to Mrs. Robert Russell; Lyndon B. Johnson to Richard B. Russell, telegrams, 14 June 1965, White House Central File, Name File, Russell, Richard B., LBJL.

58. Richard B. Russell to Harvey J. Kennedy, 16 August 1965, Dictation Series, Political Files, RBRC, RBRL.

59. Richard N. Goodwin, *Remembering America*, 403–404.

60. CR, 6 August 1975, p. 19674; the transcript of Russell's remarks on "Face the Nation" was placed in the record by Sen. Ernest Gruening, D-Alaska, one of the first Senate critics of U.S. involvement in Vietnam.

61. Richard N. Goodwin, *Remembering America*, 399–416.

62. Richard B. Russell to numerous constituents, June–December 1965, Dictation Series, Political Files, RBRC, RBRL.
63. Charles Pou, "Sanders Says He Will Run," *Atlanta Journal*, 2 September 1965, p. 1. Similar stories quickly appeared elsewhere.
64. Margaret R. Shannon, OH, 31 March 1971, RBRC, RBRL.
65. Russell note on 23 September 1965 memo, Intraoffice File, RBRC, RBRL.
66. Margaret R. Shannon, OH, 31 March 1971, RBRC, RBRL. Russell later allowed Ms. Shannon to tell part of the story of his White House dinner conversation in the *Atlanta Journal* of 1 October 1965, but not until after Russell's death did she feel free of a pledge of confidentiality and tell the whole story as related here.
67. William Tapley Bennett Jr., OH, 29 October 1977, RBRC, RBRL.
68. The wire and response are in the White House Central File, Name File, Russell Richard B., LBJL.
69. Richard B. Russell to Lyndon B. Johnson, 16 November 1965, White House Central File, Name File, Russell, Richard B., LBJL.
70. From the television series "Georgia Giant," printed with the permission of WSB-TV, Doc. #3, p. 17.
71. Ibid., p. 25. Having urged withdrawal in private (his views, as stated in the hospital and in the position of the Policy Committee, were not publicized), Russell's public criticism, once U.S. forces were fully committed, was directed at the conduct of the war.
72. Richard B. Russell to Lyndon B. Johnson, 3 November 1965, General File, Letters to Save, RBRC, RBRL.
73. Jack Bell, AP Washington, 11 November 1965.

BOARDROOM DISSENSION 1966–1967

1. In an interview with the author on 12 December 1988, Russell aide William Bates said Russell quoted Johnson as having made this statement of support.
2. Proctor Jones, OH, 3 March 1971, RBRC, RBRL. Sanders would later say that he discussed with Johnson, Russell, and Sen. Herman E. Talmadge the possibility of an appointment to the U.S. Court of Appeals for the Fifth Circuit, and that Johnson had also suggested that he serve as director of the Office of Emergency Planning and had mentioned a possible ambassadorship. Carl E. Sanders, OH, 13 May 1969, LBJL.
3. Claudia Taylor "Lady Bird" Johnson, *A White House Diary* (London: Wedenfield and Nicholson, 1970), 196. The card index of White House visitors at the Johnson Library indicates that Russell had also dined with the Johnsons ten days earlier.
4. Margaret Shannon, *Atlanta Journal*, 2 February 1966.
5. For example, Joseph A. Califano Jr., then a White House aide, writes in *The Triumph and Tragedy of Lyndon Johnson* (New York: Simon & Schuster, 1991), 87, of Johnson urging United Steelworkers Union President I. W. Abel not to take a stand against the administration's wage-price guidelines in 1965.

Johnson told Abel that when Russell said he had to take a stand against the 1964 bill, he told Russell a story about a Negro boy, discovered spreadeagled in the linen closet of a white woman he was romancing, who said, when her husband returned unexpectedly, that he had to take a stand somewhere.

6. D. W. Brooks, interview with the author, 6 December 1991.

7. "Taxing" is the word used by Bates to describe the campaigning in his oral history at the Russell Library, 17 March 1971.

8. From the television series "Georgia Giant," printed with the permission of WSB-TV, unedited tapes, RBRC, RBRL.

9. The Bates interview above is the source for this characterization of the preemptive Russell campaigning.

10. Richard B. Russell to Hon. Wilson M. Hardy, Rome, Ga., 19 January 1966, Intraoffice File, RBRC, RBRL (apparently filed there so it could be used as a model for responding to similar letters).

11. CR, 12 January 1966, p. 142.

12. Seymour M. Hersh, *The Samson Option* (New York: Random House, 1991), 151.

13. UPI, Washington, 5 January 1966.

14. Russell told Johnson that the Johns Hopkins speech was "one of your best to date." Richard B. Russell to Lyndon B. Johnson, 8 June 1965, White House Central File, Name File, Russell, Richard B., LBJL.

15. For a more extensive treatment of the Honolulu conference, see Rowland Evans and Robert Novak, *The Exercise of Power*, 566-568.

16. Lyndon B. Johnson to Richard B. Russell, 18 February 1966, White House Central File, Name Files, Russell, Richard B., LBJL.

17. Stanley Karnow, *Vietnam*, 485.

18. Rowland Evans and Robert Novak, *The Exercise of Power*, 569.

19. Quoted by Doris Kearns in *Lyndon Johnson*, 253.

20. Carl E. Sanders, OH, 13 May 1969, LBJL.

21. See, for example, Ed Rogers, *UPI*, Atlanta, 25 December 1965.

22. Charles Pou, *Atlanta Journal*, 22 March 1966, p. 1.

23. A copy of the Russell statement is in the Political File, Dictation Series, RBRC, RBRL.

24. One of the telegrams was received by Proctor Jones, who was discharging his military obligation in the marine corps. Proctor Jones, OH, RBRC, RBRL.

25. Carl Sanders, OH, 13 May 1969, LBJL.

26. Richard B. Russell to Mrs. Marie Crook, 29 December 1966, Political File, Dictation Series, RBRC, RBRL. Mrs. Crook worked for William C. (Clair) Harris, Russell's old friend and campaign treasurer in Winder. The letter thanks her for sending out "many checks" to campaign contributors.

27. William H. Jordan, letter to the author.

28. Sam Houston Johnson, *My Brother Lyndon*, 210.

29. This remark, which angered the president's critics, was apparently an ad lib added by Johnson to his prepared text, according to newsman Charles Roberts, interviewed in Merle Miller's *Lyndon*, 462.

30. Richard B. Russell to Luci Baines Johnson, 1 August 1966, Winder Files, RBRC, RBRL. The inscription is noted on the retained copy of Russell's letter.
31. Mrs. Patrick Nugent to Richard B. Russell, 22 November 1966, Winder Files, RBRC, RBRL. White House Social Files (Alpha), Russell, Richard B., LBJL.
32. Lyndon B. Johnson to Richard B. Russell, 16 May 1966, White House Central File, Name File, Russell, Richard B., LBJL.
33. William Manchester, *The Glory and the Dream: A Narrative History of America, 1932–1972, Vol. 2* (Boston: Little, Brown & Company, 1980), 1305.
34. In a memo dated 16 May 1966, Russell wrote "shall never call another conference" and "the tendency to talk to get publicity." There is a reference to "all senators from the south," but his unhappiness is not fully explained.
35. Memo, 12 September 1966, Juanita Roberts to the president, White House Central File, Name File, Russell, Richard B., LBJL.
36. Distribution of the LBJ busts is described by Protocol Chief James Symington, and the exhilarating crowd of two million by Johnson himself in Merle Miller's *Lyndon*, 455–456.
37. Lyndon B. Johnson to Richard B. Russell, 3 November 1966, White House Central File, Name File, Russell, Richard B., LBJL.
38. Jim Rowe described the mission in OH interview No. 3, 16 December 1969, LBJL.
39. Lyndon B. Johnson to Richard B. Russell, 1967, White House Central File, Name File, Russell, Richard B., LBJL.
40. The letter, in the envelope, is in the Winder Files, RBRC, RBRL.
41. CR, 6 August 1965, p. 19673.
42. Harry McPherson, *A Political Education*, 409.
43. Russell aide Charles Campbell interview with the author, 23 October 1989.
44. Russell's note does not explain why he could not accept. Memo, 4 April 1967, Intraoffice File, RBRC, RBRL.
45. Richard B. Russell, interview with Wayne Kelley, *Atlanta Journal*, 21 October 1968.
46. From the television series "Georgia Giant," printed with the permission of WSB-TV, Doc. #3, pp. 26–27.
47. Russell wrote two memos about this call from the president, one on a memo slip from the Democratic cloakroom and a later note in his office. They are in the Intraoffice File, 2 March 1967, RBRC, RBRL.
48. George Wilson, *Washington Post*, 1 April 1967, p. 1. A similar plan, begun during the Carter administration, placed floating military arsenals at the British island of Diego Garcia in the Indian Ocean.
49. John A. Goldsmith, UPI Washington, 30 June 1967.
50. Undated notes, Intraoffice File, July 1967.
51. Richard B. Russell to Lyndon B. Johnson; date assigned is 21 December 1967 but must be 21 February 1967; Political Files, Dictation Series, RBRC, RBRL. In Winder, Russell arranged to have the letter hand-delivered to the White House.

52. T. Edward Braswell, a counsel for the Senate Armed Services Committee, passed the State Department's withdrawal data to Russell in a memo, 4 August 1967, Intraoffice File, RBRC, RBRL.
53. The Southern colleague was Sam J. Ervin Jr., D-N.C., who recalled Johnson's remark, as told to him by Russell, in an OH, 28 April 1971, RBRC, RBRL.
54. Russell's thank-you note, dated 11 August 1967, is in Political File, Dictation Series, RBRC, RBRL.
55. Quoted by Doris Kearns, *Lyndon Johnson*, 270–271.
56. Eugene V. Rostow, Smithsonian LBJ Seminar, 3 December, 1990.
57. Hugh Sidey, who was present, confirmed this account in a discussion with the author, 19 November 1990.
58. Eugene McCarthy, *Up 'Til Now*, 188.
59. Noted in the White House Visitors Card File, LBJL.
60. Richard B. Russell to Lyndon B. and Lady Bird Johnson, 22 December 1967, White House Social Files (Alpha), Russell, Sen. Richard B., LBJL. The typed salutation: "Dear Mr. President and Mrs. Johnson" is amended by hand, with "Lady Bird" written over Mrs. Johnson.

SEVERANCE 1968

1. Earl Leonard Jr., OH, 15 February 1971, RBRC, RBRL.
2. Proctor Jones, discussion with the author.
3. Harry McPherson, *A Political Education*, 420.
4. Earl Leonard Jr., OH, 15 February 1971, RBRC, RBRL.
5. Stanley Karnow, *Vietnam*, 541.
6. For a detailed account of these events in March, see Stanley Karnow, *Vietnam*, 523–566.
7. Russell note, 19 January 1968, Intraoffice File, Winder Inventory, RBRC, RBRL, refers to an earlier discussion with Johnson about a replacement for McNamara. Nitze did not resign, and it would be another Georgian, Jimmy Carter, who would, in 1976, name Harold Brown to the top job in the Pentagon, where he began the military build-up usually attributed to Ronald Reagan and Casper Weinberger.
8. See Clark Clifford, *Counsel to the President*, 497–498.
9. Russell note, 8 March 1968, Intraoffice File, Winder Inventory, RBRC, RBRL. It names the participants in the meeting and cites "reserve callup" as subject matter.
10. Stanley Karnow, *Vietnam*, 555.
11. Russell note on memos, 3 April 1968, Intraoffice File, Winder Inventory, RBRC, RBRL.
12. Stanley Karnow, *Vietnam*, 559.
13. Luci Johnson Nugent, quoted by Merle Miller in *Lyndon*, 489–490.
14. Liz Carpenter, *Ruffles and Flourishes* (Garden City, N.Y.: Doubleday & Co., 1970), 326. Later, Johnson would tell Doris Kearns that he had forgotten to take the withdrawal language to the Capitol. *Lyndon Johnson*, 343.

15. Harry McPherson, A *Political Education*, 439.
16. From the television series "Georgia Giant," printed with the permission of WSB-TV, Doc. #3, p. 24.
17. Quoted in the *Washington Post*, 1 April 1968, p. 1.
18. The criticism is reported by Wayne Kelley in the *Atlanta Journal*, 1 April 1968, and Kelley reports on Russell's defense of the president in the *Journal* of 3 April 1968.
19. On 2 April 1968 the *New York Times* carried a detailed account by Max Frankl of how Johnson made his decision to withdraw. The account appears to have been written with the help of White House informants.
20. Liz Carpenter, *Ruffles and Flourishes*, 327.
21. Ibid., 328.
22. Several staff members heard Russell describe these events. The quotes are as contained in OH of Proctor Jones and press aide Powell Moore, in the RBRC, RBRL.
23. Ibid. See especially, Powell Moore, OH, 6 March 1971, RBRC, RBRL.
24. Ibid.
25. Richard B. Russell to Lyndon B. Johnson, 20 May 1968, Dictation Series, Political File, RBRC, RBRL.
26. Quoted by Larry Temple, then a White House special counsel, in OH, Tape V, 11 August 1970, LBJL. As White House liaison with the Justice Department, Temple was the aide responsible for following the Lawrence nomination.
27. Eugene McCarthy, *Up 'Til Now*, 192.
28. Ibid., 196.
29. Kennedy's colloquy with Richard M. Goodwin, then a member of the Kennedy campaign entourage, is quoted by Arthur M. Schlesinger Jr. in *Robert Kennedy and His Times* (Boston: Houghton Mifflin Company, 1978), 913.
30. Proctor Jones, in Winder with Russell, heard Russell's side of this conversation and related it to the author.
31. Griffin and Russell met privately in Russell's inner office. Proctor Jones, who saw Griffin leave the office, has told the author that Griffin did not appear displeased. In his oral history, Powell Moore says Russell told Griffin that, although the Southerners did not want to take the lead, they would join in the effort to block the Fortas nomination.
32. The account that follows, of the Russell-Johnson interplay on the Lawrence nomination, is based for the most part on the Larry Temple OH, Tape V, 11 August 1970, LBJL.
33. Years later Temple would recall, in his oral history, that he and McPherson were shocked "at how sick the man looked."
34. White House aide Tom Johnson reported to the president on the views of the two editors in a memo dated 27 June 1968, White House Social Files (Alpha), Russell, Sen. Richard B., LBJL.

35. Russell's visit is recorded in the Visitors Card File, LBJL. Wayne Kelley (OH, 6 March 1971, RBRL) says Russell had explained that Johnson said he could not get rid of Ramsey because of his (Johnson's) close relationship with Ramsey's father, fellow Texan Tom C. Clark, who had announced his retirement as an Associate Supreme Court Justice on the day Ramsey was appointed attorney general to avoid any appearance of conflict of interest. A Russell note, 14 December 1967 (Red Line File, Winder Inventory, Presidential, RBRC, RBRL) describes Johnson as "bitter against Clark" for his stance in a dispute between Hershey and civil liberties groups.

36. Wayne Kelley, OH, 6 March 1971, RBRL.

37. Richard B. Russell to Lyndon B. Johnson, 1 July 1968, Dictation Series, Patronage Files, Judgeships, Southern District, 1967–68, RBRC, RBRL. White House Aides' Files, Temple, Larry, LBJL. Russell showed a draft of the letter to his Georgia colleague, Herman Talmadge, who had joined in recommending Lawrence. Talmadge offered to cosign the letter. Russell replied that his association with Johnson had been much longer and closer than Talmadge's and that he wanted to sign the letter himself. (Talmadge, interview with the author, 5 December 1991.)

38. Richard B. Russell to Griffin Bell, 2 July 1968, Dictation Series, Patronage Files, Court Matters, 1964–69, RBRC, RBRL.

39. Johnson's call was made in the presence of Larry Temple, and the quotes are as Temple attributed them to the president in his oral history.

40. Copies of the rejected drafts are in the White House Aides' Files, Temple, Larry, at the LBJL.

41. This conversation was also made in the presence of Larry Temple, and Johnson's quotes are as reported in Temple's oral history.

42. Tom Johnson to Richard B. Russell, 3 July 1968, White House Central File, Name File, Russell, Richard B., LBJL.

43. Wayne Kelley interview, *Atlanta Journal*, 21 October 1968.

44. Lawrence became a well-respected judge who was viewed as fair and even-handed in civil rights cases.

45. The vote projection is in White House Aides' Files, Larry Temple, LBJL.

46. Richard B. Russell to Lyndon B. Johnson, 26 September 1968, White House Central File, Name File, Russell, Richard B., LBJL.

47. The meeting and Russell's comments are described by Clark Clifford in *Counsel*, 576. Russell's note on the meeting (14 October 1968, Intraoffice File, RBRC, RBRL) says it lasted all afternoon and that he had no lunch until 5:15 p.m.

48. Clifford, *Counsel*, 581.

49. Russell memo, 23 October, Intraoffice File, RBRC, RBRL.

50. In a 16 October 1968 memo, the would-be interviewer, Joe B. Frantz, advises Johnson that Russell has declined and that he, Frantz, has written to ask that Russell reconsider. On the memo, Johnson has written: "Tom J, Call Russell men and ask help." In a 13 January 1969 memo, the president is advised that Frantz has been told by a Russell aide that Russell is now personally in touch

with President and Mrs. Johnson on the matter. White House Central Files, Name File, Russell, Richard B., LBJL.

51. Lyndon B. Johnson to Richard B. Russell, 2 November 1968. White House Central Files, Name File, Russell, Richard B., LBJL.

52. William Darden, discussion with the author.

53. Published as a question-and-answer text, the interview had been conducted in October.

54. Russell note on memo, 13 November 1968, Intraoffice File, RBRC, RBRL.

55. Russell note on memo, 11 December 1968, Intraoffice File, RBRC, RBRL.

NEW MANAGEMENT 1969–1971

1. Lyndon B. Johnson to Richard B. Russell, 17 January 1969, Red Line Files, RBRC, RBRL.

2. Russell notes, 15 January 1969 (leadership meeting) and 16 January 1969 (call and reception), Intraoffice File, RBRC, RBRL.

3. Richard M. Nixon to Richard B. Russell, 25 January 1969, and Richard B. Russell to Richard M. Nixon, 30 January 1969, General Correspondence File, RBRC, RBRL.

4. Powell Moore, OH, 6 March 1971, RBRC, RBRL.

5. The Red Line Files, RBRC, RBRL, contain a series of notes reflecting courtesies and homage paid by Nixon to Russell in these final years of the senator's life.

6. On a tear-off calendar sheet, 29 January 1969, is Senate Democratic leader Mike Mansfield's message that Nixon wanted Russell to attend a meeting of leaders in the office of GOP leader Everett Dirksen and Russell's notation: "I accepted." Intraoffice File, RBRC, RBRL.

7. Russell's notes taken at the meeting, clipped to a Russell- franked envelope in which they were saved, are in the Red Line Files, RBRC, RBRL.

8. The memo, dated 20 March 1969, is in the Post Presidential Name File, Sen. Richard B. Russell, LBJL.

9. In a letter dated 29 April 1969, Tom Johnson, then with LBJ at the ranch, advised G. P. Sullivan of Boston that LBJ "was in touch with Senator Russell as soon as he heard of his illness, and you can be sure of his continuing interest in the senator's welfare." Post Presidential Name File, Russell, Richard B., LBJL.

10. Proctor Jones, OH, 4 March 1971, RBRC, RBRL.

11. Roger Mudd, OH, 4 March 1971, RBRC, RBRL.

12. Henry M. Jackson, OH, 29 April 1971, RBRC, RBRL.

13. Quoted by Merle Miller, *Lyndon*, 544.

14. Lyndon B. Johnson to Richard B. Russell, 12 August 1969, Post Presidential Name File, Russell, Sen. Richard B., LBJL.

15. Richard B. Russell to Lyndon B. Johnson, 12 August 1969, Post Presidential Name File, Russell, Sen. Richard B., LBJL.

16. Lyndon B. Johnson to Richard B. Russell, 15 December 1969, Post Presidential Name File, Russell, Sen. Richard B., LBJL.
17. Richard B. Russell to Lyndon B. Johnson, 29 December 1969, Post Presidential Name File, Russell, Sen. Richard B., LBJL.
18. A Tom Johnson memo to LBJ, clipped to Russell's 29 December letter advised LBJ that a new bowl would be hand-delivered.
19. Richard B. Russell to Lyndon B. Johnson, 19 January 1970, Post Presidential Name File, Russell, Sen. Richard B., LBJL.
20. Tom Johnson to J. Leonard Rensch, 21 January 1970, Post Presidential Name File, Russell, Sen. Richard B., LBJL.
21. For more on the Johnsons in Acapulco, see Merle Miller, *Lyndon*, 548.
22. Lyndon B. Johnson to Richard B. Russell, 16 June 1970, Post Presidential Name File, Russell, Sen. Richard B., LBJL.
23. Proctor Jones, OH, 4 March 1971, RBRC, RBRL.
24. Ibid.
25. Modine Thomas, OH, 10 February 1971, RBRC, RBRL.
26. Proctor Jones, OH, 4 March 1971, RBRC, RBRL.
27. Lyndon B. Johnson to Richard B. Russell, 26 August 1970, Post Presidential Name File, Russell, Sen. Richard B., LBJL.
28. William H. Jordan, longtime Russell aide and friend, who had observed the Russell-Johnson friendship over the years, believed it could have been rekindled if they had lived and "would have flourished in spite of these incidents." William H. Jordan, OH, 29 January 1976, LBJL.
29. Proctor Jones, discussion with the author.
30. Ina Russell Stacy, OH, 5 April 1971, RBRC, RBRL.
31. Proctor Jones, OH, 4 March 1971, RBRC, RBRL. Other Russell staff members agree that Carter exaggerated the nature of his relationship with Russell during this campaign.
32. Proctor Jones, OH, 4 March 1971, RBRC, RBRL.
33. In 1938, when FDR decided to purge a number of Southern lawmakers, including Russell's colleague Walter F. George, he called Russell to the White House, asked him to support the purge, and said Russell could select the candidate to run against George. Years later Russell would recall perspiring in mid-February as he declined the president's offer, and then telling the incumbent Georgia governor: "I don't want to have anything to do with Georgia politics." From the television series "Georgia Giant," printed with the permission of WSB-TV, Doc. #1, p. 33.
34. Modine Thomas, OH, 10 February 1971, RBRC, RBRL.
35. Ina Russell Stacy, OH, 5 April 1971, RBRC, RBRL.
36. Powell Moore, OH, 6 March 1971, RBRC, RBRL.
37. Memo, Willie Day Taylor to Lyndon B. Johnson, 19 January 1971, Post Presidential Name File, Russell, Sen. Richard B., LBJL. On the memo, advising Johnson of these events, he has written: "I'll talk to you about this—L."

38. Ina Russell Stacy, OH, 5 April 1971, RBRC, RBRL, and Proctor Jones (who was also present) discussion with the author.

39. Proctor Jones, OH, 4 March 1971, RBRC, RBRL.

40. Lady Bird and Lyndon B. Johnson to Richard B. Russell III, 11:30 a.m., 22 January 1971, Post Presidential Name File, Russell, Sen. Richard B., LBJL.

41. Proctor Jones, OH, 4 March 1971, RBRC, RBRL.

42. Richard B. Russell III, who took the author to the site.

43. The author, on the staff plane, took 20 years to reach the site.

44. Barboura Raesley, discussion with the author.

45. Proctor Jones, OH, 4 March 1971, RBRC, RBRL, and in discussions with the author.

46. Tom Johnson, the White House aide, still with the former president at the ranch, described the preparations for a trip to the Russell funeral in an interview with the author, 6 December 1991.

47. In the years since, Johnson's failure to attend the funeral of his friend has been cited by some Russell intimates as an indication of Johnson's insensitivity. At least one correspondent, who inquired at the ranch the day following Russell's funeral, was told by Mary Rather only that Johnson "is recuperating from a mild case of viral pneumonia, and he is now in Acapulco for some sun and rest." Post Presidential Name File, Russell, Sen. Richard B., LBJL. Lady Bird Johnson mentions the onset of Johnson's heart problems in talking of the Russell funeral, OH, 12 August 1977, RBRC, RBRL.

Afterword

1. Horace Busby, Smithsonian LBJ Seminar, 26 November 1991.

2. Merle Miller in Lyndon, beginning at p. 680, describes Johnson's participation in this meeting.

3. This view of Johnson's goals and his relationship with his mother is the author's own, developed from accounts of his childhood by Johnson's biographers and, importantly, from comments of his later associates, notably George Reedy. Readers who seek a pre-Freudian portrait of a man driven by the ambitions of his mother may read William Shakespeare's play Coriolanus, believed to have been written about 1607–1608.

4. Eugene McCarthy, Up 'Til Now, 82.

5. Mudd's comment, OH, 4 March 1971, RBRC, RBRL. Johnson is quoted by Harry McPherson in an interview with the author, 5 April 1991.

6. The Arch Barnes story is told by Russell's oldest sister, Mary Willie (Miss Willie) Green, OH, 29 July 1971, RBRC, RBRL.

7. From the television series "Georgia Giant," printed with the permission of WSB-TV, unedited tapes, RBRC, RBRL.

8. Russell's letter to the clergyman is at p. 105.

9. Russell himself mentioned the fall of Rome to the author. Proctor Jones, Russell's traveling companion, mentioned Russell's views on Puerto Rico in a discussion with the author. William H. Jordan mentioned Russell's view on Brazil.

10. Wayne Kelley, interview reprinted in *Atlanta Magazine*, December 1968. From the television series "Georgia Giant," printed with the permission of WSB-TV, unedited tapes, RBRC, RBRL. I did not find this "very intimate" letter.

Bibliography

Books

Abel, Elie. *The Missile Crisis.* Philadelphia: J. B. Lippincott Co., 1963.

Allen, Robert S., ed. *Our Sovereign State.* New York: The Vanguard Press, 1949.

Ashmore, Harry. *Hearts and Minds: A Personal Chronicle of Race in America.* Cabin John, Maryland/Washington, D.C.: Seven Locks Press, 1988.

Baker, Bobby, with Larry King. *Wheeling and Dealing: Confessions of a Capitol Hill Operator.* New York: W. W. Norton & Co., 1978.

Barkley, Alben W. *That Reminds Me—.* New York: W. W. Norton & Co., 1954.

Califano, Joseph A. *The Triumph and Tragedy of Lyndon Johnson.* New York: Simon & Schuster, 1991.

Caro, Robert A. *The Years of Lyndon Johnson: The Path to Power and Means of Ascent.* New York: Alfred A. Knopf, 1990.

Carpenter, Liz. *Ruffles and Flourishes.* Garden City, New York: Doubleday & Co., 1970.

Clifford, Clark, with Richard Holbrooke. *Counsel to the President.* New York: Random House, 1991.

Dallek, Robert. *Lone Star Rising: Lyndon Johnson and His Times, 1908–1960.* New York: Oxford University Press, 1991.

Donovan, Robert J. *Conflict and Crisis: The Presidency of Harry S. Truman, 1945–1948.* New York: W. W. Norton & Co., Inc., 1977.

Edwards, India. *Pulling No Punches: Memoirs of a Woman in Politics.* New York: G. P. Putnam's Sons, 1977.

Evans, Rowland, and Robert Novak. *Lyndon B. Johnson: The Exercise of Power.* New York: New American Library, 1966.

Fite, Gilbert C. *Richard B. Russell Jr.: Senator from Georgia.* Chapel Hill: University of North Carolina Press, 1991.

Geyelin, Philip. *Lyndon B. Johnson and the World.* New York: Frederick A. Praeger Publishers, 1966.

Goldman, Eric Frederick. *The Tragedy of Lyndon Johnson.* New York: Alfred A. Knopf, 1969.

Goldwater, Barry, with Jack Casserly. *Goldwater.* New York: Doubleday & Co., 1988.

Goodwin, Richard N. *Remembering America: A Voice from the Sixties.* Boston: Little, Brown & Co., 1988.

Hardeman, D. B., and Donald C. Bacon. *Rayburn: A Biography.* Austin: Texas Monthly Press, 1987.

Hersh, Seymour M. *The Samson Option.* New York: Random House, 1991.

Humphrey, Hubert H. *The Education of a Public Man: My Life and Politics.* Garden City, New York: Doubleday & Co., 1976.

Johnson, Claudia Taylor (Lady Bird). *A White House Diary.* London: Wedenfield and Nicholson, 1970.

Johnson, Sam Houston. *My Brother Lyndon.* New York: Cowles Book Company, 1969.

Karnow, Stanley. *Vietnam: A History.* Reprint, New York: Penguin Books, 1983.

Kearns, Doris. *Lyndon Johnson and the American Dream.* New York: Harper & Row, 1976.

Leighton, Frances Spatz, and Helen Baldwin. *They Call Her Lady Bird.* New York: MacFadden-Bartell Corp., 1964.

McCarthy, Eugene. *Up 'Til Now.* New York: Harcourt Brace Jovanovich, 1987.

McCullough, David. *Truman.* New York: Simon & Schuster, 1992.

McPherson, Harry. *A Political Education.* Rev. Ed. Boston: Houghton Mifflin Company, 1988.

Manchester, William. *The Glory and the Dream.* 2 vols. Boston: Little, Brown & Co., 1973.

Miller, Merle. *Lyndon: An Oral Biography.* New York: G. P. Putnam's Sons, 1980.

Mooney, Booth. *The Lyndon Johnson Story.* New York: Farrar, Straus and Cudahy, 1956.

O'Neill, Tip, with William Novak. *Man of the House: The Life and Political Memoirs of Speaker Tip O'Neill.* New York: Random House, 1987.

Oshinsky, David M. *A Conspiracy So Immense: The World of Joe McCarthy.* New York: The Free Press, 1983.

Perry, Mark. *Four Stars.* Boston: Houghton Mifflin Company, 1989.

Phipps, Joe. *Summer Stock: Behind the Scenes with LBJ in '48.* Fort Worth: Texas Christian University Press, 1992.

Reedy, George E. *Lyndon B. Johnson: A Memoir.* New York: Andrews and McMeel, 1982.

_____. *The U.S. Senate: Paralysis or a Search for Consensus.* New York: Crown Publishers, 1966.

Reidel, Richard Langham. *Halls of the Mighty: My 47 Years at the Senate.* Washington, D.C.: Robert B. Luce, Inc., 1969.

Reston, James. *Deadline: A Memoir.* New York: Random House, 1991.

Schlesinger, Arthur M., Jr. *Robert Kennedy and His Times.* Boston: Houghton Mifflin Company, 1978.

Sitkoff, Harvard. *The Struggle for Black Equality, 1954–1980.* New York: Hill and Wang, 1981.

Smith, Timothy G., ed. *Merriman Smith's Book of Presidents: A White House Memoir.* New York: W. W. Norton & Co., 1972.

Thomas, Helen. *Dateline: White House.* New York: Macmillan Publishing Co., 1975.

Truman, Harry S. *Memoirs, Vol. 2: Years of Trial and Hope.* Garden City, New York: Doubleday & Co., 1956.

Whalen, Charles and Barbara. *The Longest Debate: A Legislative History of the 1964 Civil Rights Act.* Cabin John Maryland/Washington, D.C.: Seven Locks Press, 1985.

White, Theodore H. *The Making of the President 1968.* New York: Atheneum Publishers, 1969.

White, William S. *Citadel: The Story of the U.S. Senate.* New York: Harper and Brothers, Publishers, 1956.

PAPERS AND ARTICLES

Caro, Robert A. "My Search for Coke Stevenson." *New York Times Book Review,* 3 February 1991.

Fite, Gilbert C. "Richard Russell and Lyndon B. Johnson: The Story of a Strange Friendship." Paper presented at the annual meeting of the State Historical Society of Missouri, 22 October 1988.

Gaskin, Thomas M. "Lyndon B. Johnson and Senator Richard B. Russell: Death of a Friendship." Paper presented at a meeting of the Southern Historical Association, Lexington, Kentucky, 10 November 1989.

Harrington, Walt. "Lynda: The Life and Changing Times of a Political Princess." *The Washington Post Magazine*, 9 July 1989.

Kelley, Wayne. *Atlanta Journal*, interview with Richard B. Russell, 10 October 1968, reprinted in *Atlanta* magazine and in the *Congressional Record*.

Valenti, Jack. "LBJ's Bold Gamble on a Political Revolution." *The Washington Post*, "Outlook," 5 August 1990.

Ziemke, Caroline F. "Senator Richard B. Russell and the Lost Cause in Vietnam." *The Georgia Historical Quarterly*, 72 (Spring 1988).

INDEX